Islam and International

Islam and International Development

Insights for working
with Muslim communities

Edited by
Ajaz Ahmed Khan and Affan Cheema

Practical Action Publishing Ltd
27a Albert Street, Rugby,
Warwickshire, CV21 2SG, UK
www.practicalactionpublishing.com

A catalogue record for this book is available from the British Library.
A catalogue record for this book has been requested from the Library of Congress.

ISBN 978-1-78853060-6 Paperback
ISBN 978-1-78853059-0 Hardback
ISBN 978-1-78853062-0 Epub
ISBN 978-1-78853061-3 PDF

Citation: Khan, A.A. and Cheema, A. (2020) *Islam and International Development: Insights for working with Muslim communities*, Practical Action Publishing, Rugby, UK <http://dx.doi.org/10.3362/9781788530613>.

Since 1974, Practical Action Publishing has published and disseminated books and information in support of international development work throughout the world. Practical Action Publishing is a trading name of Practical Action Publishing Ltd (Company Reg. No. 1159018), the wholly owned publishing company of Practical Action. Practical Action Publishing trades only in support of its parent charity objectives and any profits are covenanted back to Practical Action (Charity Reg. No. 247257, Group VAT Registration No. 880 9924 76).

The views and opinions in this publication are those of the editors and contributors and do not represent those of Practical Action Publishing Ltd or its parent charity Practical Action. Reasonable efforts have been made to publish reliable data and information, but the authors and publisher cannot assume responsibility for the validity of all materials or for the consequences of their use.

Cover photo: The cover photograph depicts more than 20,000 people gathering for a loan disbursement ceremony by Akhuwat Islamic Microfinance at the Badshahi Mosque in Lahore, Pakistan on 10 February 2018. Akhuwat uses mosques, and on occasions churches and temples as well, to provide training and distribute loans. In early Islamic history, as well as being places for prayer, mosques were used for administrative and community development purposes.
Courtesy of Muhammad Shakeel Ishaq.
Typeset by vPrompt eServices, India

Contents

Tables, boxes, and figures   vi

Acknowledgements   viii

About the editors   ix

Preface   x

1. An Islamic prism of poverty   1
   Affan Cheema and Mohammed R. Kroessin

2. The Islamic social sector (*zakat* and *waqf*) and development:
   principles, status, and prospects   19
   Habib Ahmed

3. The importance of spiritual capital within human development
   in Islamic teaching   43
   Atallah FitzGibbon

4. Translating faith into development: how do Islamic teachings
   advocate helping the poor?   69
   Ajaz Ahmed Khan

5. Islamic perspectives on refugees, asylum, and forced migration   87
   Sadia Najma Kidwai

6. Gender and Islam   111
   Shahin Ashraf and Najmo Abukar

7. Deconstructing Islamic perspectives on sexual and gender-based
   violence, toward a faith-inclusive approach   131
   Sandra Iman Pertek

8. Child protection and safeguarding in an Islamic context:
   understanding the critical role faith plays in supporting
   protective mechanisms in humanitarian action   153
   Neelam Fida

9. An Islamic approach to peacebuilding: putting theory into practice   173
   Sylvia Brown and Haroon Kash

10. Walking gently on the Earth: Islamic environmentalism
    and Muslim FBOs   197
    Ajaz Ahmed Khan and J.R.A. Williams

Index   215

Tables, boxes, and figures

Tables

1.1 The fundamental Islamic principles in development   10

2.1 *Zakat* estimates as a percentage of GDP   25

2.2 GDP per capita and poverty headcount in 25 countries   26

2.3 *Zakat* and poverty alleviation potentials in 2017   26

2.4 *Zakat*, income levels, and poverty alleviation   27

4.1 The relative expenditure of Muslim FBOs on emergency and longer-term development projects   72

Boxes

2.1 *Zakat* administration in Federal Territory Kuala Lumpur (FTKL)   33

2.2 Waqaf Al-Nur   36

2.3 myWakaf   37

5.1 Community-based protection in an urbanized world: the case of Muslim community sponsorship programmes in Canada   98

5.2 The freedom to be faithful: the case of promoting spiritual resilience in Jordan and Lebanon   101

5.3 Respecting rights, accepting responsibility: the case of Syrian refugees in Turkey   102

6.1 Young changemaker Salimata Togoloa refuses to accept FGM and child marriage in Mali   124

6.2 Fighting for women's and children's access to education in the Philippines   125

6.3 Engaging faith leaders in Pakistan   125

8.1 An integrated approach to gender-based violence and child protection   165

9.1   The eight Islamic principles and values of peace and
      conflict resolution   178

9.2   Conflict prevention and peacebuilding in Mandera, Kenya   185

9.3   Islamic Relief's community conflict resolution and reconciliation
      in Darfur   187

9.4   Islamic Relief's conflict transformation and peacebuilding
      programme in Yemen   188

Figures

1.1   The importance of human dignity in the fundamental
      Islamic principles   11

3.1   The objectives of Islamic law in the promotion of human dignity   51

3.2   The role of human rights in preserving human dignity   60

7.1   The 'community conversation' process   139

7.2   Process of IRE's project activities   140

7.3   A community conversation with women, an imam, and volunteers   144

9.1   Singing for peace in schools in West Darfur   188

Acknowledgements

This book is a result of the efforts of many people and they all deserve credit. Most importantly we would like to thank the authors of the individual chapters. They have done most of the work, without any renumeration, and have patiently tolerated our frequent questions and requests for further information. We are very grateful to them.

We are obliged to the various Muslim humanitarian aid and development organizations whose work is described in this book, for sharing information about their programmes and allowing us insight into their activities. We hope that they will benefit from the exposure provided through this publication.

We would like to thank CARE International and Islamic Relief Worldwide respectively for supporting us and allowing us to take the time to focus on writing this book.

Finally, we would like to thank Elise Aston for diligently reviewing the entire manuscript and her helpful comments and suggestions, Judith Forshaw for her meticulous copyediting, and Clare Tawney and Chloe Callan-Foster at Practical Action Publishing for their patience, understanding, and support in making this book possible.

Ajaz Ahmed Khan and Affan Cheema
April 2020

About the editors

Ajaz Ahmed Khan is Senior Microfinance Adviser with CARE International. He holds a PhD in Development Economics and has extensive experience of working in a diverse range of countries in Latin America, Eastern Europe, Asia and Africa. He has written widely on microfinance, Islamic microfinance in particular, as well as more generally on faith and development.

Affan Cheema is the Head of Programme Quality at Islamic Relief Worldwide. He holds a MSc in Development Planning and has worked for over two decades in the humanitarian and development sector travelling extensively in Africa, Asia and the Middle East. This experience has given him a valuable insight into the poverty related needs, demands and rights of communities, especially those of a Muslim faith.

Preface

Faith is central to the lives of many people living in poverty. It provides a lens through which they view the world and a way to make sense of life's experiences. However, this reality is rarely acknowledged, invested in, or harnessed in the strategic discourse of the international development community. Instead, faith tends to be either ignored or perceived to have a negative influence, particularly in relation to Muslim communities. We feel that these views arise from a lack of understanding. Our aim in this book is to outline Islamic teachings on a range of development issues and highlight examples of positive practice. We hope that this will help practitioners, researchers, and policymakers to better understand, explore, and utilize faith as a resource that has immense potential to promote better development outcomes in Muslim communities.

The need to adopt a more faith-inclusive approach is increasingly important. Muslims or those from Muslim backgrounds comprise 1.8 billion people, or approximately one-quarter of the world's population. However, they comprise an even greater proportion of those categorized as living in poverty, as receiving humanitarian aid, and as refugees and residing in areas of conflict. Unsurprisingly therefore, they are the focus of much of the world's international humanitarian and development assistance. According to the Organisation for Economic Co-operation and Development (OECD), nine of the top ten recipients of official development assistance are Muslim-majority countries or those with significant Muslim populations.[1] Muslims are also the principal beneficiaries of assistance provided by countries belonging to the Gulf Cooperation Council and Muslim faith-based organizations from the United Kingdom and elsewhere.

As editors, we wanted to attract a diverse set of authors to address a wide range of development issues. This presented us with a challenge. Despite the long history of Muslim charitable activities we discovered that the Muslim humanitarian and development sector has not, in general, articulated its faith approach. We also felt it was important to move beyond speaking about Islamic values and to discuss applied ethics. For this reason we encouraged all the contributors not only to explore Islamic theological perspectives and how they relate to specific issues, but also to present practical examples of how they can influence the design and delivery of development projects and advocacy. We interpret Islamic teachings as encouraging us to move beyond addressing the basic needs of those living in poverty, to also promoting rights and behavioural change, and to meeting spiritual needs – issues that are explicitly addressed in this book.

Our hope is that this book stimulates further discussion about the importance of faith in development strategies, particularly when engaging with Muslim communities, institutions, and faith leaders. We also hope that it encourages a wider range of Muslim agencies to articulate their faith perspectives and have their voices heard. If development is to succeed, we believe that more integral, inclusive, and community-appropriate strategies are critical.

Ajaz Ahmed Khan and Affan Cheema
April 2020

Note

1. See <https://public.tableau.com/views/AidAtAGlance/DACmembers?: embed=y&:display_count=no?&:showVizHome=no#1> [accessed 15 April 2020].

CHAPTER 1

An Islamic prism of poverty

Affan Cheema and Mohammed R. Kroessin

Historical and current global approaches to eradicating poverty within the international development sector have tended to focus on an income-based approach. Recently the discourse has shifted to a more holistic approach, which led to the creation of the Sustainable Development Goals (SDGs), referred to in universal terms as the 'Global Goals'. Despite an overwhelming proportion of the world's population, especially in low-income countries, regarding faith as an essential part of their well-being, the Global Goals do not explicitly recognize the importance of faith. To create a truly universal development agenda for humanity, faith (including Islam) needs to be taken seriously. Interestingly, Islam has very rich social teachings and an established practice of wealth redistribution through zakat, *which has been recognized within the aid community – for example, in attempts to use Islamic social finance to fill the humanitarian funding gap. But the dynamics of* zakat *can be effectively harnessed for the Global Goals only if Islamic approaches to addressing poverty are understood. This chapter discusses the* Maqasid al-Shari'ah *(the goals of Islamic law), which were developed almost one thousand years ago, as one such 'Islamic lens of poverty'. This can add value to the global discourse on poverty, as well as to more effective poverty eradication approaches, for example when working with grassroots Muslim communities. In a world where there is acknowledgement of the need for a multidimensional 'nexus' approach to poverty eradication,* Maqasid *provides a needs, rights, and spiritual nexus approach to viewing poverty. Islam's lens of poverty is one that focuses on material needs, human rights, and spiritual needs. An absence of basic needs, rights, and faith can be defined as a state of poverty.*

Keywords: Muslim, Islam, development, poverty, *Maqasid al-Shari'ah*, faith, spiritual, SDGs, Global Goals, dignity, triple nexus, *zakat*

Introduction

Many Muslim non-governmental organizations (NGOs) have been established since the 1980s and have grown rapidly since then, particularly around the tradition of charitable giving in the form of *zakat*, the obligatory alms tax (Benthall, 1999, 2016). However, their understanding of poverty and their conceptualization of development have often been driven primarily by theological concerns (Kroessin, 2009; Petersen, 2016)[1] rather than, for example, the Global Goals.[2]

http://dx.doi.org/10.3362/9781788530613.001

After the 2015 Global Goals agreement, the international community came together once again to focus on humanitarian crises at the World Humanitarian Summit in 2016, which gave birth to the 'Agenda for Humanity'.[3] These milestone global initiatives built upon decades of specific agreements around particular themes in tackling global poverty. Did these agreements recognize as part of their strategy the fact that 84 per cent of people around the world identify with a faith (Hackett and McClendon, 2017)? Were Islamic approaches looked for when working with poverty-affected Muslim communities?[4]

A key document regarding the Global Goals is the resolution adopted by the General Assembly on 25 September 2015, entitled 'Transforming our world: the 2030 Agenda for Sustainable Development' (UN, 2015). The document affirms the international community's broader commitment to tackling poverty. It quite rightly focuses on issues such as human rights, gender, discrimination, conflict, and climate change, while specifically outlining the importance of partnership. 'The revitalized Global Partnership will facilitate an intensive global engagement in support of implementation of all the Goals and targets, bringing together Governments, civil society, the private sector, the United Nations system and other actors and mobilizing all available resources' (ibid.: 28). The document does not explicitly mention the importance of faith communities or leaders – let alone Islam or traditional Muslim institutions such as *zakat* – both of which might be regarded as critical stakeholders if the world were to tackle global poverty successfully. It did, however, recognize the importance of religion in the context of the protection of rights and inclusion in Goal 10, within which faith communities can be interpreted as passive recipients of development work. The Agenda for Humanity declaration expanded on this, as it recognized the active role faith communities can play, particularly in creating peaceful societies. In this context an initiative named 'Charter for faith-based humanitarian action' (Agenda for Humanity) was formed.

The sector has been moving forward. For example, Lord Carey, the former Archbishop of Canterbury, pointed to 1997–8 and the World Faiths Development Dialogue as an identifiable turning point for the relationship between international organizations and 'faith-based' organizations (FBOs). The event sought to increase understanding of the role of faith, FBOs, and religious institutions in the provision of services, development, and humanitarian activities. Since the Dialogue, there has been a gradual increase in interest from the international aid architecture in the role of FBOs, faith communities, and faith leaders in the provision of humanitarian assistance, often related to questioning the 'added value' of faith. While a focus on service provision remains the most common approach by large-scale humanitarian donors towards FBOs, the nature of the conversation has developed in ways that indicate greater acceptance of the 'value' provided by FBOs and engagement with faith actors more broadly (Salek, 2016: 347). Evidence from the declaration text of the Global Goals and Agenda for Humanity suggests that global progress since 1997 has not been as dynamic as it could have been.

There appears to be a focus on secular approaches that neglect the role of faith and ignore the non-material (Kroessin, 2012: 13). During our 20 years of experience as aid sector practitioners, predominantly with Muslim international NGOs, we are used to hearing within the official Northern aid structure that they 'do not do faith' and are met with suspicion, and often unfounded views, which see faith as part of the problem. Faith agencies, particularly Muslim agencies, are deemed to be on the edge of proselytising – or, worse, are viewed through a counterterrorism lens. It would be wrong, however, to paint a completely bleak picture. There have been some great initiatives that are breaking through the iron wall of 'we do not do faith', such as the Joint Learning Initiative (JLI),[5] the UN Interagency Task Force on Religion (UNITFR),[6] and the World Bank Faith Engagement.[7] There have also been some clear examples of UN bodies engaging with Muslim scholarship to understand and outline Islamic perspectives on rights.[8]

A UN Population Fund (UNFPA) report stated:

> Development actors, both faith-based and secular, must learn how to navigate the complex world of religion rather than ignore or marginalize its significance. Secular development actors are cautioned against either ignoring the role of religion (in which case the development agenda loses a valuable interlocutor), or over-simplifying the complexities and ambiguities often found in such domains, particularly around contentious rights-related issues. (Karam, 2014: v)

On the other hand, it is noticeable that Muslim voices are limited. The reasons for this need to be understood and a thorough analysis is beyond the scope of this chapter. It does however pose some questions, such as whether Muslims' reluctance to engage within the current aid architecture is because it is perceived as culturally inappropriate. Or is the engagement seen as holding little value? Does Muslim civil society lack the current skills and resources to engage with the international aid architecture? The UNFPA does suggest that there is a need for investment in the capacity of faith agencies to engage in the relevant international forums with strong voices (Karam, 2014: 52).

There does indeed appear to be an increasing desire to engage with faith agencies, particularly Muslim organizations, as they provide inroads into the 'hearts and minds' of poverty-affected communities. Also, quite importantly, due to the massive funding gap, interest has risen in Islamic social finance, with estimates of *zakat* ranging from US$200 billion to US$1 trillion per annum across the world (cf. Ismail, 2018). There is less discussion, or perhaps less will however, to understand Islam's conceptual views on poverty and its established channels for alleviation. Harnessing the strength of traditional Islamic approaches, including the mobilization of resources that may outstrip official development aid from the 30 members of the OECD's Development Assistance Committee (totalling US$153 billion in 2018), rather than simply trying to tap into them, may significantly strengthen the international battle against poverty.

argument away from the voluntary concept of charity, which can result in unbalanced power dynamics where there is a constant demand for money. Islam makes it an obligation and moves more towards a wealth redistribution model.

With *zakat*, the alms tax – one of the five pillars of Islam – wealth redistribution is a very prominent theme in Islamic social theory and practice. The *Qur'an* states that the recipients of *zakat* should be 'the poor, the needy, those who administer them, those whose hearts need winning over, to free slaves and help those in debt, for God's cause, and travellers in need. This is ordained by God; God is all knowing and wise' (*Qur'an*, 9: 60). However, despite the numerous scriptural references to the fight against poverty there is no unanimously agreed definition of poverty in Islam. Historically, poverty was an issue of jurisprudence – vis-à-vis the individual criteria for paying and the eligibility for receiving *zakat*. The schools of Islamic law[15] did not offer an analysis of the causes of poverty. However, despite the high moral position of wealth redistribution and the practical relevance of poverty alleviation in early Islam, poverty as a challenge requiring a systematic solution is not as prominent a general theme or issue in subsequent Islamic discourses (Farooq, 2008).

This point is argued by the Turkish-American economic historian Kuran: 'The jurists who shaped Islamic law during Islam's initial few centuries touched, of course, on such questions as to how poverty should be defined, who qualifies as needy, and the extent of a poor person's *zakat* entitlement' (Kuran, 2003: 283). Their answers did not create a system for addressing structural poverty, but rather a means for identifying which individuals were eligible to receive *zakat*. Consequently, the way in which Muslim jurists define poverty is significant not only for what this discourse tells us about the distribution of charity but also for what it tells us about possible limits to their vision of changing the world around them (Mattson, 2003: 48).

Problematically, although *zakat* is acknowledged as a centrally important religious category, Islamic discourse has hinged on it for centuries without discussing it in a substantive manner outside the realm of Islamic jurisprudence. This is primarily because what we today call the realm of social sciences was dominated by Islamic jurists (Nienhaus, 2000). They adjudicated on the permissibility of human actions within the historical context of the practice established by the example of the Prophet Muhammad (PBUH),[16] rather than exploring new avenues for social or economic change. This is not to say that Muslim scholarship was devoid of broader reflection; indeed, in many ways it led human enlightenment in the Middle Ages in fields such as astronomy, medicine, and the sciences. One of the most notable scholars was Ibn Khaldun (1332–1406), who is considered by some to be the 'father of economics and of the social sciences in general' (Boulakia, 1971). In his most famous work, 'Al-Muqaddima' (translated as 'Critical introduction'), he sets out a historiography of the world known to him and analyses the rise and fall of human civilizations. The central point around which his observations are built and to which his research is directed is the study of the causation of political, social, and economic decline, including the structural foundations for wealth creation and poverty (Bearman et al., 1999).

Predating Ibn Khaldun was what perhaps turned out to be the most significant change in the way Muslim scholars constructed Islamic law (and, conversely, conceptualized poverty and development): a tool called *Maqasid al-Shari'ah* ('the goals of Islamic law'). Together with another related classical doctrine, *Maslaha* (welfare or public interest), *Maqasid al-Shari'ah* came to play an increasingly prominent role in deriving religious rulings from sources other than scriptural ones, by considering the higher objectives behind a ruling (Gleave, 2012).

However, although most classical-era jurists recognized *Maslaha* and *Maqasid* as important legal principles, they held different views regarding the role they should play in Islamic law. Some jurists viewed them as supporting tools constrained by scriptural sources (*Qur'an* and *ahadith*) and *Qiyas* (analogical reasoning), whereas others regarded them as an independent source of law whose general principles could override specific inferences based on the letter of scripture (Duderija, 2014).

The concept of *Maqasid al-Shari'ah* developed gradually over centuries from more scattered statements in the books of *Usul al-Fiqh* ('principles of jurisprudence') to become an organized, well-formulated theory of law. However it was not until the time of Abu Hamid al-Ghazali (1058–1111) that the concept was systematized and developed. He argued that *Maslaha* was God's general purpose in revealing the divine law (Opwis et al., 2007). According to al-Ghazali, the objective of the *Shari'ah* was to promote the well-being of mankind, which lies in safeguarding their faith (*din*), their human self (*nafs*), their intellect (*'aql*), their posterity (*nasl*), and their wealth (*mal*). Whatever ensures the safeguard of these five serves the public interest and is desirable.

Scholars agree about the five essential values defined by al-Ghazali, although some have added other *Maqasid* to the list. The individual components of *Maqasid al-Shari'ah* are either explicitly stated in the *Qur'an* and *Sunnah* or have been deduced, directly or indirectly, from these primary sources. Within each *Maqsad* (singular of *Maqasid*), there were three levels: the essential (*Daruriyyah*), the convenient (*Hajiyyah*), and the refined (*Tahsiniyyah*), which were defined as attainable conditions that jurisprudential analysis needed to consider in deriving a ruling or a law. Following in al-Ghazali's footsteps, Abu Ishaq Al-Shatibi (1320–88) identified two key principles to ensure that the conditions can be met – either by promoting the positive means to their enrichment, called *min Janib al-wujud*, or by blocking the means to their destruction, called *min Janib al 'adam* (Hallaq, 1997).

From this medieval school of thought, *Maqasid al-Shari'ah* was promoted as a tool for the development of Islamic law that focused on well-being. It did this through a world view built on the principles of drawing benefit and removing harm. This was beyond the traditional objective of Islamic jurisprudence of ascertaining the divine will pertaining to the permissible and the forbidden. Hence, a medieval jurisprudential tool opened up a broader debate around Islamic ethics and can be thought of as an early principle of the modern-day 'do no harm' approach.

In modern times, *Maqasid al-Shari'ah* has been championed in different forms by prominent scholars who have sought to adapt Islamic law to changing social conditions by drawing on the intellectual heritage of traditional jurisprudence (Duderija, 2014). In the contemporary *Maqasid* discourse, prominent in both reformist Islamic jurisprudence (Kamali, 2008) and Islamic economics (Chapra, 2008), poverty is conceptualized as a deficiency at the level of the absolute essential (Arabic: *Daruriyyah*). This *Daruriyyah* involves the essential key aspects for an individual to live a decent life, such as food, water, shelter, nutrition, and a society that is peaceful, safe, and fair along the lines of the original *Maqasid*. In this context, the *Maqasid* are 'to eliminate all forms of economic evils such as poverty, unemployment, underemployment etc. from society and to provide adequate and accessible incentives for all members of society to enjoy the available resources and achieve a prosperous living' (Lamido, 2016: 37).

While this sounds very much like development orthodoxy, one area where the *Maqasid* is clearly different from conventional current poverty eradication approaches is the inclusion of spiritual needs. Moreover, Chapra (1992) argues that, when al-Ghazali wrote 'faith, life, intellect, posterity, and wealth', there was an intentional hierarchy. He divides the five into three levels and concludes that faith is the most important category as it creates a moral consciousness; the second and middle category includes life, intellect, and posterity, as they relate to the human being himself or herself; and wealth is last, as Islam does not see wealth as an end, but rather as a means to an end (ibid.: 7–8). *Maqasid* is not limited to the material but is just as relevant to human rights. The Grand Imam of Al-Azhar, one of the highest authorities in Islamic thought, states:

> Muslim jurists have unanimously agreed that the Islamic legislative system is based on five purposes [of life], for which Allah has sent messengers and set legislations, namely: protecting one's religion, offspring, mind, body, and property. These five purposes constitute the foundations of any human society aiming at psychological stability and peace. The divine law protects these five pillars with strict rules – first, in order to apply them and, second, in order to protect them from what may tamper with them. As for the purpose of preserving the offspring, Islam has prohibited adultery, rape, indecent assault, killing boys and burying girls alive. Islam is pioneer in enacting a comprehensive and sufficient set of legislations concerning children's rights and interests, unmatchable in any other legal system. Islam pays due care to the children even before they form as foetuses in their mothers' wombs and continues to do so until they grow into mature men and women. (Arigatou and UNICEF, 2019: 65)

A *Maqasid al-Shari'ah* approach to poverty: Islamic Relief's 'Human Development in Islam' framework

The Qur'anic anti-poverty drive has led to the formation of many Islamic NGOs. This phenomenon also gave rise to the need for a model of development in the Islamic world that was specific to the Muslim religion. Conversely, Islamic NGOs not only saw this as a way of justifying their existence but also wanted to underline their difference to mainstream charities, and to act as an intermediary in *zakat* distribution. Historically, *zakat* was collected by the state as a religious tax, but in the contemporary Muslim world and in the Muslim diaspora in the West it has become an individualized act of charitable giving. In many ways, traditional *zakat* collection and distribution became the *raison d'*être for Islamic NGOs, which initially did not focus on development or addressing structural poverty, as the benefit of *zakat* focused on the alleviation of the poverty of individuals or groups of individuals (Benthall, 1999).

This was also the case with Islamic Relief,[17] an NGO founded in the UK in 1984 by Muslim students from the University of Birmingham in response to a famine in the Horn of Africa. For two decades the organization focused on a more traditional Islamic poverty relief model by collecting individual donations and distributing them to the needy. Gradually, over time, it moved towards a more 'project-based' format, building water wells, schools, and health facilities (Krafess, 2005).

In the early days, there was evidently a clear focus on tackling the basic needs of the poor and needy, but an exposure to the mainstream development discourse, the professionalization of the workforce, and external Western institutional funding led to a realization that a more nuanced development model was required to respond to structural poverty. The organization did not initially have a rights-based focus, although internal decision makers were aware that 'social justice' was a key element of Islam, as many Qur'anic quotes demonstrate.

The most significant development was a new organizational strategy in 2005 and a UK government-funded Programme Partnership Agreement (PPA). This unrestricted strategic funding allowed Islamic Relief to establish a Research and Policy Unit in 2007. A second PPA grant provided the space for the organization, which had become renowned for delivering humanitarian aid to hard-to-reach Muslim communities around the globe, to start thinking about how it viewed poverty and development. The result was a policy paper entitled 'An Islamic perspective on human development' (Aminu-Kano and FitzGibbon, 2014) that explicitly used a *Maqasid* approach.

Following al-Ghazali's five objectives, Aminu-Kano and FitzGibbon (2014) argued that development in Islam was primarily about safeguarding and enhancing the dignity of human beings. Thus, everyone has the right to live a life worthy of dignity and respect simply by virtue of being human, regardless of race, religion, gender, ability, age, or economic status. Humankind possesses this dignity because God has chosen to give us a special place and rank among other creations. The Islamic Relief paper defines several fundamental Islamic principles in development: namely, justice, freedom, human rights, equality, social solidarity, and sustainability. Table 1.1 outlines the scope of each of the categories.[18]

Table 1.1 The fundamental Islamic principles in development

Element	Description	Islamic underpinning
Faith	Faith is an essential element of well-being as it creates a social and moral outlook that is the basis of a drive to tackle poverty. This element also generally calls to the practice of religion, thereby ensuring freedom of religion and pluralism.	'There is no compulsion in religion: true guidance has become distinct from error' (*Qur'an*, 2: 256) 'Say, "Now the truth has come from your Lord: let those who wish to believe in it do so, and let those who wish to reject it do so"' (*Qur'an*, 18: 29)
Life	The focus is on human life and all that makes it rewarding and possible. This includes food, shelter, health, etc. Dignity is an important element here as it also includes human rights and freedom.	'The son of Adam has no better right than that he would have a house wherein he may live, and a piece of cloth whereby he may hide his nakedness, and a piece of bread and some water' (*hadith* in Tirmidhi 2341)
Intellect	This element encourages humans to develop their intellect through education but also to use it to develop society. It further encourages freedom of thought.	'Read! In the name of your Lord who created: He created man from a clinging form. Read! Your Lord is the Most Bountiful One who taught by [means of] the pen, who taught man what he did not' (*Qur'an*, 96: 1–5)
Posterity	This identifies the importance of protecting future generations. This can be through giving them a healthy lifestyle, protection from abuse, and protecting the environment that they will inherit.	'Our Lord, give us joy in our spouses and offspring. Make us good examples to those who are aware of You' (*Qur'an*, 25: 74) 'He has raised up the sky. He has set the balance so that you may not exceed in the balance: weigh with justice and do not fall short in the balance. He set down the Earth for His creatures' (*Qur'an*, 55: 7–10)
Wealth	Wealth is seen as critical to help the development of a society. Islam encourages economic endeavour and strong economic growth within ethical boundaries. It does, however, stand against greed, hoarding, and oppression while acquiring wealth. Wealth is a means, not an end in itself.	'[Prophet], tell those who hoard gold and silver instead of giving in God's cause that they will have a grievous punishment' (*Qur'an*, 9: 34) 'Man was truly created anxious: he is fretful when misfortune touches him, but tight-fisted when good fortune comes his way. Not so those who pray and are constant in their prayers; who give a due share of their wealth to beggars and the deprived' (*Qur'an*, 70: 19–25) 'Believe in God and His Messenger, and give out of what He has made pass down to you: those of you who believe and give will have a great reward' (*Qur'an*, 57: 7)

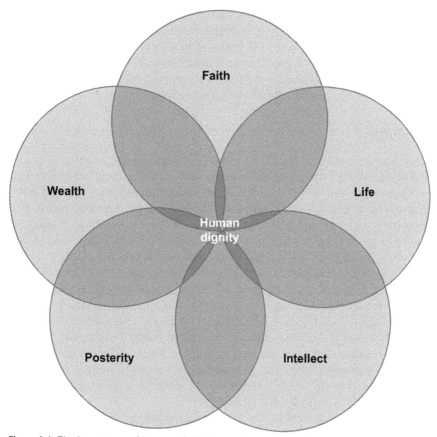

Figure 1.1 The importance of human dignity in the fundamental Islamic principles

According to Aminu-Kano and FitzGibbon (2014), human dignity was the ultimate reason for engaging in development. Hence, Islamic concepts of poverty go beyond materialistically determined outcomes, as Islam focuses on an important third pillar: that of faith or spiritual well-being.

The argument is not purely transcendental, as the authors postulate that a focus on faith creates a moral economy which supports social justice. Development is perceived as a move away from poverty – in essence, a change to a better human state – and is seen as an innate inclination towards material and moral perfection. To do this effectively, inner faith must be considered a development objective.

The focus on an individual's faith strengthens their core values and anti-poverty drive. It can be argued that this creates a virtuous cycle, resulting in a greater anti-poverty culture. By implication, not focusing on an individual's faith or fostering this virtuous cycle can represent a risk to poverty eradication.

Although Islamic Relief recognized the importance of *Maqasid*, the *Maqasid* approach lends itself to a multitude of interpretations along the depth and breadth of each principle, which need further exploration. This has left Islamic Relief with a very loose theory of change for development programmes, while also exposing the organization to criticism from more conservative Muslims that its programmes on the ground are indistinguishable from those of secular development NGOs, with the notable exceptions of Islamic microfinance or food distributions during religious festivals.

Conclusion

Islam has a traditional system of poverty alleviation in the form of *zakat*, which mobilizes billions of dollars per year as the faithful are obliged to tackle poverty and social injustice. Muslim scholars through the ages have invested in scholarly debate, primarily about eligibility for *zakat* funds, but they did not focus on or see the need to develop a structural framework approach to tackling poverty. However, one piece of work, acknowledged by most scholars, stands out: *Maqasid al-Shari'ah*. The *Maqasid al-Shari'ah*, which was developed almost 1,000 years ago, well before many of the current poverty eradication instruments, provides an Islamic lens of poverty. It is distinct from much of the current thinking around poverty as it acknowledges the key aspect of material needs and human rights, but in addition, it proposes that spiritual needs also have to be taken care of as these can create a multiplier effect on the other forms of poverty, as well as develop resilience and a community spirit at a grassroots level. The focus on material needs, human rights, and spiritual needs implies that poverty can be defined as an absence of basic needs, human rights, and spiritual support.

Maqasid-based approaches to conceptualizing poverty reduction, development, and well-being even offer a valuable addition to a 'Western' understanding of poverty reduction, which, by and large, has ignored faith, despite the fact that the vast majority of poor people see it as essential to their well-being. Over time, Christian NGOs have been more visible but far too often Muslim faith voices have been absent. The lack of Muslim faith voices in critically influential meetings, which have been predominantly located in the global North, is reflected in the resulting aid architecture.

This has started to change over the past decade, as opposition voices are beginning to recognize the potential of faith as an agent of change. The creation of UNITFR and the recognition of faith by world leaders in aid such as the UK government via its faith partnership principles (DFID, 2012) and by bodies such as JLI are very important steps and positive signs. The voice of Islam and its approaches to poverty at international level have often been limited to agencies such as the Islamic Development Bank or Islamic Relief, and often that voice has merely stated that Islam supports the ongoing mainstream poverty eradication efforts and approaches, rather than independently developing an authentic alternative. The question of whether Islam presents any alternatives or approaches to further strengthen the poverty debate is rarely posed or reflected upon when engaging with Muslim communities.

But still, in our experience, when aid structures respond to the needs of Muslim and other faith communities, they are reluctant to analyse or support the spiritual aspects of the community. This can result in aid programmes that do not engage with faith leaders, potentially resulting in conflict, as faith leaders are local and often more trusted than aid workers, and programmes that do not provide the spiritual structures that are needed. Far too often we see local aid workers recognizing this need when there is displacement, but the aid architecture's 'faith blind spot' does not allow for such funding. The initiative launched by several Muslim NGOs called the Muslim Platform for Sustainable Development is certainly a good starting point to engage with mainstream donors. But it must not just embrace and 'Islamize' mainstream topics; it also has a responsibility to develop authentic Islamic solutions that are based on the theological sources.

This inevitably poses three questions. First, should the aid system, ultimately, support mosque infrastructure, religious classes, and so on in affected Muslim communities if needs assessments indicate that this will help with poverty eradication? More fundamental is the question of whether the next set of Global Goals should not explicitly embrace faith as a force for good and include a spiritual well-being target, indicators for which could easily be developed, given the prominence of faith in poor people's lives. The last and mainly hypothetical question is whether a universal *Maqasid al-Shari'ah* approach that allows for a focus on both faith and no faith could provide the foundations for the future of conceptualizing poverty reduction.

As aid workers, we acknowledge that there is a need to further explore and develop the *Maqasid* framework via scholarship and practitioners. But we propose that utilizing this approach within Muslim communities – not to replace but to add to the current poverty discourse – will result in an appropriate basis for communication, as well as arguably improved poverty eradication results. In a world where there is acknowledgement of the need for a multidimensional 'nexus' approach to poverty eradication, *Maqasid* provides a needs, rights, and spiritual nexus approach to viewing poverty.

The following chapters will further explore aspects of the needs, rights, and spiritual approaches in relation to several subjects that are relevant to the modern drive to eliminate poverty. Each chapter outlines the Islamic principles that underline the subject matter coupled with examples of practical approaches of how to utilize them when working with Muslim communities. Chapter 2 emphasizes the importance of harnessing Islamic social finance to tackle poverty and in particular the tools of *zakat* and *waqf*. Chapter 3 highlights how spiritual capital influences and is pertinent to development workers in such areas as public health, education, social justice, and resilience. Chapter 4 analyses Islamic social teachings to understand how they advocate that poor people should be helped and in what way this might influence the design and implementation of development programmes. Chapters 5, 6, 7, and 8 focus on Islam, rights, and protection, outlining approaches to refugees, gender, gender-based violence, and child protection. Conflict is a growing challenge within the world and a major impediment to poverty eradication efforts, so Chapter 9 recognizes the importance of working with local faith leaders to foster peaceful societies with a triple nexus approach. The book concludes with one of the greatest challenges of today: the environment. Chapter 10 describes the strong environmental ethic that is inherent in Islamic teachings and how referencing such teachings may constitute an effective method to stimulate individual consciences and motivate behavioural changes among Muslim populations.

Notes

1. This is not to say that Muslim NGOs are not referring to the SDGs, but evidently more in an ex-post manner, while their programming remains largely driven by religious giving to appeals for *zakat*, to be utilized for humanitarian or development-type projects.
2. In 2015, the world convened a diverse set of stakeholders from a range of sectors including the private sector, civil society, business, governments, non-governmental agencies, and academia to tackle poverty. They agreed the SDGs. According to Ban Ki-moon, the then UN Secretary General, the goals were a 'people's agenda, a plan of action for ending poverty in all its dimensions, irreversibly, everywhere, and leaving no one behind' (Anderson, 2015). It followed the 15-year programme called the Millennium Development Goals (MDGs), which were agreed as part of the UN Millennium declaration in 2000 (UN, 2000).
3. See <https://www.agendaforhumanity.org/agendaforhumanity> [accessed 21 November 2019].
4. More than 50 per cent of the bottom 20 countries in the UNDP HDI ranking are Muslim-majority countries.
5. The JLI is an international collaboration on evidence for faith groups' activities, contribution, and challenges to achieving humanitarian and development goals (see <https://jliflc.com/>).
6. See UNITFR (2018).
7. See <https://www.worldbank.org/en/news/press-release/2015/07/12/global-conference-religion-sustainable-development>.
8. See <https://www.unicef.org/eg_Azhar_book_high_res_Eng.(1).pdf>; <https://egypt.unfpa.org/sites/default/files/pub-pdf/Islamic%20 perspectives%20on%20GBV.pdf> (in Arabic).
9. See <http://hdr.undp.org/en/content/human-development-index-hdi>.
10. https://www.un.org/en/sections/issues-depth/poverty/ (accessed 3rd January 2020)
11. See <https://www.islamic-relief.org/about-us/>.
12. See <https://www.wvi.org/our-approaches-change/our-promise>.
13. See <https://www.caritas.org/what-we-do/development/>.
14. Quotes are taken from M.A.S. Abdel Haleem, *The Qur'an*, Oxford University Press, Oxford, 2005.
15. Islamic schools of law were formed as rulings deduced from the primary sources of Islam: the *Qur'an* and *ahadith* (sayings of the Prophet Muhammad (PBUH)). As different methodological approaches were developed,

they resulted in distinct schools of thought. Over history, the most famous and dominant ones have been Hanafi, Shafi'i, Hanbali, Maliki, and Jafari.

16. The sayings, actions, and silent endorsements of the Prophet are referred to as '*Sunnah*' and, together with the *Qur'an*, are a key source of Islamic law.

17. Both authors are employees of Islamic Relief (see <https://www.islamic-relief.org>).

18. Adapted mainly from Aminu-Kano and FitzGibbon (2014) and Lamido (2016).

References

Aminu-Kano, M. and FitzGibbon, A. (2014) *An Islamic Perspective on Human Development*, Islamic Relief Worldwide, Birmingham.

Anderson, M. (2015) 'Ban Ki-moon: Sustainable Development Goals – leave no-one behind', *Guardian*, 3 August <https://www.theguardian.com/global-development/2015/aug/03/ban-ki-moon-hails-sdgs-agreed-by-193-nations-as-leaving-no-one-behind> [accessed 21 November 2019].

Arigatou and UNICEF (2019) *Faith and Children's Rights: A Multi-religious Study on the Convention on the Rights of the Child*, Arigatou International, New York.

Bearman, P., Bianquis, T., Bosworth, C.E., van Donzel, E. and Heinrichs, W.P. (eds) (1999) *Encyclopaedia of Islam*, Brill, Leiden <https://referenceworks.brillonline.com/browse/encyclopaedia-of-islam-2>.

Benthall, J. (1999) 'Financial worship: the Quranic injunction to almsgiving', *Journal of the Royal Anthropological Institute* 27 (1): 27–42.

Benthall, J. (2016) *Islamic Charities and Islamic Humanism in Troubled Times*, Manchester University Press, Manchester.

Boulakia, J.D.C. (1971) 'Ibn Khaldoun: a fourteenth-century economist', *Journal of Political Economy* 79: 1105–18.

Chambers, R. (2006) 'What is poverty? Who asks? Who answers?', *Poverty in Focus* (UNDP International Poverty Centre), December, pp. 3–4.

Chapra, M.U. (1992) *Islam and the Economic Challenge*, Islamic Foundation, Leicester.

Chapra, M.U. (2008) 'The Islamic vision of development in light of the *Maqasid al-Shari'ah*', Occasional Papers Series 15, International Institute of Islamic Thought, London.

Dariah, A.R., Salleh, M.S. and Shafiai, H.M. (2016) 'A new approach for Sustainable Development Goals in Islamic perspective', *Procedia: Social and Behavioral Sciences* 219: 159–66.

DFID (2012) *Faith Partnership Principles: Working Effectively with Faith Groups to Fight Global Poverty*, Department for International Development (DFID), London <https://assets.publishing.service.gov.uk/government/uploads/system/uploads/attachment_data/file/67352/faith-partnership-principles.pdf> [accessed 3rd January 2020].

Duderija, A. (2014) *Maqasid al-Shari'a and Contemporary Reformist Muslim Thought: An Examination*, Palgrave Macmillan, New York.

Farooq, M.O. (2008) 'The challenge of poverty and the poverty of Islamic economics', *Journal of Islamic Economics, Banking and Finance* 4 (2): 35–58.

Fukuda-Parr, S. (2006) 'The Human Poverty Index: a multidimensional measure', *Poverty in Focus* (UNDP International Poverty Centre), December, pp. 7–9.

Gleave, R.M. (2012) 'Maḳāṣid al-Sharīʿa', in P. Bearman, T. Bianquis, C.E. Bosworth, E. van Donzel, and W.P. Heinrichs (eds), *Encyclopaedia of Islam*, 2nd edn, Brill, Leiden.

Hackett, C. and McClendon, D. (2017) 'Christians remain world's largest religious group, but they are declining in Europe', Pew Research Center, Washington DC <https://www.pewresearch.org/fact-tank/2017/04/05/christians-remain-worlds-largest-religious-group-but-they-are-declining-in-europe/> [3rd January 2020].

Hallaq, W.B. (1997) *A History of Islamic Legal Theories: An Introduction to the Sunni Usul Al-Fiqh*, Cambridge University Press, Cambridge.

IsDB (2007) *Policy Paper on Poverty Reduction*, Islamic Development Bank (IsDB), Jeddah.

Ismail, Z. (2018) *Using Zakat for International Development*, K4D Helpdesk Report, University of Birmingham, Birmingham.

Kamali, H. (2008) *Maqasid al-Shari'ah Made Simple*, International Institute of Islamic Thought, London.

Karam, A. (2014) *Religion and Development Post-2015*, United Nations Population Fund, New York.

Krafess, J. (2005) 'The influence of the Muslim religion in humanitarian aid', *International Review of the Red Cross* 87 (858): 327–42.

Kroessin, M.R. (2009) *Mapping UK Muslim Development NGOs*, Working Paper 30, Religions and Development Research Programme Consortium, University of Birmingham, Birmingham.

Kroessin, M.R. (2012) '*An exploratory study of the discourse of Islam and development: the case of the Islami Bank Bangladesh*', PhD thesis, University of Birmingham <https://www.etheses.bham.ac.uk/3670/2/Kroessin_12_PhD.pdf> [accessed 5 December 2019].

Kuran, T. (2003) 'Islamic redistribution through *zakat*: historical record and modern realities', in M. Bonner, M. Ener, and A. Singer (eds), *Poverty and Charity in Middle Eastern Contexts*, State University of New York Press, Albany NY.

Lamido, A.A. (2016) '*Maqasid al-Shari'ah* as a framework for economic development theorization', *International Journal of Islamic Economics and Finance Studies* 2 (1): 27–49.

Mattson, I. (2003) 'Status-based definitions of need in early Islamic *zakat* and maintenance laws', in M. Bonner, M. Ener, and A. Singer (eds), *Poverty and Charity in Middle Eastern Contexts*, State University of New York Press, Albany NY.

Narayan, D. and Petesch, P. (2002) *Voices of the Poor from Many Lands*, World Bank, Washington DC.

Nienhaus, V. (2000) 'Islamic economics: dogma or science?', in K. Hafiz (ed.), *The Islamic World and the West: An Introduction to Political Culture and Political Relations*, translated by M.A. Kenny, Brill, Leiden.

Opwis, F., Abbas, A. and Frank, G. (eds) (2007) *Shari'a: Islamic Law in the Contemporary Context*, Stanford University Press, Stanford CA.

Petersen, M.J. (2016*) For Humanity or for the Umma?: Aid and Islam in Transnational Muslim NGOs*, Oxford University Press, Oxford.

Ranis, G., Stewart, F. and Samman, E. (2006) 'Human development: beyond the HDI', *Poverty in Focus* (UNDP International Poverty Centre), December, pp. 12–14.

Salek, L. (2016) 'Faith inspiration in a secular world: an Islamic perspective on humanitarian principles', *International Review of the Red Cross* 97: 345–70.

Sirageldin, I. (2000) 'Elimination of poverty: challenges and Islamic strategies', *Islamic Economic Studies* 8 (1): 1–16.

UN (2000) 'Millennium Declaration', Millennium Summit of the United Nations (UN), New York, 6–8 September <https://www.un.org/en/development/devagenda/millennium.shtml> [accessed 21 November 2019].

UN (2015) 'Resolution adopted by the General Assembly on 25 September 2015. Transforming our world: the 2030 Agenda for Sustainable Development', United Nations (UN) General Assembly, 21 October <https://www.un.org/ga/search/view_doc.asp?symbol=A/RES/70/1&Lang=E> [access 21 November 2020].

UNITFR (2018) *Annual Report of the United Nations Inter-Agency Task Force on Engaging Faith-based Actors for Sustainable Development*, United Nations Interagency Task Force on Religion (UNITFR), New York.

About the authors

Affan Cheema is the Head of Programme Quality at Islamic Relief Worldwide. He holds a MSc in Development Planning and has worked for over two decades in the humanitarian and development sector, travelling extensively in Africa, Asia, and the Middle East. This experience has given him a valuable insight into the poverty-related needs, demands, and rights of communities, especially those of a Muslim faith.

Mohammed R. Kroessin is a development economist with over 20 years of experience in working with and researching Islamic development and financial institutions. He was a research associate with the DFID-funded 'Religions and Development' research programme at the University of Birmingham, where he also completed his PhD on the political economy of Islam. He is now heading Islamic Relief's microfinance programme.

CHAPTER 2

The Islamic social sector (*zakat* and *waqf*) and development: principles, status, and prospects

Habib Ahmed

Resolving the problem of poverty and achieving sustainable development requires mobilizing funds from various sources. A potential source of funds in Muslim societies would be to tap into Islamic social finance institutions of zakat and waqf. While these Islamic social finance institutions played an important role histori-cally, they are not contributing to socio-economic development in contemporary times. This chapter provides an overview of the concepts of zakat and waqf and then presents ways in which these institutions can be revived to create a positive impact on development. This can be done by increasing mobilization of zakat and waqf funds by expanding the scope of jurisprudential interpretations and introducing innovative instruments and institutional formats. There is also a need to improve the governance and management of zakat and waqf institutions to increase their efficiency and effectiveness in alleviating poverty and enhance their social impact.

Keywords: zakat, waqf, poverty alleviation, development, social finance, governance and management

Introduction

The launch of the Sustainable Development Goals (SDGs) in 2015 aimed to bring about balanced sustainable development in all countries and is a global attempt to tackle the problem of underdevelopment and poverty. However, the first SDG, which focuses on ending poverty in all forms everywhere, remains the greatest global challenge (UN, 2017). One of the key constraints in achieving the SDGs is funding the huge investments necessary. UNCTAD (2014) estimates that at the current levels of investment, developing countries will face an annual gap of US$2.5 trillion to achieve the SDGs. Given the scale of funding requirements, promoting sustainable development will need 'significant mobilization of resources from a variety of sources and the effective use of financing' (UN, 2012: 48). It will also require engaging different stakeholders, including entities from the public, private, and non-profit sectors.

http://dx.doi.org/10.3362/9781788530613.002

In the last few decades, various policies have tried to mitigate the menace of poverty. However it continues to plague large segments of humanity, particularly in many Muslim-majority countries, where poverty is pervasive and 700 million people live on less than US$2 a day (World Bank, 2014: 38). Historically the Islamic social finance sector played an important role in promoting overall development and alleviating poverty in Muslim societies. *Zakat* is one of the fundamental pillars of Islam and requires Muslims to distribute a part of their income or wealth to the poor and deprived. Similarly, *waqf* is a voluntary charitable act that used to have wide economic implications and contributed to alleviating poverty and promoting social welfare. While these institutions were able to mitigate the problems of poverty and extend social services in Muslim societies in the past, nowadays they are not being used extensively and have limited impact.

Given the huge funding needs and gaps to achieve the SDGs, this chapter examines the role and scope of Islamic social finance in addressing some of the problems of poverty and underdevelopment. Specifically, the objective is to investigate how *zakat* and *waqf* can be used in contemporary times to alleviate poverty in Muslim societies. The chapter is organized as follows. The first section provides an overview of charitable giving in Islam and then presents the concepts and principles of *zakat* and *waqf*. The current status and potential of using *zakat* and *waqf* to mitigate poverty and enhance social welfare are then presented, while the subsequent section discusses the jurisprudential issues that could expand *zakat* and *waqf* funding. A discussion follows on the governance and management frameworks that could improve the efficiency and effectiveness of these social finance institutions, including three case studies as examples.

Islamic social finance: a conceptual framework

Islamic teachings instil religious motivation among Muslims to perform charitable acts as an expression of love of God. Citing various verses from the *Qur'an* and prophetic sayings, Siddiqi (1991: 6) asserts that Muslims are encouraged to care for others to enhance 'their spiritual wellbeing, material welfare, individual needs and their collective or social good'. The objective of doing good to others is to seek the pleasure of Allah (God) and to reap rewards in the hereafter (Siddiqi, 1991). A comprehensive concept of compassionate giving in Islamic teachings is *infaq* (or spending), which means 'giving away for the betterment of the society and family members' (Kahf, 2009). *Infaq fi sabil Allah* (giving for the sake of God), which appears frequently in the *Qur'an* and *ahadith* (prophetic sayings), signifies charitable spending that benefits God's creation.

Infaq can be broadly classified as obligatory and voluntary. Obligatory *infaq* can be further categorized into three types: first, *infaq* as personal religious absolute obligation, which is obligatory for every eligible Muslim (Kahf, 2009). Examples of this type of *infaq* would be *zakat* on assets/income and *zakat al fitr* paid before the festival of *Eid al fitr*, which marks the end of the month of fasting of Ramadan. Second, *infaq* as a personal religious circumstantial obligation relates to spending arising from certain circumstances or relationships. Examples of this category of *infaq* include a man's obligations to spend on his family and on needy relatives and neighbours. A third type of obligatory *infaq* is the community obligation, which requires spending by society to achieve certain social objectives. Falling under the doctrine of *fard kifaya* (collective obligation), the communal religious obligation is not mandatory for each individual but needs to be carried out by some members of society. Activities that are deemed necessary to protect the vital needs of people to survive and live in an Islamic way are considered socially obligatory (Siddiqi, 1991: 19). Examples of this kind of *infaq* would be spending to build civil and religious infrastructure such as mosques, roads, public utilities, and for public safety. While the role of discharging these functions can be ensured by the state, in many cases the non-profit or voluntary sector could also play an important role in performing these socially obligatory duties.

The second broad category of *infaq* is voluntary; this includes spending on beneficial causes. The objectives of voluntary charitable acts are not limited to the provision of economic goods and services; they can also serve non-material needs, such as protecting the environment and animals, enhancing information provision, social cohesion, and so on (Kahf, 2009; Siddiqi, 1991). Voluntary *infaq* or *sadaqah* (charity) can take two forms. First, *infaq* can relate to current spending that provides a one-time benefit to the recipients. Examples of this include spending on a charitable act to fulfil a need, such as feeding the poor. A second form of voluntary *infaq* is continuous *infaq/sadaqah*, which takes the form of donating assets to produce a constant stream of benefits over time. A key type of continuous voluntary *infaq* is *waqf*, which is an endowment that provides benefits over a period of time. Note that continuous charity such as *waqf* can perform some societal obligations, by providing services that fall under communal religious obligation.

This chapter focuses on two key types of *infaq* – zakat and *waqf* – that historically played important roles in Muslim societies. The principles and background of these Islamic social-sector instruments are discussed below.

Zakat: *principles and background*

Zakat is one of the five pillars of Islam and requires Muslims to distribute a part of their income and wealth among the poor and needy. Specifically, *zakat* is an obligation on eligible persons to pay specific percentages of their assets/income every lunar year (*hawl*) if they satisfy the threshold condition of *nisab*. *Nisab* is the minimum amount of wealth that makes a person eligible to pay *zakat* and is equal to the value of 87.48 grams of gold or 612.36 grams of silver. If an adult Muslim owns assets above *nisab*, *zakat* is payable on the value of all assets. A key condition of *zakat* is *tamlik* (ownership of *zakat* by the recipient), which requires that alms be distributed so that the recipient has full ownership of and authority over the proceeds.

There are two types of items eligible for *zakat*. The first is assets on which *zakat* is paid at the end of *hawl* and would include items such as cash, gold, silver, livestock, and goods for trade. The rate of *zakat* on these items is 2.5 per cent of the value of the assets. The second type is items to which *hawl* does not apply; these include agricultural produce on which *zakat* is due at harvest time rather than at the end of the year. The *zakat* rate for agricultural products that use water from rain, rivers, or springs or that are not watered at all is 10 per cent; this decreases to 5 per cent if the crops are irrigated by water obtained from wells or other sources.

The *Qur'an* (9: 60) identifies eight categories of beneficiaries of *zakat* as indicated in the following verse: '*sadaqat* are exclusively for the poor, and the needy, and the workers on it, and those whose hearts have been reconciled, and for [liberating] necks, and for those [burdened] under debts, and for the cause of God, and for the wayfarer. An obligation [ordained] from God; and God is full of knowledge and wisdom.' It should be noted that while the wayfarers (travellers) may be rich, they can be temporarily poor when travelling since they are not able to access their assets. 'Liberating necks' refers to freeing slaves who do not have enough money or assets to buy their own freedom.

Since the time of the Prophet Muhammad (Peace Be Upon Him), *zakat* management was implemented by state-appointed *zakat* collectors and distributors. Islamic scholars agree that the state should be responsible for administering *zakat* in Muslim societies (al-Qaradawi, n.d.).[1] While there are no historical data on the amount of *zakat* collected and distributed, two accounts give some indication about the effect on its status and impact. Narrations from the time of the second Muslim Caliph Umar ibn al-Khattab (13–22 H, 635–43 CE) and the period of the eighth Umayyad Caliph Umar ibn Abd al-Aziz (99–101 H, 718–20 CE) indicate that *zakat* collected in some regions could not be disbursed due to a lack of poor recipients (Ahmed, 2004).

Waqf: *principles and background*

The inspiration behind the creation of *waqf* comes from the saying of the Prophet Muhammad (PBUH) as narrated by Abu Hurairah and reported in Muslim (Book 13, *Hadith* 8).[2] This states: 'When a man dies, his deeds come to an end except for three things: *Sadaqah Jariyah* [ceaseless charity]; a knowledge which is beneficial; or a virtuous descendant who prays for him [the deceased].' One form of continuous *sadaqah* (*sadaqah jariyah*) is *waqf*, which is created by dedicating an asset through a *waqf* deed. The deed specifies the attributes of the *waqf* (such as an asset that becomes the corpus of the endowment), the beneficiaries, and the way in which it will be managed. Since the donor has the freedom and authority to structure the *waqf* in the ways he or she deems desirable, issues relating to its management or the type of beneficiary are flexible. The only condition that a *waqf* should satisfy is that its purpose should be to serve goodness (*birr*) (Kahf, 2004).

Waqf can be categorized in various ways. First, it can be distinguished according to its asset type, which can be broadly classified as movable or immovable. While the former usually takes the form of real estate, the latter would include *waqf* of books, horses, cash, and so on. A cash investment *waqf* as a key form of immovable assets-based endowment dates back to as early as the turn of the first century of *Hijrah*, or the migration of Prophet Muhammad (PBUH) and his followers from Mecca to Medina in the year 622 AD. Malik ibn Anas (93–179 H, 711–95 CE) mentions cash *waqf*, while Bukhari narrates an incident of cash *waqf* given to a merchant to use for trade, with the profits to be used for charity (Kahf, 2004). This practice continued in the later stages of the Ottoman Empire, when cash *waqf* was used for lending to help consumers and producers with liquidity and investment, with the revenue spent on beneficiaries.

A related classification of *waqf* is the type of benefit that can be either direct or indirect. In the former, services are provided directly from *waqf* assets (such as hospitals, schools, or private guest houses), while in the latter the *waqf* assets take the form of investments that generate revenue that is then used on beneficiaries (Kahf, 2004). In cash *waqf*, the direct benefits can take the form of cash used for interest-free lending to beneficiaries.[3] Indirect benefits of cash *waqf* would be derived from investing the funds and assigning the net return to the beneficiaries.

Waqf can also be classified according to its purpose, which can be philan-thropic/public (*khayri* or *aam*), family/private (*ahli* or *khass*), or combined/mixed *waqf* (*waqf mushtarak*). While the public *waqf* serves some social cause and the private *waqf* serves family members, the mixed *waqf* serves the dual objectives of serving both the family/descendants and the public. A final classification of *waqf*, which relates to its purpose, is religious or social/philanthropic. Whereas a religious *waqf* would include mosques and cemeteries that people use, beneficiaries of a social *waqf* would be society at large. The latter can take various forms, such as *waqf* providing socio-economic relief to the needy and the poor; providing education and health services; spending on the environment, scientific research, and other purposes, such as preserving forests; helping newlyweds; and even caring for animals (Ahmed, 2004).

The Prophet Muhammad (PBUH) established *waqf* himself and encouraged his companions to do the same. As a result, many *waqf* were established during the Prophet's time and continue to the present. The result was that the *waqf* sector became significant in many Muslim societies, with *waqf* covering more than a third of total cultivable land and other properties in some countries (Schoenblum, 1999). For example, Kahf (2003, n.d.) reveals that at the turn of the twentieth century in Palestine there were 233 recorded *waqf* deeds containing 890 properties, compared with only 92 private ownership deeds containing 108 properties. Similarly, one of the first land surveys in Egypt carried out during Muhammad Ali's rule in the early nineteenth century showed that 600,000 *feddan* (one *feddan* is slightly greater than one acre) out of a total of 2.5 million feddan of cultivable land was *waqf* (Kahf, 2003, n.d.).

The *waqf* sector developed significantly and became the most important institution for poverty alleviation in many Muslim societies (Cizakca, 2002).

The sector transformed society by serving the immediate needs of the poor and the deprived and empowered and equipped them by providing education and healthcare, increasing their productive and income-earning capacities. For example, during the Ottoman Empire, there were *waqf* complexes (*kulliye*), collections of buildings that included mosques, colleges, hospices, hospitals, public food kitchens, and caravanserais. These services were provided by the revenue generated by *waqf* through shops, markets, baths, and agricultural properties (Singer, 2005).

Islamic social finance: current status and potential

Although *zakat* and *waqf* have historically played an important role in fulfilling essential economic needs and in providing social services in Muslims societies, these institutions have become dormant and have not been performing these roles in recent times. The current status and the potential of the Islamic social instruments of *zakat* and *waqf* are presented below.

Zakat

There is a gap between the actual global *zakat* collection and disbursement and its potential reach. While this is due to various reasons, the key factors are jurisprudential interpretations and management issues. Although traditionally *zakat* was managed by the government, current practice shows that *zakat* is administered through three key channels: the government, non-profit organizations, and individuals. Unlike in the past, governments of most present-day Muslim countries do not play an active role in *zakat* administration. While governments in a few countries, such as Saudi Arabia and Pakistan, collect and distribute *zakat*, the amount is very small and has little impact on the beneficiaries. For example, citing various studies, Ahmed (2004: 71) reports that the *zakat* collected in different countries ranges from 0.01 per cent of gross domestic product (GDP) in Saudi Arabia (1975–6), 0.02 per cent in Egypt and Jordan (1985), and 0.08 per cent in Kuwait (1985) and Malaysia (2001) to 0.30 per cent in Pakistan (1985). One of the reasons for the low *zakat* collection is misman- agement, which discourages individuals from paying *zakat* to state institutions.[4] In the absence of credible public *zakat* institutions, people give their dues either directly to people they know or to non-profit welfare organizations they trust. The bulk of the *zakat* is distributed by individuals to people they know in an ad hoc manner. Since this *zakat* is given out in small amounts without any planning, it does not address the long-term needs of the recipients and produces negligible effects (Lessy, 2013: 2).

Potential *zakat* proceeds that could be used for socio-economic development depend on the size of wealth and income in any society. However, the size of the *zakat* collection also depends on the jurisprudential interpretations that define 'zakatable' assets or property. For example, the traditional view captured in historical texts gives a narrow definition of *zakat*able assets and property, thereby excluding most contemporary income sources and assets (Kahf, 1989). Scholars counter that forms of wealth have changed, and *zakat* should include modern types of asset and income. While the narrow perspective identifies traditional *zakat*able items (such as agricultural output, livestock, trade inventory, and cash holdings), some contemporary scholars include returns on fixed assets, salary, and wages, and the capital value of fixed assets in the *zakat* base (Kahf, 1989, 1999). Furthermore, since the bulk of modern-day wealth takes the form of investments in the financial sector, financial assets such as investment accounts, stocks, and *sukuk* (Islamic securities or bonds) should also be included as *zakat*able wealth. By including these *zakat*able assets, there is the potential to increase the collections that can be used to mitigate poverty and enhance social welfare.

Islamic scholars have different views on the potential *zakat* that can be collected, based on the assumptions on what constitutes *zakat*able assets. For example, Salama (1982) assesses the estimates of *zakat* collection to be in the range of 2 to 4 per cent of GDP, whereas al-Tahir (1997) suggests that the figure could be 14 per cent. Kahf (1989, 1999) provides a comprehensive analysis of the potential of *zakat* collection for a sample of eight countries, based on three opinions on the *zakat* base. The first opinion takes the traditional view and includes only agricultural output, livestock, trade inventory, and cash holdings as *zakat*able items. The second includes returns on fixed assets, salary and wages. The third is the broadest and also includes the capital value of fixed assets as a *zakat*able item.

Table 2.1 shows the estimates of *zakat* collection as a percentage of GDP based on these opinions for different countries. The table shows that the average potential *zakat* collection ranges from 1.8 per cent for the narrow view (A) to 4.3 per cent of GDP for the broader view (C). Given that the GDP of the 57 Organisation of Islamic Cooperation (OIC) member countries was valued at US$6,671 billion in 2017, the potential annual *zakat* collection could have been in the range of US$120 billion to US$287 billion.[5]

Table 2.1 *Zakat* estimates as a percentage of GDP

Country	Opinion A	Opinion B	Opinion C
Egypt	2.0	3.9	4.9
Pakistan	1.6	3.5	4.4
Indonesia	1.0	1.7	2.0
Qatar	0.9	3.7	3.2
Saudi Arabia	1.2	3.7	3.4
Sudan	4.3	6.3	6.2
Syria	1.5	3.1	3.1
Turkey	1.9	4.9	7.5
Average	**1.8**	**3.9**	**4.3**

Source: Kahf (1989).

Table 2.2 GDP per capita and poverty headcount in 25 countries

	GDP per capita 2017 (US$ constant 2010)	Poverty headcount ratio at $1.90 per day (2011 PPP) (% of population)
Average	3,382.90	11.1
Minimum	395.90	0.0
Maximum	14,936.40	62.4
Standard deviation	4,168.30	19.7

Note: The countries are Bangladesh, Benin, Burkina Faso, Cameroon, Cote d'Ivoire, Djibouti, Egypt, Gabon, Gambia, Indonesia, Iran, Kazakhstan, Kyrgyz Republic, Malaysia, Mauritania, Mozambique, Niger, Pakistan, Palestine, Tajikistan, Togo, Tunisia, Turkey, Uganda, and Yemen. PPP is purchasing power parity.
Source: Estimated using data from the World Bank Databank at <https://databank.worldbank.org/data/source/world-development-indicators#>.

Table 2.3 *Zakat* and poverty alleviation potentials in 2017

Variables	
Total population (million)	1,184.41
Population living under US$1.90/day (million)	131.68
GDP (US$ million)	3,857,908.5
Potential *zakat* collection (1.8% of GDP) (US$ million)	69,442.4
Annual distribution per poor person/day (US$)	1.44
Potential *zakat* collection (4.3% of GDP) (US$ million)	165,890.1
Annual distribution per poor person/day (US$)	3.45

Source: Estimated using data from World Bank Databank at <https://databank.worldbank.org/data/source/world-development-indicators#>.

This amount is significant, given that the total official development assistance from Development Assistance Committee member countries of the Organisation for Economic Co-operation and Development (OECD) was US$146.6 billion in 2017 (OECD, 2018: 266).

Data on poverty are available on 25 OIC member countries. This information is used to examine the potential of *zakat* in reducing poverty levels. The statistics in Table 2.2, summarizing the GDP per capita and poverty in these countries, show wide variations. The average per capita GDP for the sample countries is US$3,382.90, with a minimum of US$395.90 and a maximum of US$14,936.40. Similarly, variations in the occurrence of poverty in different countries range from 0.0 per cent to 62.4 per cent of the population, with an average of 11.1 per cent and standard deviation of 19.7 per cent.

Table 2.3 shows that 25 countries had a population of 1,184.41 million in 2017, of which 131.68 million people live under US$1.90 per day. The estimates of the potential *zakat* collection are calculated on the average rates of narrow and broad opinions on *zakat*able items identified in Table 2.1. With a *zakat*

Table 2.4 *Zakat*, income levels, and poverty alleviation

Variables	Turkey	Mozambique
Total population (million)	80,745,020	29,668,834
Population living under US$1.90/day (million)	161,490	18,513,352
GDP (US$ billion)	851.5	12.65
GDP per capita (US$)	14,936.4	519.1
Zakat collection (1.8% of GDP) (US$ billion)	15.33	0.228
Number of poor who can be paid $1.90/day	22,102,217	328,218

Source: Estimated using data from World Bank Databank at <https://databank.worldbank. org/data/source/world-development-indicators#>.

rate of 1.8 per cent of GDP, the total *zakat* collections in these countries would be US$69.4 billion, and with a *zakat* rate of 4.3 per cent of GDP the total *zakat* collections would be US$165.9 billion. Taking a global view for all the sample countries, this translates to US$1.44 per poor person per day. Assuming that the average earnings of the poor is more than US$0.50 per day, the global *zakat* proceeds could potentially mitigate poverty in the sample 25 countries. If the broader *zakat* rate of 4.3 per cent were used, the US$3.45 could be distributed to each poor individual per day, which would move them above the poverty line.

The impact of *zakat* on poverty in each country, however, would depend on its specific income and poverty levels. In general, the higher the income and the lower the poverty level, the more likely that a country will be able to mitigate poverty with *zakat* funds. Table 2.4 shows examples of the impact of *zakat* in countries with different income and poverty levels. With a GDP of US$851.5 billion, Turkey's per capita income of US$14,936.40 is the highest in the sample, with 0.2 per cent of the population (or 161,490 persons) living under US$1.90 per day. With a *zakat* rate of 1.8 per cent of GDP, the total *zakat* collections would equal US$15.3 billion, which could be used to pay US$1.90 per day to 22.1 million people – much higher than the number of poor people living in the country. However, Mozambique has a GDP of US$12.65 billion and has one of the lowest per capita incomes in the sample at US$519.90, with a poverty rate of 62.4 per cent (or 18.5 million of the 29.7 million population). At a *zakat* rate of 1.8 per cent of GDP, the country would be able to collect US$227.6 million. The number of people to whom US$1.90/day could be distributed from the *zakat* proceeds would be 328,614 persons, which is only 1.8 per cent of the poor population.

The above examples indicate that, given the variations in national income and poverty, the impact of *zakat* would be maximized if it were implemented at a global level. Since *zakat* may not be enough to mitigate poverty in countries that have relatively low income levels and high incidences of poverty, transferring *zakat* proceeds from higher-income countries to countries with low income and higher poverty rates could play an important role in significantly decreasing overall poverty incidences. This is apparent in the examples shown in Table 2.4. When taken together, the total *zakat* collection is US$15.558 billion, which can provide US$1.90 per day to 22.43 million people. With the total number of poor people in both countries at 18.675 million, the *zakat* funds could provide US$1.90 to all the poor in both countries and still have an excess.

Waqf

There is a large number of *waqf* assets in most Muslim countries beyond religious institutions such as mosques and cemeteries. For example, the Islamic Research and Training Institute and Thomson Reuters report that Indonesia has 1,400 square kilometres of *waqf* land valued at US$60 billion (IRTI and TR, 2014). If these assets yield a return of 5 per cent per annum, US$3 billion could be generated for various socio-economic purposes. Considering the other forms of *waqf* assets, such as cash, the potential of utilizing *waqf* for effective social development schemes is huge but remains untapped. While no specific figures are available for the size of the *waqf* sector, Finterra estimates that the endowed land assets constitute over US$3 trillion.[6] With an estimated return of 5 per cent, this would translate to US$150 billion in returns that could be used for various socio-economic goals.

Most of the pool of public *waqf* assets in many Muslim countries however are dormant and are not being used for socio-economic development purposes. While the causes of the stagnancy of *waqf* have been attributed to various factors such as the loss of *waqf* deeds, mismanagement, corruption among the *mutawallis* (the managers or custodians of the *waqf*), and the sale and liquidation of *waqf* assets, a key element is the involvement and management of governments in the *waqf* sector. Although *waqf* is a non-government entity in essence, historically different states have attempted to take control of *waqf* assets. Cizacka (2009) maintains that Muslim rulers have attempted to confiscate *waqf* and transform them into state assets from as far back as the times of the Fatimid period in the tenth century CE. This reached a peak during the Ottoman rule of Sultan Mehmed II in the 1470s, when all arable land, including *waqf*, was brought under the ownership of the Sultanate. The trends continued under the modern states of the twentieth century with *waqf* being controlled by the states in most jurisdictions by either government ministries or public administrators of *waqf*.

While in most countries the *waqf* remains undeveloped, making little contribution to socio-economic development, a few have taken initiatives to revitalize the sector. Sudan created an autonomous Awqaf Corporation in 1986 that had an investment/construction department to develop existing *waqf* properties to make them more productive; it also initiated new *waqf* projects by soliciting fresh donations (Kahf, 2004). Similarly, the General Secretariat of Awqaf was established in Kuwait in 1993 to initiate specialized investment funds for different objectives and also to solicit donations. While the investment of the resources of all these funds is the responsibility of a specialized investment department, an autonomous managerial board for each fund takes decisions about how to use the revenue. The Secretariat also has an investment and construction/development department to renovate and develop existing *waqf* properties (Kahf, 2004). A few other countries, including Qatar and Bahrain, reorganized their *waqf* sector following Kuwait's model. There are other developments in regenerating the *waqf* sector in countries with Muslim minorities. For example, in the UK, Islamic Relief has established a *waqf* where supporters can donate *waqf* shares to be invested and where the returns are used in various social and developmental projects. Islamic Relief Waqf disbursed a total of £407,814 in 2018 to fund six projects globally (Islamic Relief, 2019).

Expanding the Islamic social sector: jurisprudential considerations

As indicated above, key factors in the development of both *zakat* and *waqf* are the jurisprudential rulings that limit the scope and operations of these institutions. The views of contemporary scholars that can help expand the utilization of these Islamic social finance instruments and increase their impact are presented below.

Zakat

Since the nature of the economy and wealth has changed significantly compared with the early era of Islam, there is a need to review the principles of *zakat* for modern times. There are diverse *Shari'ah* opinions and views on the application of *zakat* on some of the new items or entities. For example, there is no consensus on some types of income and wealth, such as company stocks and shares, economic enterprises either wholly or partly owned by the government, mineral resources including petroleum, income from service-sector businesses that have very little capital, and inventory investments (such as travel agencies, law firms, and real-estate agents). Views on applying *zakat* to legal entities such as corporations also vary (Kahf, 2004).

Al-Qaradawi (n.d.) provides a comprehensive analysis of the implications of *zakat* in modern economies and addresses some of the issues. To come up with *zakat* payable on different modern income sources and assets, he finds similarities with traditional *zakat*able items and then applies the same rates. For example, al-Qaradawi asserts that salaries and professional income should be subject to *zakat* on condition that the total annual income reaches *nisab* after deducting the amount needed for normal personal expenses. The applicable rate for *zakat* on salaries and income would be 2.5 per cent, which is similar to the rates on money and trade inventory. Using the same rates as on returns on agricultural land, al-Qaradawi maintains that rental income on properties and revenues from businesses, including agricultural and livestock industries, are *zakat*able at a rate of 5 per cent on the gross returns or 10 per cent on the net returns.[7]

Kahf (2004) discusses the opinions of the International *Shari'ah* Board of *Zakat* (ISBOZ) of the *Zakat* House of Kuwait, which developed a standard to identify recipients of *zakat*. This standard identifies the objectives of *zakat* as meeting basic human needs and providing adequate living standards, guided by the principles of social solidarity and mutual responsibility among all Muslims. Accordingly, *zakat* can be used to support full-time student expenses, as they could be considered poor and needy since they do not have sufficient means to finance their living and study needs. Similarly, ISBOZ ruled that medical care for the poor and needy, including the cost of surgery, within the country or overseas, can also be covered by *zakat*. *Zakat* can also be used to pay lawyers' fees for poor people trying to get their legitimate rights in court.

Several *Shari'ah* rulings also permit the establishment of various institutions for the poor and needy. For example, the Islamic Fiqh Academy permits investment of *zakat* funds in projects that will eventually be owned by the *zakat*'s beneficiaries, provided their basic and immediate needs are satisfied and there are guarantees against loss.[8] Similarly, the Fatwa Committee of the Ministry of Awqaf in Kuwait permits the spending of *zakat* funds on charitable organizations specializing in providing medical care to poor Muslims. ISBOZ also allows the use of *zakat* proceeds for the construction and operation of orphanages, hospitals, clinics, refugee centres, and rehabilitation centres that provide apprentice training for jobs such as sewing, embroidery, carpentry, word processing, car repair, and so on, as long as the beneficiaries are the poor and needy (Kahf, 2004). It also maintains that *zakat* can be used to purchase equipment or tools and provide stipends to students.

When *zakat* is used in investments, ISBOZ identifies the conditions that investments should comply with to satisfy the condition of *tamlik*, or transfer of ownership. First, the owner of the principal or equity in the project will be someone deserving of *zakat*. However, projects will be managed by either the government or a public agency. Second, the beneficiaries of the project should be those who deserve *zakat*. While non-deserving persons can also use the facilities they should pay fees that compensate for the price of the services, and the fees are then used to benefit the deserving beneficiaries. Finally, if the project is sold or liquidated, the proceeds are considered *zakat* funds and must be used accordingly (Kahf, 2004).

An accepted principle of *zakat* is that it should be disbursed in areas where it is collected. However if there are no deserving beneficiaries in the area of collection it is permitted to transfer *zakat* funds to other regions that have deserving beneficiaries or more dire needs.[9] The discussion below shows that the collection and distribution of *zakat* at the global level by transferring the surplus *zakat* from high-income countries to low-income countries can help solve the problem of poverty more effectively.

There are some views that *zakat* can even be used for microfinancing. Quoting scholars such as Muhammad Abu Zahrah, 'Abd al Rahman Hasan, and 'Abd al Wahhab Khallaf Muhammad Hamidullah, al-Qaradawi (n.d.: 53–4) argues that giving interest-free loans from *zakat* to those who are temporarily poor and will be able to return it after a while is permissible. The Fatwa Committee of the Ministry of Awqaf and Islamic Affairs in Kuwait also permits giving loans with *zakat* funds, provided there is adequate collateral and/or material or personal guarantees (Kahf, 2004).

Waqf

Although there are some claims that the *waqf* sector has stagnated due to its rigid rules, in principle the jurisprudence of *waqf* has greater flexibility compared with *zakat* since there are no clear guidelines in the *Qur'an* or *Sunnah*. This is confirmed by Zarqa (1947: 15), who asserts that in *waqf* nothing is outside the realm of *ijtihad* (rational thinking/deduction) except that the objective of *waqf* should be *birr* (righteousness/benevolence). Kahf (2004) recommends developing new rulings and ideas on *waqf* to enable the inclusion of a variety of forms and activities to serve society. His suggestions include *waqf* that could be temporary and based on newer types of assets or services, such as providing periodical publications to schools and libraries, and *waqf* of usufructs, such as free or discounted travel for disabled people and the elderly. This is also reflected in a recent OIC Fiqh Academy resolution that has acknowledged various novel features of *waqf*.[10] For example, while traditionally *waqf* were created with immovable assets and were considered perpetual, the Fiqh Academy resolution permits the creation of *waqf* with different types of assets, such as cash and shares, and also allows temporary *waqf*. However, a key feature of *waqf* that can make existing *waqf* inflexible is the supremacy of the founder's intentions as set out in the *waqf* deed, which governs different aspects of the endowment. Given this condition, to a large extent the rigidity of *waqf*'s role in development is determined by the specifications made by the founder of *waqf*, rather than by jurisprudence.

The OIC Fiqh Academy also allowed the investment of cash *waqf* through various *Shari'ah*-compliant means.[11] Cash investment *waqf* enables small donors to contribute and is currently found in countries such as Kuwait, Saudi Arabia, and Sudan (Kahf, 2004). For example, a ruling of the *Shari'ah* Board of the *Zakat* House in Kuwait established a 'continuous' *sadaqah* fund that accepts cash donations that are invested in various revenue-generating fixed assets.[12] The returns from these investments are spent on various charitable activities, including establishing hospitals and schools for poor Muslims, and giving stipends to poor students and orphans. Unlike the classical understanding that *waqf* property cannot be sold or exchanged, the fund is more flexible since it can alter the composition of its assets by selling existing assets and buying new ones.

Improving governance and management to enhance social impact

Moore (2003) identifies the building blocks of a successful non-profit organization as a clear social mission, legitimacy and support, and organizational capabilities. While a social mission defines the public value objective of organization, legitimacy and support relate to increasing credibility to enhance the trust of donors. The organizational capabilities reflect the ability to achieve the objectives efficiently and effectively. The operational issues that can enhance the impact of *zakat* and *waqf* are discussed below.

Zakat

As indicated, the current practice of *zakat* administration is carried out by government, non-profit organizations, and individuals themselves. However, as mentioned above, *zakat* is collected by the state in only a few countries and even in these countries the *zakat* collected is much less than the potential. Due to a lack of credible public *zakat* institutions, people opt to give *zakat* either personally or to non-profit organizations they can trust. Since the bulk of the *zakat* is distributed by individuals themselves, and this is done in an ad hoc manner and given out in small amounts, there is little impact on society. There is therefore a need to come up with efficient models of *zakat* governance and management to increase its social impact and effectiveness. Various aspects that can make a *zakat* organization efficient and effective are discussed below.

Governance and management
One option is to establish specialized organizations to manage *zakat* collection and disbursement. Learning from the governance and management practices of non-profit organizations, *zakat* organizations need to implement governance structures and management procedures that increase their organizational capabilities to fulfil their social objectives. This would require having an effective and supportive board of trustees that pays attention to strategic planning, human resources management, and ensures that the relevant systems, processes, and procedures are in place. The board should also provide oversight over the management of the organization to enhance the operational capacity of raising funds and using them efficiently to achieve their goals. Governance structures and management procedures need to cover various aspects, such as decision-making processes, operational implementation, cost efficiency, and organizational flexibility to promote innovation.

Increasing zakat *revenues*
Zakat revenue can be increased by introducing systems and processes related to marketing, building trust by providing information and making it easy for *zakat* payers to contribute. A key factor that determines the inflow of funds in non-profit organizations is their credibility and reputation. Factors that affect credibility and reputation include maintaining financial integrity by establishing internal control mechanisms to avoid misappropriation of funds, fraud, waste, and abuse of resources. Operational transparency can be ensured by having independent auditors prepare annual audits of the accounts and making these audits available to the public. Reporting on the positive impact on beneficiaries improves the reputation and goodwill of an institution, which makes it easier to increase both the number and size of *zakat* accounts.

Improving the impact of zakat

The value of a non-profit organization ultimately lies in the extent to which it can fulfil its social mission of having a positive impact on its beneficiaries. Since the main objective of *zakat* is to eliminate poverty there is a need to ensure effective disbursement of *zakat* funds to achieve socio-economic goals. This requires identifying beneficiaries, establishing efficient delivery systems, having access to volunteers, and networking and coordinating with other similar organizations to enhance impact. Assessing and reporting the impact of *zakat* disbursements on beneficiaries would add to an organization's credibility and have a positive influence on raising further funds. The implication of this is that the *zakat* system should be able to eliminate poverty by enabling the poor to be productive so that they can earn adequate income to satisfy their basic needs. This can be done not only by distributing cash to be used for consumption, but also by using the proceeds to provide the necessary skills and capital to engage in income-generating activities. *Zakat* can also be used to mitigate the dire conditions, meet the urgent needs, and save the lives of vulnerable people in conflicts zones. In this regard, the United Nations High Commissioner for Refugees (UNHCR) established the Refugee *Zakat* Fund in 2019 to rehabilitate refugees and internally displaced families, a situation that affects Muslim countries disproportionately.[13]

Box 2.1 *Zakat* administration in Federal Territory Kuala Lumpur (FTKL)

In Malaysia, the Islamic Religious Councils at the state level are responsible for religious matters including *zakat* and *waqf*. Accordingly, religious issues in the FTKL are administered by the Islamic Religious Council of the Federal Territory (IRCFT), while its operations relating to *zakat* and *waqf* are implemented by the Federal Territory Islamic Department. *Baitulmal* of the Federal Territory, one of the divisions of the Islamic Department, is responsible for enhancing the welfare of Muslims by solving social and economic problems. While IRCFT determines the overall strategy and policies of the disbursements, *Baitulmal* is responsible for implementing these policies, which includes dealing with *zakat*, charities, donations, income from *waqf*, wills, trusts, etc., and using these to enhance the welfare of recipients.

Collection and disbursement of *zakat* funds are separate functions in the FTKL. The IRCFT established a subsidiary corporation, Hartasici Private Limited, in 1991 to manage the *Zakat* Collection Centre (ZCC).[14] Set up with an initial capital of MYR 1.2 million (equivalent at the time to approximately US$441,000), the objective of establishing ZCC was to create an independent institution to collect *zakat* revenue efficiently by using modern technologies and methods. The IRCFT selects a board of directors to oversee ZCC's operations. The corporation replaced bureaucracy with a professional management team and introduced a proactive and customer-oriented approach to collecting *zakat*. Employing people from various backgrounds, ZCC operates like a corporate entity. For transparency, ZCC provides daily, weekly, monthly, and annual reports directly to the collectors and through the media. Using computerized systems, ZCC employs modern management techniques for its finance, audit, and reporting systems. In recognition of the quality of its management, the Federal Territory's ZCC received International Organization for Standardization (ISO) certifications in 1994 and 2015.

The revenue of ZCC is one-twelfth (or 8.3 per cent) of the total collections. Since the revenue of ZCC is directly linked to *zakat* collections, it has incentives to devise

---

(Continued)

Box 2.1 Continued

processes and procedures to increase the amount collected. This is done by providing various facilities for contributors to pay zakat and also by raising public awareness of zakat through a marketing strategy. Various aspects of zakat, including its assessment, are advertised on TV and radio, in newspapers and magazines, and through sermons in mosques and newsletters. There is a computerized online zakat assessment system that makes payment of zakat easier. Zakat can be paid through different channels, such as in cash, by cheque, via bank transfer, through salary deductions, and via internet and phone banking. Furthermore, special zakat collection counters are opened in shopping centres and malls during the month of Ramadan. In 2018, a total of MYR 651.2 million (approximately US$158.4 million) zakat was collected, up from MYR 615.2 million (US$149.7 million) in 2017 (PPZ, 2018).[15]

While zakat is collected by ZCC, Baitulmal is responsible for distributing the proceeds. The zakat funds disbursed by Baitulmal are categorized as direct and indirect. Direct disbursements are paid to the eight categories of beneficiaries stipulated in the Qur'an: monthly financial aid, emergency aid, medical aid, marriage aid, rental aid, natural hazard aid, aid for settling debt, and aid to travellers. Other forms of support to help beneficiaries include scholarships at various levels of education, entrepreneurial aid, taxi hire-purchase deposits, and house purchase deposits. One of the direct expenditure items is payments made to ZCC as administrator (amil) as fees for collecting zakat. In 2018, zakat was distributed to a total of 196,589 beneficiaries, up from 184,377 in 2017 (PPZ, 2018).

Indirect distribution takes place through financing and building projects for the beneficiaries. After direct payments are made to the beneficiaries, the surplus is put in a special fund. The accumulated amount from surpluses is spent on large projects such as hospitals, educational institutions, and orphanages, after an interval of a few years. From these funds, Baitulmal has built a vocational training institute, a shelter complex for widows, and an orphanage centre to serve the poor. While Baitulmal runs these institutions directly, it has also created companies that provide services to the poor at subsidized rates. These include a MYR 29 million (approximately US$7.1 million) Baitulmal professional institute that has 1,500 students enrolled and the 285-bed Pusrawi hospital, built at a cost of MYR 100 million (approximately US$24.3 million) to serve the poor at subsidized rates.

Waqf

There are three broad ways in which the waqf sector could be revived to increase its impact today: first, by increasing the productivity of existing waqf assets that have become stagnant and unproductive due to lack of development; second, by increasing new waqf that can promote socio-economic development; and finally, by improving the management of waqf to remedy mismanagement by mutawallis and governments.

Development of existing waqf

As mentioned above, there are huge numbers of waqf assets in the form of land and real-estate properties in most Muslim countries that were established over the centuries. However, after years of neglect and misman-agement, most of these assets are now dilapidated and unproductive, generating insignificant income. Since many waqf assets are located in prime locations there is huge potential to increase this revenue by investing in and developing these properties. For example, a study carried out on a sample of 30 *awqaf* (the plural of *waqf*) in India shows that an average investment of US$660,896 in these properties has the potential to yield an average rate of return of 19.2 per cent per annum and to increase their income by an average of US$126,547 per annum.[16]

With appropriate investment, many *waqf* properties could be developed and their income increased significantly. This could be done either through Islamic financial institutions or by raising funds from Islamic capital markets. An example of the former is the Awqaf Properties Investment Fund (APIF), which was established by the Islamic Development Bank in 2001 with the objective of investing in the commercial development of *waqf* properties. APIF raises funds from other stakeholders and uses these to invest in under-developed *waqf* lands and/or to renovate existing *waqf* buildings to transform them into productive income-generating assets. The investments increase the income of *waqf* assets which are used for beneficiaries.

An alternative to raising funds for the development of *waqf* properties is from the capital market, by issuing *sukuk* or a *Shari'ah*-compliant bond. One of the first cases of using *sukuk* to develop *waqf* assets was the Singapore $35 million (approximately US$25.7 million) raised by Majlis Ugama Islam Singapore (MUIS) to develop a *waqf* property on Bencoolen Street in Singapore (Abdul-Karim, 2010). The *waqf* constituted a mosque with adjacent shops, which were earning S$400 per month (approximately US$295) as rental income. The property was located in a central area with great commercial potential. A plan to develop the property as a mosque and a six-storey commercial complex required an investment of S$35 million, which was raised by issuing a *musharakah* (profit and loss sharing) *sukuk*. The result of the investment was that the monthly income of the *waqf* increased to S$20,000 per month (approximately US$14,700).

Establishing new waqf

Most of the new *waqf* being created now are mainly for religious purposes. There is a need to establish new *waqf* for socio-economic purposes and to create opportunities for people from all economic backgrounds to contribute to the development of the *waqf* sector. Historically real estate formed the basis of *waqf*, which only the relatively wealthy were able to donate. Since land has become scarce and expensive in modern times, few wealthy people are able to create new *waqf*. Furthermore, focusing on real-estate-based *waqf* deprives a large segment of the population from performing the religious act of *sadaqah jariyah* or ongoing charity. Revitalizing the institution of *waqf* and enabling a larger section of the population to contribute to *sadaqah jariyah* would require coming up with new and innovative models of *waqf*. Opportunities could be created for retail donors from all income groups to invest in existing *waqf* and create new assets to increase the sector's capacity to contribute to social objectives. This could be done by issuing *waqf* shares/certificates and the proceeds could be added to the corpus of the income-generating endowment.

Box 2.2 Waqaf Al-Nur

Johor Corporation (JCorp), the state investment entity for the state of Johor Malaysia, established a corporate *waqf*, Waqaf Al-Nur Corporation Berhad (WANCorp), in 2006 with an initial contribution of MYR 200 million (approximately US$48.6 million). WANCorp carries out various income-generating activities and the resulting income is spent on various socio-economic projects. It holds equity in several listed companies in the endowment and part of the income generated is in the form of dividends, which are reinvested in the endowment. The remaining income is distributed for social purposes. WANCorp has also established a network of Waqaf An-Nur clinics and hospitals to serve the healthcare needs of the poor.

One of WANCorp's social infrastructure initiatives is the Waqaf Saham Larkin Sentral (Larkin Sentral), which has a target to raise a total of MYR 85 million (US$20.68 million)[17] to finance the upgrade and refurbishment of the Larkin Sentral transportation terminal and the wet market at Johor Bahru. JCorp implemented a retail scheme to raise funds in the form of cash *waqf*. The funds raised were used to purchase land and construct multi-storey parking and shops targeting single mothers and lower-income groups. *Waqf* funds were raised by offering Larkin Sentral shares to individuals and institutions, who can purchase shares with a minimum value of MYR 100 (US$24.3 million) or 1,000 unit shares at MYR 0.10 per share (JCorp, 2017).

Improving waqf *management*

A key factor that has led to the stagnation of the *waqf* sector is the misman-agement of assets by both private *mutawallis* and the government. The revival of *waqf* would require the adoption of modern governance and management techniques. There is a need to develop capabilities at an organizational level that can enhance the professional management of *waqf* institutions. The services required to both manage existing *waqf* assets and help create new ones can be provided by corporate management entities. This is similar to trust services offered to different individuals and organizations to meet various current and future financial needs related to wealth and asset management in the conventional finance sector. Corporate trust services exist to protect wealth by planning for the future, protecting interests in accordance with rules and regulations, and ensuring returns and managing risks (Ahmed, 2018).

Similar to trust management services, a *waqf* management company can provide various services that could revive the *waqf* sector in two ways. First, *waqf* management companies can manage existing *waqf* that are currently managed by high net worth individuals and by charitable organizations or institutions. *Waqf* management services companies can ensure efficient and professional operations of *awqaf* institutions that would yield a good return. The company managing the *awqaf* properties would do so professionally and get a percentage of the income or assets managed as its fee. The benefits of using a corporate entity to manage *waqf* include expertise to ensure profes-sional and expert management of the assets, objectivity, and administration of the assets without any bias; and permanence, which ensures continuity in case of death or disability of the originator of the *waqf*.

Another type of service that the *waqf* management company can provide is to assist individuals to set up new *waqf*. Since one-third of properties can

---

Box 2.3 myWakaf

An innovative way in which individuals can contribute *sadaqah jariyah* is to establish a mechanism through which cash *waqf* of small denominations can be donated to be invested in developing new or existing *waqf* assets. A good example is the establishment of the crowd-funding platform myWakaf by six Islamic banks in Malaysia in 2017.[18] myWakaf liaises with different state Islamic religious councils (SIRCs) in the country to identify priority *waqf* projects for development. These projects are then listed on the myWakaf platform and opened up for crowd-based donations. Individuals and institutions can donate any amount through ATMs and other digital payments channels such as Internet Biller or JomPAY.

The operations are governed in a transparent and efficient manner under the guidance of the Joint Management Committee, which comprises key leaders from six banks. The Joint Management Committee manages the financing and development of the *waqf* properties in consultation with the respective SIRC partner. An example of a project financed through myWakaf is the renovation of the Mualaf Centre in Kelantan state, a transit centre for new converts to Islam who are rejected by their family, neighbours, and friends. The project provides converts with basic shelter and the means to become self-sufficient. While the goal was to raise MYR 369,632 (US$90,000) for the project, the campaign ended up raising over MYR 878,000 (over US$213,500), well over twice the requested amount.

---

be given away as charity under Islamic inheritance law, the corporate entity can provide advisory services that help with *waqf* formation, investment advice, and *waqf* accounts or funds. Thus, the *waqf* management company can help establish new *waqf* by providing services relating to wills and legacy management to individuals. The specific services provided by the company to individuals could include will writing and custodian services, creating trusts with movable or immovable assets, and legacy management whereby the organization is appointed as an administrator or executor for the estate and to implement the will after the demise of the client (Ahmed, 2018).

Conclusion

This chapter has shown that Islamic social finance has great potential for generating resources that can be used for poverty alleviation and development. It has also shown that the impact of Islamic social finance instruments on overall development depends on two broad factors.

First, there is a need to increase the mobilization of funds in order to have more resources that can be used for socio-economic development. A key factor that would determine the size of both *zakat* and *waqf* would be to expand their jurisprudential interpretations to increase both revenue and returns. This would require identifying various modern assets as *zakat*able wealth and introducing innovative instruments that would enable people from all income groups to contribute to cash *waqf*.

Second, the governance and management of Islamic social finance institutions must be efficient and effective to enhance their social impact. In this regard there is a need to introduce newer models of *zakat* institutions that are professionally managed and show the impact of *zakat* in a transparent way.

Using innovative products and services that can uplift the poorer sections of the population will improve the credibility of the institutions and raise funds from those who pay *zakat*. The *waqf* sector can be revived by investing in existing *waqf* assets to enhance their productive capacities, increasing the creation of new *waqf*, and improving the overall management of *waqf* assets.

Notes

1. While this is the traditional view of scholars, this perspective is not a strict requirement. During contemporary times, *zakat* is also disbursed by individuals and non-governmental organizations.
2. See <https://sunnah.com/riyadussaliheen/13/8>.
3. Since the corpus of *waqf* needs to be protected it cannot be used for cash transfers. However, the returns from cash *waqf* can be transferred to deserving beneficiaries.
4. Lessy (2013) reports that, in a survey carried out in Indonesia, 39 per cent of *zakat* payers preferred to give *zakat* to individuals due to a lack of trust in institutions. Similarly, Shaikh (2014) attributes the low collection of *zakat* by the government to a trust deficit and the weak administration of the *zakat* system.
5. The GDP of the OIC is calculated from data gathered from the World Bank Databank at <https://databank.worldbank.org/data/source/world-development-indicators#>.
6. See '*Waqf* chain: the social economic solutions', Finterra <https://www.finterra.org>.
7. See al-Qaradawi (n.d.: Volume 1, Chapters 8 and 9).
8. Islamic Fiqh Academy Resolution No. 15 (3/3), dated 13 Safar 1407 H (16 October 1986).
9. Resolutions of different *Shari'ah* bodies, such as IZBOS, Al Azhar, and the Permanent Committee for Research and Fatwa in Saudi Arabia *Zakat* House, support this view (Kahf, 2004).
10. Islamic Fiqh Academy Resolution No. 181 (19/7).
11. Islamic Fiqh Academy Resolution No. 140 (15/6).
12. The House of *Zakat* Fatwa No. 38/84 (1999), pp. 169–70.
13. See <https://zakat.unhcr.org/en/about-zakat>.
14. Information on the ZCC is taken from Alias (2004).
15. Exchange rate: US$1 = MYR 4.109 (as of 19 July 2019).
16. The study was carried out by the author to assess the scope and feasibility of investing in *waqf* assets commercially before Awqaf Properties Investment Fund (APIF) was established by the Islamic Development Bank.
17. Exchange rate: US$1 = MYR 4.109 as of 19 July 2019.
18. See <https://www.mywakaf.com.my/>.

References

Abdul-Karim, S. (2010) 'Contemporary *Shari'ah* structuring for the development and management of *waqf* assets in Singapore', DPhil thesis, Durham University <http://etheses.dur.ac.uk/778/>.

Ahmed, H. (2004) *Role of Zakat and Awqaf in Poverty Alleviation*, Islamic Research and Training Institute, Islamic Development Bank Group, Jeddah.

Ahmed, H. (2018) 'Integrating *waqf* and Islamic finance: creating synergies for social impact', paper presented at the Global Conference on *Awqaf* and Endowments: Case Studies and Analysis of Management, Performance, and Trust Law, Hamad bin Khalifa University, Doha, 4–6 December.

Alias, M.R. (2004) 'Efficient *zakat* collection system: the case of Malaysia', paper presented at the International Seminar on 'Nonbank Financial Institutions: Islamic Alternatives', Kuala Lumpur, 1–3 March.

al-Qaradawi, Y. (n.d.) *Fiqh al Zakah: A Comparative Study of Zakah, Regulations and Philosophy in Light of Quran and Sunnah*, Volume I, translated by M. Kahf, Scientific Publishing Centre, King Abdulaziz University, Jeddah.

al-Tahir, A. (1997) '*Zakah* proceeds and developments of society', in M. Kahf (ed.), *Economics of Zakah*, pp. 507–64, Book of Reading No. 2, Islamic Research and Training Institute, Islamic Development Bank, Jeddah.

Cizakca, M. (2002) 'Latest developments in the Western non-profit sector and the implications for Islamic *Awqaf*', in M. Iqbal (ed.), *Islamic Economic Institutions and the Elimination of Poverty*, Islamic Foundation, Leicester.

Cizakca, M. (2009) '*Waqf* and its role in the Islamic economic system', in M. Kahf, A. Brahimi, and K. Ahmad (eds), *Encyclopaedia of Islamic Economics*, Volume II, Yildiz A.S., Istanbul.

IRTI and TR (2014) *Islamic Social Finance Report 2014*, Islamic Research and Training Institute (IRTI) and Thomson Reuters (TR), Jeddah and Dubai.

Islamic Relief (2019) *Islamic Relief Worldwide Annual Report 2018*, Islamic Relief Worldwide, Birmingham <https://www.islamic-relief.org/annual-reports/> [accessed 8 May 2020].

JCorp (2017) *Annual Report 2016*, Johor Corporation (JCorp), Johor, Malaysia <http://www.jcorp.com.my/userfiles/file/JCorpAR17(Eng).pdf>.

Kahf, M. (n.d.) '*Waqf* and its sociopolitical aspects', mimeo <http://monzer.kahf.com/papers/english/WAQF_and_its_Sociopolitical_Aspects.pdf>.

Kahf, M. (1989) '*Zakat*: unresolved issues in the contemporary *Fiqh*', *Journal of Islamic Economics* 2 (1): 1–22.

Kahf, M. (1999) '*Zakah*: performance in theory and practice', paper presented at the International Conference on Islamic Economics Towards the Twenty-first Century, Kuala Lumpur, August.

Kahf, M. (2003) 'The role of *waqf* in improving the Ummah welfare', paper presented at the International Seminar on Waqf as a Private Legal Body, Islamic University of North Sumatra, Medan, Indonesia, 6–7 January.

Kahf, M. (2004) '*Shari'ah* and historical aspects of *zakat* and *awqaf*', background paper prepared for Islamic Research and Training Institute, Islamic Development Bank.

Kahf, M. (2009) '*Infaq* in the Islamic economic system', in M. Kahf, A. Brahimi, and K. Ahmad (eds), *Encyclopaedia of Islamic Economics*, Volume II, Yildiz A.S., Istanbul.

Lessy, Z. (2013) 'Philanthropic *zakat* for empowering Indonesia's poor: a qualitative study of recipient experiences at Rumah *Zakat*', PhD thesis, Indiana University <https://core.ac.uk/download/pdf/46957789.pdf>.

Moore, M.H. (2003) 'The public value scorecard: a rejoinder and an alternative to "Strategic Performance Measurement and Management in Nonprofit Organizations" by Robert Kaplan', Working Paper 18, Hauser Center for Nonprofit Organizations, Harvard University, Cambridge MA.

OECD (2018) *Development Co-operation Report 2018: Joining Forces to Leave No One Behind*, Organisation for Economic Cooperation and Development (OECD), Paris <https://www.oecd-ilibrary.org/docserver/dcr-2018-en.pdf?e xpires=1563543915&id=id&accname=guest&checksum=8DC14CF9B7442 89D1AC20F77C9881DF4> [accessed 9th May 2020].

PPZ (2018) *Ringkasan Laporan Zakat 2018* [Summary of *Zakat* Report 2018], PPZ-MAIWP, Kuala Lumpur.

Salama, A.A. (1982) 'Fiscal analysis of *zakat* with special reference to Saudi Arabia's experience in *zakah*', in M. Ariff (ed.), *Monetary and Fiscal Policy of Islam*, pp. 341–64, International Centre for Research in Islamic Economics, King Abdul Aziz University, Jeddah.

Schoenblum, J.A. (1999) 'The role of legal doctrine in the decline of the Islamic *waqf*: a comparison with the trust', *Vanderbilt Journal of Transnational Law* 32: 1191–227.

Shaikh, S.A. (2014) 'Welfare potential of *zakat*: an attempt to estimate economy-wide *zakat* collection in Pakistan', MPRA Paper 68752 <https://mpra.ub.uni-muenchen.de/68752/1/MPRA_paper_68752.pdf> [accessed 9th May 2020].

Siddiqi, M.N. (1991) 'The role of voluntary sector in Islam: a conceptual framework', in M. Ariff (ed.), *The Islamic Voluntary Sector in Southeast Asia*, pp. 6–30, Institute of Southeast Asian Studies, Singapore.

Singer, A. (2005) 'Serving up charity: the Ottoman public kitchen', *Journal of Interdisciplinary History* 25 (3): 481–500.

UN (2012) 'The future we want', resolution adopted by the General Assembly, 17 July <https://www.un.org/ga/search/view_doc.asp?symbol=A/RES/66/ 288&Lang=E> [accessed 8 May 2020].

UN (2017) 'Task of eradicating poverty must be met "with a sense of urgency," says deputy UN chief', UN News Centre <https://www.un.org/sustain-abledevelopment/blog/2017/05/task-of-eradicating-poverty-must-be-met-with-a-sense-of-urgency-says-deputy-un-chief/> [accessed 9th May 2020].

UNCTAD (2014) *World Investment Report 2014: Investing in the SDGs: An Action Plan*, United Nations Conference on Trade and Development (UNCTAD), Geneva.

World Bank (2014) *World Financial Development Report 2014: Financial Inclusion*, World Bank, Washington DC.

Zarqa, S.M. (1947) *Ahkam al Waqf* [*Rulings on Waqf*], University of Damascus Press, Damascus.

About the author

Habib Ahmed is Professor and Sharjah Chair in Islamic Law and Finance at Durham University Business School. Prior to joining Durham University in 2008 he worked at the National Commercial Bank and Islamic Development Bank Group (IRTI) in Saudi Arabia. He has taught at the University of Connecticut, National University of Singapore, and

University of Bahrain, and has also worked as Visiting Professor at Hamad bin Khalifa University, Qatar. Professor Ahmed has authored or edited more than 100 publications, including books, articles in international refereed journals, and other academic papers and monographs on various topics of Islamic law and finance, financial inclusion, and risk management and governance.

CHAPTER 3

The importance of spiritual capital within human development in Islamic teaching

Atallah FitzGibbon

The role of spirituality and organized religion in contributing to sustainable development has been a subject of increasing interest to development workers and sociologists. Quite apart from the merits of spiritual well-being in its own right, which for Muslims, like other religious communities, forms the cornerstone of their existence, there is now increased understanding of its crucial influence within other dimensions of human development. This chapter defines spiritual capital in the context of Islam and explores how, in its crucial relationship to revelation and social values, it influences and is pertinent to development workers in such areas as public health, education, social justice, and resilience.

Keywords: spiritual capital, *Maqasid*, *Shari'ah*, development, human dignity, Islam, Muslim, well-being

Introduction

Over recent decades a more subjective understanding of human development has prioritized the concept of well-being, enabling the overseas aid and development sector to break free from materialistic and secular definitions to a more universally accessible one. Religion and faith became recognized as valid contributions as researchers started evidencing faith communities' prioritization of their faith being, in some cases, of paramount importance to their life satisfaction and resilience (Abdel-Khalek, 2011; Masten, 2009). In the last 20 years academics have recognized religious and spiritual capital as a distinctive and dynamic component of the broader concept of social capital (Baker and Smith, 2010). In 2003, the Metanexus Institute conducted a substantial research programme into spiritual capital. Its working definition was 'the effects of religious and spiritual practices, beliefs, networks and institutions that have a measurable impact on individuals, communities and societies'.[1] Berger and Hefner more precisely defined it as 'the power, influence, knowledge and dispositions created by participation in a particular religious tradition' (Berger and Hefner, 2003: 03). In many ways these definitions summarize well the complexity and influence of spiritual capital which, certainly in the case of Islam, directly contributes to other forms of human,

http://dx.doi.org/10.3362/9781788530613.003

economic, and intellectual capital, including, as we shall explore, the notion of its transference to the next life.

While secular and atheist commentators may continue to use secularization theses to explain the persistent adherence to religion, others welcome the fact that human development now includes discovering and celebrating all possibilities of humanness, including our capacity to know and experience the Divine. Narayan et al. (2000) argue that many people are not simply interested in seeking the means to improve their quality of life on a material level, but are also interested in the end itself, which is feeling psychologically well. An important component of this, he argues, is believing in a God and being connected to one's community through shared rituals and celebrations. In effect, spirituality is central to many of the daily decisions people in the 'global South' make about their own and their community's development. With the increasing emphasis on development studies within research centres in the Muslim world, several paradigms have been presented that emphasize spirituality to differing degrees as a critical component of multidimensional models, affecting such areas as social values, activism, and self-development (Dariah, 2016). Within Islamic teaching, the system of ethics that underpins revealed law identifies the protection of religion and faith as the first priority of human development (Chapra, 2008). This reflects the importance placed on worship in the fulfilment of life's meaning and of human purpose, as well as the importance of an eternal afterlife. 'And I did not create the jinn or mankind except to worship Me' (Qur'an, 51: 56). For those who discover the human heart's capacity to experience and be cognisant of the presence of the Divine, all other meanings are rendered subservient.

This chapter provides the reader with an understanding of why Islam, and religion more widely, emphasizes spirituality. We define this in development terminology as 'spiritual capital', which for many Muslims is the most important cornerstone of human development. It explains the huge social investment in such areas as Qur'anic education, public and private acts of redistribution of wealth, provision of social services by faith-based organizations (FBOs), public and private worship, and ethical finance. Importantly, spiritual capital provides the bedrock of social solidarity and the moral economy, through the fulfilment of rights, obligations, and understandings of human equality and accountability. The growth of the role of the state in northern Europe to encompass collective responsibility for the comprehensive provision of social care, while an admirable culmination of good governance, to a considerable extent has shifted the social contract away from the individual duty to exercise human responsibility, and as a result has had an impact on the moral economy. Spirituality, like all human faculties, withers if it is not exercised. In many societies today, people's meaning and purpose are increasingly defined and measured by their economic and social function and as consumers of goods and services. The inevitable and inherent deficits in equity and dissatisfaction that this entails can lead to a sense of obsolescence and a narrowing experience of existence.

Interestingly, in a recent chapter entitled 'The changing soul of Europe' (Pace, 2019), following a period in Europe in which religion and spirituality were ideologically repressed, Enzo Pace charts their increasing practice and influence, and a shift in the nature of secularism and the role of religion in a 'post-secular' Europe. Post-secularism is a concept underpinned both by religious communities' increasing competition for expression and influence within the public sphere, and also by an increasing willingness by government at different levels to be inclusive of their contribution to society, for example in the provision of social services, other forms of social capital, and influence (Baker and Smith, 2010). Pace found that many people in Europe, following this recent period of repression, now seem more willing to admit to a need for spiritual satisfaction and to find ways of life and communities of practice to fulfil this need. Very often this is outside formal religion and in more individualistic expressions, but it is coupled with a greater acceptance of the value and validity of religion in other communities. Secularization theses such as those of Berger, Marx, and Weber state that improvements in rationality and science, rising living standards, and increased social diversity would lead to developed societies dispensing with religion and replacing its function to explain existence and provide solace. Their argument that this would occur, together with the collapse of the influence of broad social affirmation, which they claim contributes to societies' maintenance of religious traditions, now seems partially discredited. Thomas Luckmann argued that religion has become more privatized and thereby 'invisible' (Luckmann, 1967). However, even this trend is challenged by the changing and increasingly visible role of organized religion within European society, particularly among new and Eastern religions, but also in indigenous religious communities.

The alienation of religion and religious communities from development practice was first driven by colonial and postcolonial governments, and then compounded by secular development agencies. It has become widely recognized that this has led, in many countries, to a vacuum of shared values in the public space and a failure for large groups to identify with the newly formed states created in the process of colonial withdrawal. In joint research carried out in 2016 into the faith sensitivity of their programmes, Islamic Relief and the Lutheran World Federation found that the humanitarian values of impartiality and neutrality[2] so beloved by the aid sector are commonly used by aid workers to justify the exclusion of and lack of engagement with faith-based actors, although these are arguably the most influential forces within many societies. This exclusion can contribute to a failure to harmonize values and bring society together around a common meaning and interpretation of events.

However, over the last 15 years there has been an increase in confidence and assertion in faith-inspired NGOs seeking to build social change based on faith values and teaching, and a growth in the influential mediating role that faith leaders can represent when included. This is being matched by bilateral and multilateral aid actors' recognition of the reach, influence, long-term presence, and sustainable resources that the participation of faith communities can provide. The United Nations (UN) Environment Programme's 'Faith for Earth' initiative, launched in 2017, assertively states its support to mobilize faith communities to protect the environment:

> The networks of faith-based organizations and faith leaders cross continents and political boundaries, making it a viable and practical means to achieve sustainable development. *Tapping into the spiritual wealth of people and their beliefs* accelerates people's engagement and the organizational drive to contribute.[3]

Agencies such as the UN High Commission for Refugees (UNHCR) have started to realize the important distinction between a service-led approach, which agencies provide, and a community-based response, which local faith-based actors can contribute towards. Crucially, the latter includes elements of acceptance, accompaniment, sharing, and protection to complement the delivery of services.

This is particularly helpful when working in many Muslim communities, where religion influences people's understanding and behaviour in all institutions and social practices, including their attitudes to newcomers and people of other faiths.

An important understanding of spiritual capital is in its relation to law and cultural practice. If one considers an act or practice as the body and the intention as its spirit, then one can understand that, when religious cultures lose connection or misunderstand the original purpose of their law, their practice can become malign and destructive. This process of revitalizing and addressing the meaning or intention behind law and social practice emerging from revelation is vital for development workers and activists tackling areas such as harmful social practices. Such practices may be, at least in part, the result of confused and misunderstood interpretations of religious teaching, manifest in phenomena such as discrimination, oppression, social exclusion, female genital mutilation (FGM), early/forced marriage, and domestic violence. Just as the body dies when the spirit leaves it, so too does social practice within religious communities ossify when it becomes disconnected from its original benevolent intention. Understanding this original meaning or intention is an important component of spiritual capital and a lived faith, and with it religions in their pure and original form can continue to be a liberating force from human oppression and a driver of human development. Over the last 12 years, this connection between the spiritual and the temporal has increasingly led faith-based NGOs such as World Vision, Tearfund, and Islamic Relief to use ways of working and tools such as Channels of Hope, which empower faith leaders as vital interlocutors within their communities, ensuring that issues are addressed within communities' own language of meaning. We examine later in this chapter how Islamic jurisprudence developed to ensure that this role is maintained dynamically.

As a development practitioner, one can argue for the importance of understanding how spiritual capital is stored and utilized in communities and cultures – irrespective of the merits of any particular religion or no religion – and how it feeds and influences more conventional values and assets that constitute human, social, and financial capital. Spirituality is not exclusive to religious people: it is present and manifests in all people and groups. It ebbs and flows and, in the absence of organized religion, takes other forms of expression, always inspiring us and very often triumphing in the darkest of moments.

There are a number of questions raised by religious belief and practice and their relationship to human development. How are the other dimensions of human development affected by collective and individual religious practice and enhanced spirituality, or a lack thereof? How should this affect our approach to development programming? How can we tangibly describe, measure, and evidence the presence of spiritual capital, as we do with other assets? To understand the answer to these questions from an Islamic perspective, we must first define what we mean by the spirit and spirituality.

The spirit

In the *Qur'an* the spirit, or *'ruh'*, is referred to in several contexts. As narrated in the *Qur'an*, human life is created by the spirit being breathed into the foetus (*Qur'an*, 38: 72) and death is brought on by its departure. The word 'spirit' is used in connection with angels on several occasions: for example, the Angel Gabriel is described as the Holy Spirit (*Ruh'ul Qudoos*). Revelation is also described as 'spirit' coming from the divine presence to human messengers, and, through its recitation, into people's hearts.

In Qur'anic Arabic – which, like its cousin, Hebrew, is a language of revelation – much can be deduced from the root meanings of words. Derivative meanings of the root *'ruh'* include 'cool delightful breeze', 'to be lively or active', 'to feel joy', 'to feel solace and relief', 'to put forth leaves', 'to smell a sweet scent', 'to feel at ease', 'life breath', 'vital principle', and 'universal life energy' (Bewley, 2014).

At birth, the spirit forms part of the human soul, or *'nafs'* in Arabic. The word *nafs* is also used to describe self-identity and, in some verses of the *Qur'an*, is interpreted as referring to the heart. All this points to the complexity of the human soul, which contains both angelic and spiritual influence from the spirit's presence in the body, as well as the physical desires and appetites of the flesh. The soul is generally not predetermined predominantly by genetic disposition in its nature but is transformed and moulded according to upbringing, education, and social influence (Bewley, 2014). A well-nurtured soul displays gratitude, humility, kindness, and generosity – in fact, all that we associate with humanness and humanitarian characteristics. The *Qur'an* describes souls as falling into three main categories. The *'nafs ul mutma'inna'* is the translucent soul at peace and in compliance with its Lord. The *'nafs ul Lawama'* is the self-accusing soul that wavers between good and evil. And the '*nafs ul amara bi su*' is the undisciplined soul that has given reign to the lower animalistic desires and appetites and is often self-serving, arrogant, and selfish. In the last two categories, as a result of evil acts and diseases of the soul such as pride, envy, and greed, the spirit will often remain dormant, inaccessible, and unable to emerge and be known. However, with the disciplining of the soul and deeper self-knowledge, it becomes translucent and communicative of its unlimited treasures.

The important transformative organ that determines the soul's nature is the human heart. In Islam this forms the most important centre of consciousness in understanding the unseen world of spiritual meaning, while the intellect located in the brain is essentially computative, external-facing, and rational. Both organs working together in harmony ensure that our decision making and our behaviour are balanced, rooted in a deeper consciousness of ourselves, of the consequences of our actions, and of the true nature of reality. Modern science has evidenced this two-way internal conversation within the self and has also identified neurons located in the heart that enable this (Lacey and Lacey, 1978).

Referring to the function of the spirit with regard to the human being, the great thirteenth-century scholar and teacher Shaykh Muhyideen Ibn Arabi said: 'It is applied to what casts knowledge of the Unseen to the heart in a particular aspect' (Bewley, 2014). This sums up the link between the spirit and the soul and the body; it is the vital source code of life itself – the means of experiencing the presence of God. The great twentieth-century North African scholar Shaykh Muhammed Ibn al Habib wrote in his revered *Diwan* (poetry anthology): 'My *ruh* [spirit] speaks to me and says, "My reality is the light of God, so do not see other-than-Him"' (Ibn al Habib, 1980: 129).

The *Qur'an* unambiguously declares: 'We have bestowed dignity on the progeny of Adam ... and conferred on them special favours, above a great part of Our creation' (*Qur'an*, 17: 70). Muslims believe that humankind possesses this inherent dignity because God has chosen to give us a special place and rank among other creations as His khalif (custodian or steward) of creation. 'It is He who has made you His vicegerents of the Earth' (*Qur'an*, 6: 165).

Muslims believe that life occurs as a result of God breathing His spirit into us and that through it, God manifests many of His noble attributes in human beings. Discovering this Adamic self-form that is at the root of our human dignity and deepening our knowledge of it define our human development in a very real way (Aminu-Kano and FitzGibbon, 2014). The concept of human dignity being rooted in the divine manifestation within humans is also present in the other Abrahamic religions, often referred to in Christianity in relation to humankind being created in the 'image of God' (Genesis, 1: 27). While this is too anthropomorphic a statement for most Muslims, both understandings share a similar meaning and theology.

The relationship between religion and faith and other development priorities within the multidimensional framework defined by Islamic legal ethics is critical. It provides an understanding of why spiritual capital underpins not just the nature of knowledge and worship of the Divine, but also the protection of, and benefit to, health, education, wealth, social protection, and justice. Indeed, material and social development is viewed by Muslims as part of what the Divine intended to promote through revelation and prophetic guidance. Understanding this symbiotic relationship between the material and the spiritual is vital and forms the main theme of this chapter.

Before exploring this important question, let us first look at how Islamic jurisprudence has developed in order to define this multidimensional framework that provides Muslims with an extraordinary insight into how they should prioritize their development needs.

Maqasid al-Shari'ah: the purpose and priorities of divine law

The two basic sources of guidance for Muslims are the revelation of the *Qur'an* and the *Sunnah* (life practice of the Prophet Muhammad (Peace Be Upon Him)). This guidance was sent in the seventh century AD to a community in a particular cultural, economic, climatic, and social context, but was, as Muslims believe, intended as guidance for all mankind until the end of time. It contains within it moral and ethical guidance in almost all areas of human existence. As the Muslim community expanded out of Arabia into southern Europe, Africa, and central Asia, it became necessary for scholars to interpret the divine guidance in the light of new situations, cultures, scientific discoveries, and environments.

To enable Muslim scholarship and jurisprudence to remain meaningful, relevant, and responsive to these changing needs, scholars, led by the great twelfth-century religious revivalist Imam Ghazali and followed by Imam Shatibi (fourteenth century AD) in Spain and others, began the process of defining what is the divine intent (*maqsad*) of revelation and religion – in other words, the spirit or intention that gives life and meaning to the law. This enabled interpretation of the law to adapt, where necessary, and still remain linked to the mercy, compassion, and beneficial intent of God's revelation. It also enabled Muslims to differentiate and mediate between culture and religion. For instance, the definition of adulthood and the marriageable age in sixth-century Arabia, with the social conditions and life expectancy of that time, may not be appropriate to another people in another time. It is therefore important that Muslim scholars and people understand that law and custom can be adapted in many cases in order to remain within the original purpose of the divine guidance.

In relation to our discussion, spiritual capital can therefore be described as the understanding of, and connection to, the intent or 'spirit' of revelation and the knowledge of God that influences the correct forms of behaviour and social practice. This was summed up by Imam Malik (eighth century AD), one of the greatest Muslim scholars in history: 'He who takes the spiritual reality [*haqiqah*] without the revealed law [*Shari'ah*] has left this religion, but he who takes the revealed law without its spiritual reality has become corrupted' (Keller, 1991: 862).

Understanding the symbiosis of both of these components enables the 'maslaha' of the community – its practical interests and benefit – to be respected and promoted. For instance, one of the fundamental Islamic legal principles is to benefit health. Therefore, considering the considerable evidence of the harmful health and social effects of early marriage to women, girls, and society in general, many countries practising Islamic family law, such as Morocco, Pakistan, and the United Arab Emirates, have outlawed marriage below the age of 18. On a similar basis, the concept of *maslaha* has enabled scholars to decide, based on the intent of the law banning alcohol, that other intoxicants should also be avoided by Muslims. If the intent of the law is not understood or appreciated, respect for the law can quickly die. General levels of public education on the impact of particular behaviours as well as basic faith literacy surrounding such behaviours are therefore critical to achieving behavioural change in Muslim communities. This explains the priority of intellect (*'aql*) and knowledge within the *Maqasid* (plural of *maqsad*) ethical framework underpinning religious law, as a critical component of spiritual capital and human dignity. Returning to the practical examples of protection and human rights work mentioned earlier, we can therefore make a direct connection between spiritual capital, as understanding and motivation, and support for the achievement of human rights.

The underlying ethics informing Islamic law have been termed the *Maqasid*, or the objectives or purpose of divine law. *Maqasid* are important for our discussion here, not principally because they enable adaptation to development needs, but because they provide us with an indication of what the Divine wants for humankind: His prioritization of our development through particular guidance, and the understanding that all of *Shari'ah* is for the protection of mankind and our spiritual and physical state and not to unnecessarily prevent benefit or provide unhelpful obstacles. This process of reconciling social practice with religious ethics is relevant to many contemporary development practitioners' ways of working in traditional Muslim communities. The Islamic Foundation for Ecology and Environmental Science (IFEES) (Khalid and Thani, 2007) successfully spearheaded its model of behavioural change in environmental protection by engaging fishing communities on Pemba Island, Zanzibar on theological imperatives and environmental teachings from the *Qur'an*. Islamic Relief and World Vision jointly developed the Channels of Hope toolkit for working with Muslim religious and traditional leaders on harmful social practices relating to a range of issues, including FGM, child protection, maternal health, and attitudes towards HIV/AIDS sufferers, enabling them to develop a faith-sensitive approach to mobilizing social change.

The *Maqasid*, or objectives of *Shari'ah*, were categorized under five headings (see Figure 3.1) in the Middle Ages and have been used for centuries by Muslims worldwide to decide how their faith guides them. While more recent and even

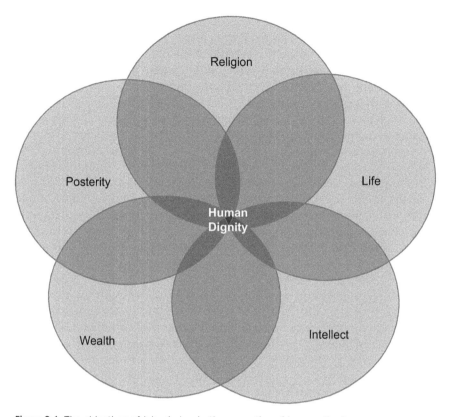

Figure 3.1 The objectives of Islamic law in the promotion of human dignity

contemporary scholars have suggested additions, there remains a consensus on these five original core objectives. Through this multidimensional under-standing of God's purpose in sending revelation to the human race, we can deduce how poverty and development might be conceptualized beyond a very simplistic material definition.

The emphasis on preserving spiritual life

As we can see from the diagram of the *Maqasid al-Shari'ah* (Figure 3.1), paramount importance is given to the uppermost priority entitled '*Deen*'. This is often translated as religion, but is more specifically understood as the life transaction that binds us to our Creator.

Earthly life for Muslims is conceptualized as a short journey in preparation for the eternal life to come. The Prophet Muhammad (PBUH) described the believer's attitude to life as one of a traveller who stops briefly under a tree, knowing that they must move on. The priority above all else is to meet their Creator with a sound heart, full of faith and love, and at peace with their Lord. Central to this is a healthy account of our deeds and their consequences, which will be in their favour at the great questioning in the next life (*yawm ul hisab*). Spiritual capital can be described as several things, but perhaps of most importance to Muslims is this sense of their good actions as the wealth or '*hisab*' (account) of the soul, which is ultimately more meaningful and useful to them than any worldly wealth. In this sense, Muslims believe that humans only really receive the value of their money when they give it away or use it to their community's benefit. Every action has both a worldly and a spiritual consequence. The two are reciprocal but it is the spiritual capital that represents ultimate value. The famous saying about the value of wealth – 'You can't take it with you' – is not true; it can be transferred to spiritual capital, where it remains the property of the soul. 'He knoweth that which each soul earneth' (*Qur'an*, 13: 42). This is one of the primary motivations of the huge traditional concentration on charitable giving and endowment in Islam. It is believed that one's gifts bring repeated good actions and benefit to the soul beyond death. Therefore for Muslims, in a very real sense development is a vision of redemptive transformation, with the other objectives of divine law ultimately serving the spiritual one.

For humanitarian and development agencies there is now an increasing recognition of the contribution of spiritual capital to resilience, defined as individuals' and families' ability to achieve emotional adjustment and social functioning at times of crisis: 'good adaptation in a context of risk'. People of faith often find enormous comfort and tangible relief from trauma and loss in prayer and in places of worship. Faith enables patience and the unburdening of stress when facing both short- and long-term challenges. More specifically in an Islamic context, coming to terms with and patient acceptance of what they perceive as God's decree promises a divine reward and atonement for wrong actions. Belief in the next life and in the ultimate and merciful justice of the Divine is central to Muslims' acceptance and closure following the trauma of loss and suffering. For instance, those believers who suffer sudden traumatic death, such as drowning, plague, or being burnt alive, are believed to have all their sins expiated. In faith-sensitive guidelines developed in 2016 for improved management of mental health and psychosocial provision in humanitarian settings, Ager et al. (2018) recommended the integration of faith-based support and institutions throughout the programme cycle. Faith-based support can range from access to faith leaders for pastoral support, to provision of prayer space for individual and communal prayers, to access to books of scripture, and to proper burial arrangements.

Faith teaching and leadership have also been shown to be effective in resolving conflict and addressing prejudice, particularly when fostering forgiveness and reconciliation (Kadayifci-Orellana et al., 2014). Religion more generally, but Islam specifically, references the equality of all before God, thus contributing to the breaking down of cultural traditions of ethnic, tribal, and social hierarchies and at least preventing the open legitimation of racism and prejudice.

Preservation of life itself

The second objective (*maqsad*) of divine law is respect for the sanctity of life and the inherent recognition of life and health as gifts from God, only to be taken under very strict circumstances. One of God's attributes is that He is The Living (*Al Hayy*) and the life-giver. This forms the basis of Muslims' respect for life, the right to life, and humanitarian support and security. Honour, dignity, public health, and self-respect, as well as social equality, are also included in this objective, along with freedom from fear, shame, and social exclusion. Life, of both animals and humans, may be taken only under very strict conditions.

The obligation to protect life and the right to life form the basis of Islam's enormous humanitarian tradition, which takes the form of welfare institutions including endowments (*awqaf*) for the provision of hospitals, schools, shelter, and fresh food and water, *Zakat* agencies, and charity at all levels. The humanitarian motivation is, among other things, a recognition of one's divinely ordained responsibility as a human being and as a *custodian* of wealth (*Mustakhlafeen fih*), and it forms a critical component of spiritual capital. From an Islamic perspective, wealth and capabilities of any kind that we possess are not strictly ours; they belong to those who have rights over them, including family members, neighbours, and the needy. In the next life we will have to account for how we managed them. The *Qur'an* refers to this in several verses: 'And those in whose wealth is a recognized right; for the needy who asks and those who are deprived' (*Qur'an*, 70: 24–5).

Understanding the rights of the poor and the suffering and their relationship to God is well summed up in the following extract from a famous *hadith*:

> Allah (mighty and sublime be He) will say on the Day of Resurrection: O son of Adam, I fell ill and you visited Me not. He will say: O Lord, and how should I visit You when You are the Lord of the worlds? He will say: Did you not know that My servant So-and-so had fallen ill and you visited him not? Did you not know that had you visited him you would have found Me with him? (Muslim, Book 45, *Hadith* 54)

We can infer from this *hadith* that God is manifest through His creation and manifests His rights through the rights of created beings. This understanding forms an important distinction in Islamic understanding of human rights, which we will explore later.

The contribution of religion and spiritual capital to human health is a subject of increasing interest. In 2015, the leading British journal for health professionals, *The Lancet*, devoted a whole edition to this subject, referencing and acknowledging the huge contribution of faith and FBOs to the provision of healthcare in many countries and their contribution to traditional services to the sick, as well as to supporting healthy behaviours and lifestyles. Some researchers have identified a clear relationship between those who report a closer connection to God and both mental and physical health, including lower rates of depression, higher self-esteem, less loneliness, greater relational maturity, greater psychological competence, greater well-being, hope, and optimism, as well as more purpose and meaning in life and higher levels of social support (Abdel-Khalek, 2017).

Furthermore, Hill and Hood Jr (1999) and Koenig (1997) state that, in addition to the impacts on mental health mentioned above, religious beliefs and practices are associated with a wide range of improved physical health indicators as well as better health behaviours. Clearly, there are also controversies, such as abortion and end-of-life decisions in relation to medical ethics, and where harmful cultural norms and stigma have become embedded in religious traditions, as with early marriage.

Intellectual development

The third objective of divine law is the preservation and development of the intellect, which relates to the need for education, both from a spiritual perspective and for the pursuit of worldly knowledge and the means to earn a livelihood to maintain one's dignity. Knowledge of religion and of the Divine is defined as the crown of all knowledge in Islamic tradition. There remains no greater demonstration of this than the prioritization among Muslims of religious instruction over paying for other forms of education. Another manifestation of spiritual capital is the massive investment in the institutions of religious sciences, which are primarily there to build the wider sense of human development that we have discussed.

In the secular educational environment found in some parts of the postcolonial Muslim world, where religion is taught in separate institutions, this can unfortunately lead to an unhelpful disconnection of religion from other subjects. Traditionally, both spiritual and temporal education would have otherwise coexisted and enhanced each other in the same space as they traditionally did, and as they still do in countries such as Morocco. Evidence of this influence can be found in the huge growth in science that Muslim universities inspired in the Middle Ages. This was driven in part by the scientific integrity of the Qur'an, with its impeccable accuracy in describing ecological, geological, and cosmic processes, revealed well before these were established by scientists. This has helped retain respect for Qur'anic education and its pertinence to development more generally among Muslims and has contributed to staving off the European 'Enlightenment' process, which contributed to European secularism.

Equally important is the notion that intellect ('aql) must coexist with spiritual intuition (hads and firāsah), providing correct meaning and interpretation of both the outer and inner worlds.

> These [intuitive] terms imply a 'participation' in a knowledge that is not simply rational but not opposed to the intellectual as the term is understood in its traditional sense. Another set of terms more prevalent

in texts of philosophy, theology, and Sufism are *dhawq* [taste], *ishrāq* [illumination], *mukāshafah* [unveiling], *basīrah* [inner sight], *nazar* [in this context, meaning 'a glance that conveys a spiritual force'] and *badīhah* [intuition]. These terms are all related to the direct vision and participation in the knowledge of the truth, in contrast to indirect knowledge upon which all reasoning is based. This contrast is also emphasized in the usage of the term *al-'ilm al-hudūrī* or 'presential knowledge' as opposed to *al-ilm al-husūlī*, or 'attained knowledge', but these terms refer to the difference between intuition as a form of a knowledge based upon immediate experience and ratiocination as indirect knowledge based upon mental concepts. (Nasr, 1979)

The *Qur'an* refers consistently to those who possess divinely inspired or 'presential' understanding as the '*Ulul albaab*'. The word '*albaab*' is the plural of the noun '*lub*', describing the innermost core or 'eye' of the heart, through which those who have purified their hearts gain immersion in spiritual illumination and understanding, emanating from revelation and from God's timeless presence. Through this is gained an enlightened interpretation of events and issues. 'He gives wisdom to whom He wills, and whoever has been given wisdom has certainly been given much good. And none will pay heed except those of understanding [*Ulul albaab*]' (*Qur'an*, 2: 269).

Here we see another aspect of spiritual capital – spiritually illuminated understanding, ensuring that one's faith is a lived experience emanating from the heart. In Islamic understanding, faith (*iman*) and worship (*ibadah*) should not be blind; they should be informed and enriched by intuition and a state of certainty (*yaqin*). Illuminated faith is actually one of our faculties that remains dormant and undeveloped unless the heart is stimulated and brought to life. Most people will profess some level of spiritual experience, sometimes prompted by heightened emotion – for example, through experiences such as listening to music, experiencing feelings of love, or seeing the beauty of nature or a manifestation of justice. They sense an underlying presence or depth of meaning, sometimes in a fleeting, inspirational, and perhaps subconscious way. Muslims believe that God is manifest at all times but it is our hearts that are blind to His presence. 'Have they not travelled in the land and have they not hearts wherewith to feel and ears wherewith to hear, for indeed it is not the eyes that are blind but the hearts which are in the breasts' (*Qur'an*, 22: 46).

The protection of wealth

The fourth objective of divine law is preserving and generating wealth, primarily to maintain human dignity and to enjoy the bounty that God has given us. Wealth is the lifeblood of a community and must flow, circulate, and increase fairly among all groups to ensure general welfare. This is no doubt the reason for the emphasis placed on it by financial legal ethics and the more general moral guidance given in Islamic revelation and jurisprudence.

Worship, on one level, is defined as the enjoyment of all that God has provided within the parameters of righteous action and with the remembrance of God, while ensuring that the rights of humanity and creation are provided for. Interestingly, in Islamic tradition economics and development were never considered a science in their own right but were dealt with under various subjects such as law, statecraft, and social behaviour. The reason for this was the difficulty in separating material development from non-economic issues in a political economy where human development was dominated by the spiritual imperative (Zaman and Asutay, 2009).

The attitude and laws relating to wealth however, are based on the benefit and harm it can confer. At one end of the spectrum, the Prophet Muhammad (PBUH) described extreme poverty (*fakhr*) as detrimental to faith because it drives people to desperate acts and indignity. He advocated the provision of means to the poor. The *Qur'an*, while advocating the appreciation and enjoyment of the providence of God with humility and gratitude, warned that love of wealth and possessions and unbridled greed are dangerous distractions for the believer and detrimental to one's relationship with the Divine. 'O you who have attained to faith! Let not your worldly goods or your children make you oblivious of the remembrance of God: for if any behave thus – it is they, they who are the losers!' (*Qur'an*, 63: 9–11); 'Wealth and children are an adornment of this world's life: but good deeds, the fruit whereof endures forever, are of far greater merit in thy Sustainer's sight, and a far better source of hope' (*Qur'an*, 18: 46).

Wealth and resources are considered to be the dominion of and a trust from God, over which humans have been given custodianship (*mustakhlafina fi*) so that they can meet the needs and obligations of their family, the human community in general, the Earth, and wider communities of beings. The Prophet Muhammad's (PBUH) own example was to practise what has been called the 'charity of excess': to take from his wealth what was required for the dignity of his family and to distribute the remainder. He taught that: 'He is not a believer who goes to bed with a full stomach while his neighbour is hungry' (Bukhari, *Al-Adab al-Mufrad*, Book 6, *Hadith* 12). Muslims today often forget that their Prophet chose a path of asceticism. Although he never insisted on it for his companions, he lived very simply, sleeping on a straw mat on the floor, repairing his clothes when worn out, and eating little. This was despite the considerable power and wealth that the Muslim community possessed in the latter part of his life. Today, when rising consumption is seen as critical to economic growth and development status, Muslims must reflect on this often overlooked life practice (*Sunnah*).

Abu al-Darda said: 'I heard the Messenger of Allah (PBUH) say, "Seek me among the poor and weak. Truly, you are given success and provided for on account of the poor and weak among you"' (Tirmidhi, Book 23, *Hadith* 33). The Prophet Muhammad (PBUH) said: 'O Allah, cause me to live as a needy person [*miskeen*] and cause me to die as a needy person [*miskeen*], and gather me among the needy on the Day of Resurrection.' His wife asked him why he said that, and he replied: 'Because the poor will enter Paradise before the rich. Do not turn away a poor man even if all you can give is half a date. If you love the poor and bring them near you, God will bring you near Him on the Day of Resurrection' (Tirmidhi, Book 36, *Hadith* 49). This prophetic guidance is consistent with earlier revelation in the Gospels: 'Blessed are the Meek, for they shall inherit the Earth' (Matthew, 5: 5).

This tension in relation to guidance on how Muslims should approach wealth is important and central to understanding a lived faith. What is clear from Islamic teaching is that, while it is acceptable and even meritorious to be wealthy, as long as it is not prejudicial to one's relationship with God, and if one uses one's wealth to communal benefit, it is also a spiritual test because it imposes social obligations. Indeed, it is clear from the *ahadith* quoted that, in a general sense, the poor possess greater spiritual capital than those with means – no doubt, at least in part, a result of the humility and reliance that poverty engenders among them with regard to their relationship to God. 'O mankind, you are the ones that have need of God; He is the All-sufficient, the All-laudable' (*Qur'an*, 35: 15). From a 'resilience' perspective, the poor have learned to live with little and have experienced trials. The illusion that they are autonomous has been diminished, either willingly or unwillingly.

Despite this important discourse on poverty, the economic legacy that Islam has gifted to the world is unique and hugely influential. Its revelation descended on a desert nation for whom trade and exchange were vital, resulting in a huge body of revealed law and jurisprudence concerning commerce, contracts, investment, and taxation. Lenders, for instance, are forced to share risks as investors. They share in either the success or failure of joint ventures, which leads to more responsible investment. Between the eighth and eleventh century AD, when Europe was feudal and church law strictly forbade the practice of usurious investment and credit, these systems enabled the Islamic community to develop and dominate the world economy. Non-usurious systems of credit, exchange, coinage, and law were hugely respected and fostered trade, investment, and economic development in Europe, Africa, and much of the known world. Today, one of the legacies of this is the rich trading and entrepreneurial tradition within Muslim communities, a legacy of how the practice of Islam spread through trade routes in much of Africa, China, and the Far East. Islamic finance is once again re-emerging today as a formidable force within both Islamic and non-Muslim finance houses, inspiring a generation of Muslims who are disillusioned by the social, economic, and environmental damage and injustice inflicted by fractional-reserve banking.

Research has recently shown that there is enormous disparity in wealth ownership today. Just 1 per cent of the world's population owns the same amount as 82 per cent of the rest of the population (Oxfam, 2018). National taxation systems and off-shore tax havens allow large corporations and the very rich to prevent any redistribution of their wealth. In fact, it is calculated that, if only 0.5 per cent of that hoarded wealth were to be redistributed, it would be more than enough to fulfil the development needs of all the world's poorer nations. In Islam, it is legally required to transfer 2.5 per cent of your standing wealth to address social inequality and injustice in the form of the wealth tax or *zakat*. Today, Islamic social finance is also attracting huge attention in relation to fulfilling development and humanitarian needs, including the UN's Sustainable Development Goals.

Another important tradition learned from the Prophet Muhammad (PBUH) is the concept of transforming one's personal spiritual capital of good deeds into development capital. *Awqaf* is the tradition of endowments, left either during an individual's life or on one's death, to serve the community in the form of land, fruit trees, wells, and property. Interestingly, this led to an early emergence of what has been described as a thriving 'third sector', or what we would describe today as the civil society sector. The concept of endowment (*waqf*) indicates how an Islamic system recognizes the importance of the non-profit sector in social and economic development and offers the required legal and institutional protection for this sector to function (Suleiman, 2016). Over the years this tradition grew significantly, to the extent that in the more developed economies of Turkey and Egypt the bulk of public services were provided through this third sector.

> At its creation in 1923, three-quarters of the arable land in the Republic of Turkey belonged to endowments. Also, one-eighth of all cultivated soil in Egypt and one-seventh of that in Iran were known to be *waqf* property. In the middle of the 19th century, one-half of the agricultural land in Algeria, and in 1883 one-third of that in Tunisia, was owned by *awqaf*. (Suleiman, 2016)

This sense of an obligation to redistribute wealth and to use it ethically is one of the primary forms of spiritual capital and leads very directly to the removal of destitution.

It has also been suggested more broadly within academia that faith, religion, and, by extension, spiritual capital all influence economic culture. There is a conjecture that higher religious beliefs stimulate growth because they help sustain aspects of individual behaviour that enhance productivity (Barro and McCleary, 2003). There is much evidence cited, for instance, of a 'Protestant work ethic' positively impacting attitudes towards economic output among this particular Christian grouping. Research has indicated similar traits within Muslim communities. For instance, research on resilience in Afghanistan found that 'by and large, Afghan families suffer great material poverty, but not a poverty of aspirations: on the contrary, hard work and education are seen as the gateway to economic security and social respectability' (Eggerman and Panter-Brick, 2010). One may make a connection through the element of spiritual capital understood as '*Tawakkul*' (trust in God's providence), which is undoubtedly a factor in entrepreneurial motivation as well as in resilience among Muslim and other faith communities.

Protecting our posterity

The fifth and final dimension is posterity, defined as the welfare of the community and those generations that will come after us. Some scholars have replaced the term with family, lineage, progeny, or offspring. Posterity embraces all of these. Its focus is the welfare and social protection of future generations and the family as the basic unit of society. It includes the right to family life and the rights of the child. The religious basis of the family, with its obligations of care and protection, and in its wider manifestation of community and *Ummah* as family, is the cornerstone of society in Islamic teaching. In fact, it also tends to make up a large part of the wider secular definition of social capital.

One related aspect of this dimension is intergenerational concern for the environment. Islam teaches that mankind is the 'custodian' of this Earth and its surroundings, which have been given to us as a sacred trust from God. As custodians (*kulafaa*), we do not have the right to abuse or destroy the Earth. We have to take active steps to ensure its health and longevity. There is a wealth of Islamic teaching that advocates living in harmony with the environment, not being wasteful, and respecting life in all its forms.

> It is He who produces gardens, both cultivated and wild, and palm trees and crops of diverse kinds, and olives and pomegranates, both similar and dissimilar. Eat of their fruits when they bear fruit and pay their due on the day of their harvest, and do not be profligate. He does not love the profligate. (*Qur'an*, 6: 141)

The *Qur'an* teaches that the cosmos is set up in a perfect balance and equilibrium (*mizan*). *Mizan* refers to the universal law of nature that takes into account the reciprocal relationships between every element in the universe, including living creatures, in providing harmony, stability, and complementarity. In a chilling warning that echoes our current catastrophic pollution of the environment, the *Qur'an* states: 'Corruption has appeared throughout the land and sea, by [reason of] what the hands of people have earned so He may let them taste part of [the consequence of] what they have done that perhaps they will return [to righteousness]' *(Qur'an*, 30: 41).

There is evidence that mobilizing and sensitizing Muslim communities through religious leadership can be effective in altering harmful behaviours, such as over-fishing, and in fostering the protection of species (Khalid and Thani, 2007). Ultimately, it is often spiritual capital, in the form of our moral obligations to other life forms and future generations that determines our willingness to change our practice, although self-preservation is increasingly playing a part as communities of humans and animals face extinction. Development actors must harness the important influencing role of spirituality, particularly where poorly educated communities are not aware of the ecological implications of their behaviours. In 2014, IFEES and Islamic Relief cooperatively produced a toolkit to mobilize Muslim communities to protect the environment. In 2018, Islamic Relief produced materials and resources containing reference to Qur'anic teaching that were used to run sustainable consumption campaigns in local Muslim communities around the world.

Establishing social justice

As the reader will have discerned, all of these development priorities are driven and protected by rights and obligations contained within revealed guidance (see Figure 3.2). As we have explored, there are important distinctions in the Islamic understandings of human rights – indeed, in the rights of all living creatures – that differ from secular understanding. Similar to Catholic social teaching, there is an understanding of subsidiarity and moral autonomy at an individual and community level. In contrast, the Universal Declaration of Human Rights tends to focus heavily on the social contract between the state and its citizens. Within *Shari'ah*, more rights are initially defined at a family and community level between the various parties, with detailed obligations

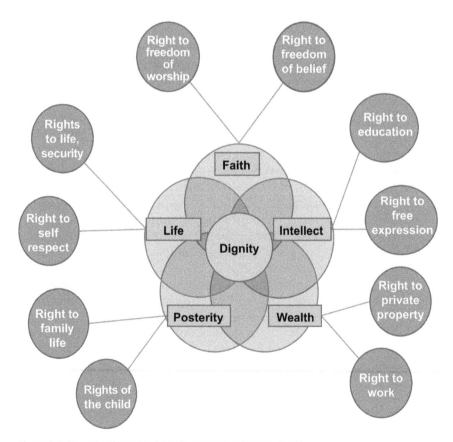

Figure 3.2 The role of human rights in preserving human dignity

between spouses, and between parents and children, and between wider family members, as well as with neighbours and those living in proximity. Because revelation gives greater definition in terms of absolute truth and moral parameters, there are inevitably more widely accepted limitations of public space and behaviour within the Islamic tradition. This has inevitably led to criticism by secularists of the infringement of certain freedoms, such as freedom of speech and the right to blaspheme. This phenomenon is just one example within Islamic law of the protection of the rights of God through upholding people's right to the protection of the common good and the fabric of society. The concept of the legal protection of the common good is also central in secular society, but remains more open to change and relative interpretation, as social and moral values move with the times. In relation to spiritual capital, it is important to emphasize here that, for Muslims, human rights are rooted in our vertical relationship to God, who is the transcendent value. It is God who bestowed dignity on humankind and who makes it unacceptable for anyone to violate human rights or take away a person's dignity.

Implications for development practice

From this short discussion of the objectives of religion, one can see that in reality, faith and spirituality contribute to essential elements regarding distributive justice, protection from destitution, the preservation of rights, and human dignity. There are a number of implications for aid agencies here. Broadly speaking, we can identify four critical areas where development organizations can engage with and leverage spiritual capital:

1. **Inclusion:** Ensuring that local faith actors, institutions, and communities are mainstreamed and enabled to participate in aid processes and decision making throughout the programme cycle.
2. **Harmonization**: Ensuring support for human rights and sustainable development by integrating a faith-literate approach that harnesses spiritual capital while being respectful of diversity.
3. **Localization**: By addressing the historic issues of alienation from formal partnerships caused by mutual distrust and misunderstanding, governmental and non-governmental aid actors must move to a point where they see faith communities as potential allies in the war against poverty and suffering. FBOs are often the first responders in humanitarian settings and provide sustainable development services such as savings and loans, health, and education services which achieve reach, influence, and ownership within the community.
4. **Additionality**: Faith communities do not simply provide services; they often provide a community-based model of support in which people feel included, accepted, and appreciated unconditionally within a human family. This has been recognized as extremely valuable,

particularly in the context of forced migrants. Alongside the myriad forms of social finance and support mobilized by faith communities, this presents huge opportunities for additionality, sustainability, and meaningful partnership with aid actors.

Let us examine each of these in more detail.

Inclusion

Spiritual capital must be recognized as a bulwark against poverty and a contributor to social justice, social capital, and the broader moral economy. For the last 50 years, Europe among other areas, has exported an essentially secular model of administration to its former colonies and the rest of the world and continues to train administrators and development workers to essentially delegitimize and alienate faith as a development factor. As a consequence, religion and faith institutions have often been pushed into a more peripheral role, dealing only with worship and religious instruction and losing their traditionally broader role in providing an informed moral compass as well as social and development services. A new secular development language has developed, which has little or no connection to its equivalent in religious discourse. In many cases, religious institutions have been marginalized and alienated by the state, and, in the case of huge religious endowments, they have often been nationalized, swallowed up, and lost by corrupt state governments. Burdened by national government debt, state services rarely compensate. People in poor developing nations have often fallen back on their faith communities and the spiritual capital that powers them to provide education, welfare services, savings and loans, health, and in some cases protection. Meanwhile, some communities, feeling that the state delegitimizes their faith, reciprocate by delegitimizing the secular edifice of government. This contributes fundamentally to the fragility of states. Ethics in the public sector have often deteriorated – for example, with teachers sometimes turning up for just an hour or two a day, and rampant corruption eating away at the public purse. In other words, the public sector has somehow cut out the mobilization of spiritual capital, with disastrous results.

Inclusion can be enabled by supporting FBOs to understand humanitarian and development concepts through the lens of their own value system, way of life, and world view. This needs to start with participatory assessments, both of their spiritual needs and of the role belief, practice, and faith institutions play in affecting the situation. Importantly, engagement should not be value-free but should enable both aid actors and FBOs to reflect on and share their practice and values in the light of this discourse, which in some cases may be challenging. Engagement should enable participation within a broad spectrum of partnership models with the ultimate aim of ensuring that faith and FBOs are valued and included as a crucial part of civil society and the wider humanitarian and development community.

Harmonization

For those of us who take a rights-based approach and who believe that the denial of basic rights constitutes poverty and is the primary cause of poverty, this has very real implications and presents a difficult dilemma. The denial of just treatment – for instance of women, children, and minorities – often stems from a poor understanding of rights and obligations, and, for many Muslims, a lack of awareness of the ultimate consequences of their behaviour when they are held accountable in the next life. In the Muslim world, rights and obligations are viewed through a faith-teaching lens. Poor understanding of their faith often leads to an abuse of rights. Various UN agencies, such as UNHCR, the UN Development Programme (UNDP) and the United Nations Children's Fund (UNICEF), increasingly engage with and mobilize religious actors and faith teaching to improve protection for affected populations. In doing so they directly tap into and engage with spiritual capital, for example when tackling violent extremism or xenophobia against forced migrants, as well as encouraging behavioural change (UNDP, 2017; UNHCR, 2014).

While UN and other multilateral agencies have often instrumentalized religion and religious communities to achieve particular humanitarian and development outcomes, there is an increasing shift by aid agencies such as World Vision, Tearfund, CAFOD, Islamic Relief, and others to encourage faith and faith communities to take a much more central role in leading change. Interestingly, this represents a reclaiming of the original social reforming characteristic and role of some religions, which, in their earliest phases, overthrew ingrained social injustice. It also represents a seismic ethical shift in a sector traditionally dominated by antipathy and distrust of religion towards a more inclusive, respectful, and less prejudicial mindset.

In theories of change, we must recognize that spiritual capital is often foundational to justice and protection. Where relevant and necessary, we must engage with faith teaching in support of spiritual capital. In the Muslim context, that does not mean distributing *Qur'ans*, building mosques, or conversion. It means that, rather than alienating faith teachings and traditions relating to issues such as transforming conflict peacefully, protecting children, preserving the environment, building civil society, providing financial services, and fulfilling women's rights through the lens of people's own faith and leadership, we harness them and tap into their greatest priorities: their faith and the meaning it gives them.

For many societies around the world today, religion wields little influence. Governments and development actors base their mobilization around universal human rights values. There is emerging understanding of secular spirituality among non-believers, which, in many cases, enables very similar inspiration for social action. This can provide the important bridge between faith and non-faith communities.

Interestingly, the UK Conservative government's recent austerity programme, which attempted to roll back the welfare state, talked openly about moving back to a 'Big Society', in which religious and civil society actors are contro-versially encouraged or forced to provide more social and welfare services in a reawakening of civic 'social' responsibility. As a result, there has been an increase in non-governmental services such as food banks and refugee services, often provided by faith communities. However, this is fairly marginal in relation to the much broader role that religion had previously played a century earlier within British society, not least in relation to maintaining social cohesion and social obligations within the family and the community. The mainstream faiths have tended to maintain a belief in the divinely ordained sanctity of marriage as the building block of society, and, in the least economically and materially developed societies, the family is still usually the social safety net mechanism. In many 'developed' nations, the traditional notion of the family is experiencing rapid change and taking on more hybrid forms, with very high rates of family breakdown (including a divorce rate of 47 per cent in the UK), leading inevitably to a greater welfare role for the state.

Localization

A major priority within aid operations in traditional religious societies is to increase partnerships with local religious institutions such as faith schools, clinics, faith-inspired NGOs, and community-based organizations. If done sensitively, and with sufficient time given for exchange of ideas and reflection, this should provide these organizations with the vital bridging capital to integrate into the wider development movement and harness their spiritual and material capital, reducing the divide that imposed secularism has created in their perceived role. For example, in recent times Islamic Relief has worked in Kenya to build the capability of *madrassas* (Qur'anic schools) to provide basic literacy and numeracy. They have worked with mosques and faith leaders in Yemen to improve faith understanding around conflict, and are actively promoting the reintroduction of *awqaf* or endowments built on Islamic principles as a way of encouraging the sustainable redistribution of wealth and improved services to poor communities. Islamic social finance modalities of various kinds need to be integrated with contemporary aid and development activities, expertise, and innovation. Islamic insurance (*takaful*), for instance, has enormous potential for providing disaster and health insurance for, among others, poor and vulnerable communities.

A re-evaluation of our theories of change is needed in the light of the emerging evidence that, within many contexts, religion and spiritual capital must not be alienated intellectually or operationally from attempts to raise living standards.

Additionality

Can building spiritual capital be a specific development aim? This is a justified question, to which we would have to resoundingly answer yes, because of its foundational developmental impact on human and social capital. This means that places of worship, religious schools, and agencies built on furthering faith all have their place in contributing to humanitarian and development outcomes. Whether one believes they play a positive or negative role may depend on several factors, but what must be accepted is that they inevitably have an influence on human development and are therefore a stakeholder to be engaged with. Generally, faith-based aid and development actors have tended to leave the specific promotion of faith to specialist agencies. There are, however, many faith institutions that combine humanitarian and development work with faith teaching, and this can be completely appropriate in terms of humanitarian ethics. For instance, it is very common in Indonesia and Pakistan for microfinance organizations to operate through mosques, and this lack of separation between the temporal and the spiritual is a tradition rooted in Muslims' belief in the oneness of God and His presence everywhere.

Some Muslim and Christian development agencies use faith teaching and theology as a key element in enabling internal reflection and change on critical issues relating to social justice such as FGM, HIV/AIDS, early and forced marriage, xenophobia, and discrimination (for example, World Vision's Channels of Hope programme). Critical to this is reference to the underlying ethics that inform religious law, enabling a deeper theology to take root in people's hearts and minds. Similarly, the Christian Community of Sant'Egidio builds refugee protection by inviting refugees to participate as members of its local church community. It recognizes that refugees do not only need services; they need to feel part of a community in which people are also afforded unconditional love and companionship, based on shared humanity.

Theory or theology of change?

It is fashionable for development agencies today to invest a great deal of energy in understanding poverty and suffering, and in theorizing and strategizing how they should best alleviate them. For faith-based agencies there is an added complication in also attempting to understand how God changes people and communities for the better and issues around divine cause and effect. Central to this, for Muslims, is the belief in God as an all-powerful being, the provider, and as responsive to His servants.

There are some basic principles that point towards the mobilizing impact of building spiritual capital to improve the outward condition of a people. Central to this is the understanding of the agency that God places in us. In an important verse, the *Qur'an* says: 'Allah will not change the condition of a people until they change what is within their souls' (*Qur'an*, 13: 11). This verse clearly places the onus for change on us, and confirms that our outward behaviour is ultimately a reflection of our inward change. In another important saying of the Prophet Muhammad (PBUH), God said: 'When My servant comes towards Me walking, I come towards him running' (Bukhari, Book 97, *Hadith* 34).

Generally, Islamic teaching indicates that societies undergo lasting change for the better when:

- they establish social justice (*adalah*) by promoting right and preventing wrong;
- they nurture the family's ability to provide an environment in which human values and morals can develop and grow in the new generation; and
- individuals strive for inner transformation.

Interestingly, it is clear from research using multiple indices of development that these factors operate universally, irrespective of religion and religiosity. Social justice, in particular, is heavily dependent on the strengthening of social accountability and equality among social groups. Some secular countries, such as Sweden, do particularly well using these indices. From a theological perspective, this would indicate that God rewards the practical deployment and implementation of these values, as opposed to their mere profession within a belief system. It is likely, therefore, that, from an Islamic perspective, our 'theology' of change must rely heavily on supporting a 'lived faith' in which social justice in its various forms – including good governance, accountability, and the promotion of human dignity – transforms society.

Notes

1. See <https://www.metanexus.net/spiritual_capital>.
2. Impartiality and neutrality are two of the four humanitarian principles derived from the core principles of the International Federation of Red Cross and Red Crescent code of conduct, ensuring humanitarian aid priorities are calculated on the basis of need alone.
3. See <https://www.unenvironment.org/about-un-environment/faith-earth-initiative/why-faith-and-environment-matters> [accessed 17 May 2020].

References

Abdel-Khalek, A.M. (2011) 'Subjective well-being and religiosity in Egyptian college students', *Psychological Reports* 108 (1): 54–8 <https://doi.org/10.2466/07.17.PR0.108.1.54-58>.

Abdel-Khalek, A.M. (2017) 'The construction and validation of the Arabic Scale of Intrinsic Religiosity (ASIR)', *Psychology and Behavioral Science* 4 (4): 555644 <https://doi.org/10.19080/PBSIJ.2017.04.555644>.

Ager, W., Horn, R. and Ager, A. (2018) *A Faith-sensitive Approach in Humanitarian Response*, Lutheran World Federation and Islamic Relief, Geneva.

Aminu-Kano, M. and FitzGibbon, A. (2014) *An Islamic Perspective on Human Development*, Islamic Relief Worldwide, Birmingham.

Baker, C. and Smith, G. (2010) 'Spiritual, religious and social capital: exploring their dimensions and their relationship with faith-based motivation and participation in UK civil society', paper presented at the BSA Sociology of Religion Group Conference, Edinburgh, April.

Barro, R.J. and McCleary, R.M. (2003) 'Religion and economic growth', Working Paper 9682, National Bureau of Economic Research, Cambridge MA <http://www.nber.org/papers/w9682>.

Berger, P. and Hefner, R. (2003) 'Spiritual capital in comparative perspective', paper prepared for the Spiritual Capital Planning Meeting <https://www.metanexus.net/spiritual_capital/pdf/Berger.pdf> [accessed 29 March 2006].

Bewley, A. (2014) *Understanding Spirituality in Islam*, Reflection Network.

Chapra, M.U. (2008) 'The Islamic vision of development in light of the *Maqasid al-Shariah*', Occasional Papers Series 15, International Institute of Islamic Thought, London.

Dariah, A.R. (2016) 'The shape of Islamic sustainable development', in S.M. Saniff and R.M. Ramli (eds), *Islamic Perspectives on Sustainable Development*, ISDEV, USM, and Islamic Relief Academy, Pulau Pinang.

Eggerman, M. and Panter-Brick, C. (2010) 'Suffering, hope, and entrapment: resilience and cultural values in Afghanistan', *Social Science Medicine* 71 (1–2): 71–83.

Hill, P.C. and Hood Jr, R.W. (1999) *Measures of Religiosity*, Religious Education Press, Birmingham AL.

Ibn al Habib (1980) *Diwan of Shaykh Muhammed Ibn-ul Habib*, Diwan Press, Bradford.

Kadayifci-Orellana, S.A., Abu-Nimer, M. and Saleem, A.M. (2014) *Understanding an Islamic Framework for Peacebuilding*, Islamic Relief Worldwide, Birmingham.

Keller, N.H.M. (1991) *Reliance of the Traveller*, Sunna Books, Evanston IL.

Khalid, F. and Thani, A.K. (2007) *Promoting Conservation of Misali Island, Pemba, Tanzania: Teachers Guide Book for Islamic Environmental Education*, Islamic Foundation for Ecology and Environmental Sciences (IFEES), Birmingham.

Koenig, H.G. (1997) 'Religion, spirituality, and medicine: research findings and implications for clinical practice', *Southern Medical Journal* 97 (12): 1194–200.

Lacey, B.C. and Lacey, J.I. (1978) 'Two-way communication between the heart and the brain: significance of time within the cardiac cycle', *American Psychologist* 33 (2): 99–113.

Lancet (2015) 'Faith-based health-care', *The Lancet* 386 (10005).

Luckmann, T. (1967) *The Invisible Religion: The Problem of Religion in Modern Society*, Macmillan, New York.

Masten, A.S. (2009) 'Ordinary magic: lessons from research in resilience in human development', *Education Canada* 49 (3): 28–32.

Narayan, D., Patel, R., Schafft, K., Rademacher, A. and S. Koch-Schulte (2000) *Can Anyone Hear Us?: Voices of the Poor*, World Bank, Washington DC.

Nasr, S.H. (1979) 'Intellect and intuition: their relationship from the Islamic perspective', *Studies in Comparative Religion* 13 (1/2).

Oxfam (2018) *Reward Work, Not Wealth*, Oxfam GB for Oxfam International, Oxford.

Pace, E. (2019) 'The changing soul of Europe: the challenge to the secular state', in F. Cadeddu (ed.), *EUARE Lectures: European Academy of Religion Annual Conference 2017–2018*, European Academy of Religion, Bologna.

Suleiman, H. (2016) 'The Islamic Trust *waqf*: a stagnant or reviving legal institution?', *EJIMEL: Electronic Journal of Islamic and Middle Eastern Law* 4: 27–43.

UNDP (2017) *Journey to Extremism in Africa Drivers, Incentives and the Tipping Point for Recruitment*, United Nations Development Programme (UNDP) Regional Bureau Africa, New York.

UNHCR (2014) *Welcoming the Stranger: Affirmations for Faith Leaders*, United Nations High Commissioner for Refugees (UNHCR), New York.

Zaman, N. and Asutay, M. (2009) 'Divergence between aspiration and realities of Islamic economics: a political economy approach to bridging the divide', *IIUM Journal of Economics and Management* 17 (1): 73–96.

About the author

Atallah FitzGibbon has worked in local economic development both in the public and voluntary sector in the UK. Over the last 20 years he has served at Islamic Relief Worldwide (IRW) as Programmes Director, Performance Improvement Manager, Head of Policy and Strategy, and Head of Global Advocacy. Currently the Faith and Partnerships Advisor, he leads IRW's engagement and partnerships on faith-based approaches to tackling the major challenges of our time. Atallah has led the development of IRW's last two global strategies, between 2009 and 2021, which has involved improving faith literacy and localization within IRW's work and the development of a conceptual framework and theory of change on human development. As Global Advocacy Manager, Atallah focused on the faith community contribution to the Sustainable Development Goals and refugee protection. He co-chairs the Joint Learning Initiative Hub on Forced Migration and leads IRW's work on faith-based approaches to peacebuilding. He has been active in recent initiatives and research on the role of faith-based actors in refugee protection and conflict transformation. He is involved in both the World of Neighbours initiative in Europe and KAICID's Network for Dialogue, which explores the role of interreligious and intercultural dialogue for the social inclusion of migrants and people seeking refuge in Europe.

CHAPTER 4

Translating faith into development: how do Islamic teachings advocate helping the poor?

Ajaz Ahmed Khan

The number of Muslim faith-based aid and development organizations (FBOs) in the United Kingdom has grown significantly over recent years. Much of their income is the result of religiously motivated giving from individual Muslim donors. The focus of Muslim FBOs is largely on providing humanitarian aid, supporting orphans, and seasonal food distribution. This chapter analyses Islamic social teachings to understand how they advocate that poor people should be helped and in what way this can influence the design and implementation of development programmes. It concludes that, in contrast to the current focus of many Muslim FBOs, an 'Islamic approach' to development should emphasize enabling poor people to become self-reliant. It should also encourage Muslims to advocate on social and economic issues that impact on the lives of the poor.

Keywords: Muslim faith-based organizations, self-reliance, Islamic micro-finance, *qard hasan*, advocacy

Introduction

The number of Muslim faith-based organizations (FBOs)[1] with a specific focus on providing humanitarian aid and promoting development in poor countries has grown rapidly since the 1980s. The Muslim Charities Forum (MCF) was established in 2007 and is the network for British Muslim charities working in the United Kingdom and abroad. The MCF currently has 17 members, which include most of the larger and more established Muslim FBOs in the UK.[2] According to the accounts presented to the Charity Commission (the regulatory body for charities in England and Wales), the combined income of the MCF's members was approximately £310 million.[3] Islamic Relief is the largest Muslim FBO with a reported income of £128 million, followed by Human Appeal (£60 million), Ummah Welfare Trust (£35 million), Penny Appeal (£33 million), Muslim Aid (£25 million), Al-Khair Foundation (£21 million), and Muslim Hands (£21 million). Unlike the other organizations, Ummah Welfare Trust and Penny Appeal are not members of the

http://dx.doi.org/10.3362/9781788530613.004

MCF. The MCF estimates that there are 129 Muslim FBOs in the UK with a focus on providing humanitarian aid and promoting development in poor countries (Imtiaz, 2020), and that their combined income in 2018 was just under £500 million (Itani, 2019). Most are relatively small organizations with incomes of less than £100,000 per year.[4]

The importance attached to charitable giving in Islam is a key factor in establishing Muslim FBOs and in their ability to attract funding from Muslim donors. The principles of charitable giving and compassion enshrined in the *Qur'an* and *ahadith*,[5] or sayings of the Prophet Muhammad (Peace Be Upon Him[6]), are well established. All Muslims who meet the necessary criteria of wealth are obliged to provide for the poor and other eligible recipients by paying 2.5 per cent of their standing wealth as *zakat*, or obligatory almsgiving. According to the *Qur'an* (9: 60), there are eight categories of people who are eligible to receive *zakat*: the poor, the needy, the administrators of *zakat*, persons who are inclined to or have recently embraced Islam, persons trapped in bonded labour, those who are heavily indebted, those promoting the cause of God, and finally travellers who have few resources or do not have enough money to return home. Neither the *Qur'an* nor *ahadith* specify the relative division of *zakat* between the above eight categories.

The importance of *zakat* is such that, after the *shahada* or declaration of faith, and *salat* or five daily prayers, it is the third pillar of Islam. The purpose of *zakat* is to promote equality by redistributing wealth from the rich to the poor, as well as keeping wealth clear of greed and selfishness. In addition to this compulsory payment, Muslims are encouraged to make voluntary charitable donations or *sadaqah* to help the poor and needy. Both *zakat* and *sadaqah* play a key role in the religious beliefs of Muslims. Indeed, as Singer (2008: 218) observes, 'without them, faith is incomplete'. Traditionally, Muslims have also established *waqf*, which is an endowment (usually a building or plot of land) or a trust set up for charitable purposes, typically for education or health. It involves ensuring that a property cannot be sold, inherited, or donated to anyone.[7]

Muslim FBOs have drawn upon this rich charitable tradition and much of their income is a result of religiously motivated donations from individual Muslim supporters. Indeed, their fundraising strategies use overtly 'religious' language, frequently referencing the *Qur'an* and *ahadith*, and emphasize the importance of charity as well as solidarity with other Muslims. For example, 'Indeed, the men who practise charity and the women who practise charity … it will be multiplied for them, and they will have a noble reward' (*Qur'an*, 57: 18);[8] 'And whosoever saves one life, it is as if they have saved the lives of all humankind' (*Qur'an*, 5: 32);[9] and 'The believers, in their love, mutual kindness, and close ties, are like one body; when any part complains, the whole body responds to it with wakefulness and fever' (Muslim, Book 45, *Hadith* 83).[10]

To facilitate this process of religious giving, most of the leading Muslim FBOs offer practical information on their websites, including online '*zakat* calculators'[11] for donors to assess their *zakat*. Furthermore, their key marketing campaigns coincide with Muslim festivals such as *Eid-al-Adha* and particularly the month of Ramadan, when Muslim FBOs can receive as much as one-third of their total annual income (Khan, 2012). Although it can be paid at any time during the year, many Muslims calculate and give their *zakat* during Ramadan, as they believe that charitable giving during Ramadan attracts more merit. This is supported by the following *ahadith*. When asked 'Which charity is best?', the Prophet Muhammad (PBUH) replied 'Charity in Ramadan' (Tirmidhi, Book 7, *Hadith* 47). It is also reported that the Prophet Muhammad (PBUH) 'was the most generous of people in charity, and he was generous to the utmost in the month of Ramadan' (Muslim, Book 43, *Hadith* 68).

In contrast to their secular and non-Muslim FBO counterparts, only a relatively small proportion of the income of Muslim FBOs is from institutional sources such as the Department for International Development (DFID) of the UK government, the European Union or the various United Nations (UN) agencies. For example, according to their most recent accounts, only 13 per cent of Islamic Relief's income is from institutional sources (Islamic Relief, 2019), and this is the highest proportion of any of the leading Muslim FBOs.[12] In contrast, during the same year, the proportion of income received from institutional donors for secular and non-Muslims FBOs was higher: for example, CAFOD (31.5 per cent), Oxfam (48.5 per cent), Christian Aid (53 per cent), and Save the Children UK (65 per cent). Most of the income of all the leading Muslim FBOs is from private individual donors.

As the preceding analysis has highlighted, faith has played a key role in establishing Muslim FBOs and exerts a strong influence on their ability to attract funding. The remainder of this chapter explores the extent to which faith influences the way in which Muslim FBOs design and structure their development programmes. It also analyses Islamic teachings to see how they advocate that the 'poor and needy' should be helped and their implications for Muslim FBOs in terms of the types of development activities they pursue.

The programme focus of Muslim FBOs

The emphasis of Muslim FBOs has been on providing emergency relief and basic services such as education, health, and water and sanitation, particularly following natural disasters such as earthquakes and flooding, as well as war and civil conflict. In fact, most Muslim FBOs were founded from a desire to respond to a specific natural disaster or conflict, particularly one that disproportionately affected Muslims. For example, Islamic Relief was established in 1984 and Muslim Aid one year later, both in response to the famines in the Horn of Africa, while Muslim Hands was founded in 1993 in response to the conflict in Bosnia and Herzegovina. In more recent years, the Kashmir earthquake in 2005, the conflict in Syria, which began in 2011, and the exodus of Rohingya refugees from Myanmar, which started in 2015, have stimulated the growth of a second wave of Muslim FBOs.

Although quite diverse in the ways in which they express their faith identity, all the leading Muslim FBOs claim to support 'all in need, regardless of race, religion, gender, nationality and political opinion'.[13] Unlike leading secular and non-Muslim FBOs though, none refers to a person's 'sexual orientation'. In recent years, some Muslim FBOs have responded to natural disasters in which those affected were not Muslims. For example, Islamic Relief and Al-Khair Foundation both provided humanitarian aid to survivors of the earthquake in Haiti in January 2010, while Muslim Aid has maintained a field office in overwhelmingly non-Muslim Cambodia since 2007. While the leading Muslim FBOs have assisted non-Muslims in Muslim-majority countries, the predominant focus of both their emergency and longer-term programmes remains on assisting other Muslims.

Providing aid to refugees is a widely recognized priority, especially since the issue of forced migration holds a particular resonance in Islamic history. The Prophet Muhammad (PBUH) was a refugee who, to escape persecution, fled with his followers in 622 AD from Mecca to Yathrib (later renamed Medina), both located in present-day Saudi Arabia. In fact, this event, known as the *Hijra*, marks the beginning of the Islamic calendar. The *Qur'an* is quite explicit about the issue of asylum seekers and refugees: 'And if any one of the disbelievers seeks your protection, then grant him protection so that he may hear the word of Allah, and then escort him to where he will be secure' (*Qur'an*, 9: 6).

While Muslim FBOs were generally established with the aim of providing humanitarian relief, their expressed strategic objectives have evolved and now also include promoting longer-term development. For example, Human Appeal aims to assist poor people to 'generate a sustainable income and be self-sufficient' (Human Appeal, 2015: 6); Muslim Aid believes 'one of the foremost ways out of poverty is to focus on building sustainable livelihoods, to reduce dependency on aid and to allow individuals and their families to become self-sufficient' (Muslim Aid, 2018: 8); while Muslim Hands targets 'addressing the root causes of poverty and empowering communities'.[14] Despite this change in strategic objectives, though, their emphasis remains on providing humanitarian aid and basic services. Table 4.1 shows the most recent available data regarding the amount of spending by the seven largest UK-based Muslim FBOs

Table 4.1 The relative expenditure of Muslim FBOs on emergency and longer-term development projects

Organization	Expenditure on emergency relief and basic services projects	Expenditure on longer-term sustainable livelihoods projects
Islamic Relief Worldwide[15]	£73,292,508	£6,652,545
Human Appeal[16]	£40,750,436	£874,149
Ummah Welfare Trust[17]	£27,921,967	£467,612
Muslim Aid[18]	£8,614,969	£3,014,088
Penny Appeal[19]	£9,721,811	£2,678,860
Al-Khair Foundation[20]	£6,532,447	£95,966
Muslim Hands[21]	£9,313,360	£0

on emergency relief and basic service projects, compared with programmes categorized as promoting sustainable livelihoods – these include activities such as vocational training, income generation projects, microfinance services, and provision of livestock and other assets. In all cases, a large share of each organization's *operational* expenditure, ranging from 65 per cent in the case of Muslim Aid to 100 per cent for Muslim Hands, is dedicated to emergency relief and projects that provide basic services.

Among the non-emergency programmes implemented by Muslim FBOs, there is a special emphasis on providing food parcels during the month of Ramadan when Muslims are obliged to fast between sunrise and sunset, and meat during *Qurbani*;[22] supporting orphans,[23] particularly through child sponsorship; providing access to clean water by digging wells; and for some organizations, supporting the construction and rehabilitation of mosques. There are theological reasons for this, as each of these activities is clearly encouraged in the *Qur'an* and *ahadith*. For example, during the festival of *Eid-al-Adha*, each Muslim family that is financially able sacrifices an animal, most commonly a sheep. Prophetic tradition recommends that the family eat one-third of the meat themselves, offer another one-third to friends and neighbours, and donate one-third to the poor. As Singer has observed, not only does charity accompany many Islamic festivals but it is also 'a canonically acceptable substitute to replace a variety of ritual obligations' (2008: 73). Thus, if a Muslim is unable to fast during the month of Ramadan, for example due to illness, he or she must feed a needy person every day and thus, under certain circumstances, the obligation of fasting can be replaced by an act of charity.

There are several verses in the *Qur'an* that demand kindness towards orphans, promising rewards for those who care for them and warning of punishment for those who mistreat them. Indeed, the *Qur'an* even compares the person who mistreats an orphan with a non-believer: 'See the one who denies the religion, then such is the man who repulses the orphan with harshness and does not help feed the poor' (*Qur'an*, 107: 1–3). This message is reinforced by various *ahadith*. The Prophet Muhammad (PBUH), whose mother passed away when he was six years old and whose father died a few months before the Prophet Muhammad (PBUH) was born, said, 'I and the person who looks after an orphan and provides for him will be in Paradise like this,' putting his index and middle fingers together (Bukhari, Book 78, *Hadith* 36); and 'The best house among the Muslims is a house in which there is an orphan who is treated well. And the worst house among the Muslims is a house in which there is an orphan who is treated badly' (Ibn Majah, Book 33, *Hadith* 23). Therefore, supporting orphans and vulnerable children is a core component of the work of most Muslim FBOs, typically through enabling individual donors to sponsor orphans. Almost one-quarter (23 per cent) of the expenditure of Muslim Hands is allocated to supporting orphans (Muslims Hands, 2018), while almost one-fifth (18.5 per cent) of Islamic Relief's total expenditure is directed at 'orphans and vulnerable children' (Islamic Relief Worldwide, 2018).

There are numerous references to water and cleanliness in Islamic teachings. Water is also a necessary element of regular Muslim purification rituals, most commonly those performed before prayer. It is unsurprising therefore that programmes that provide safe and clean water to poor communities have a particular significance among Muslims. The digging of a well is regarded as an act of merit and promoted by many Muslim FBOs. When the Prophet Muhammad (PBUH) came to Medina, he found only one well, from which Muslims bought drinking water. His companions purchased the well and made it *waqf*. Indeed, when asked 'What sort of *sadaqah* is best?', the Prophet (PBUH) replied 'Water' (Abu Dawud, Book 9, *Hadith* 126). In addition to encouraging donors to fund the construction of drinking water wells, over recent years Muslim FBOs have extended their activities to improving sanitation and developing health and hygiene awareness.

While recognizing that it can be very important to have a place of worship, particularly for displaced Muslims, the larger and more established Muslim FBOs such as Islamic Relief, Human Appeal, and Muslim Aid do not generally fund the construction of mosques or *masjids*. In part, this is because they consider such activities may be interpreted as proselytizing. It is also because mosques 'are difficult to maintain and the quality of Islamic teaching can be poor'.[24] In contrast, other organizations, including Ummah Welfare Trust, Muslim Hands, Penny Appeal, and Al-Khair Foundation, actively support the construction of new *masjids* or the reconstruction of damaged ones. They stress that in addition to being places of worship and thereby addressing people's spiritual needs, mosques also serve as local community centres 'where people gather, learn and are kept informed about local news'.[25] They can also act as places where NGOs can deliver aid. The most notable example of using religious infrastructure for development purposes is Akhuwat Islamic Microfinance in Pakistan, the world's largest interest-free microfinance organization, which routinely uses mosques (and, on occasion, churches and temples as well) to provide training and distribute loans (Khan et al., 2017). Supporting the construction of mosques is particularly attractive for some Muslim donors because it is reported that the Prophet Muhammad (PBUH) said, 'Whoever builds a *Masjid* for [the sake of] Allah, be it small or large, then Allah will build a house for him in Paradise' (Tirmidhi, Book 2, *Hadith* 171). Although Ummah Welfare Trust translates and distributes *Qur'ans*, and supports young students to memorize the *Qur'an*, overt *da'wah*[26] activities are uncommon among Muslim FBOs.

In general, and in contrast to the development programmes of secular and non-Muslim FBOs, Muslim FBOs are less involved in longer-term development activities, particularly advocacy. In 2018, only Islamic Relief reported any spending on campaigning: £1.94 million, or approximately 1.5 per cent of its overall expenditure (Islamic Relief, 2019). All other Muslim FBOs reported no expenditure on advocacy. In contrast, Oxfam UK allocated £12.1 million, or 3.6 per cent of its total expenditure, in 2018 on advocacy;[27] Save the Children UK dedicated £15.2 million, or 3.7 per cent of its total expenditure;[28] and CAFOD reported £2.4 million or 4.6 per cent of total spending.[29]

There are several factors that may explain this trend. First, there is a perception among many Muslim FBOs that their private individual donors will not fund such activities – particularly if they are considered to be in 'controversial' areas, such as reproductive health and HIV/AIDS. Rather, they believe that traditional Muslim donors hold very conservative beliefs, and they wish to see a large part (or preferably all) of their donations being used directly in 'visible' projects such as wells and schools, rather than more intangible projects and overheads. Indeed, Ummah Welfare Trust has been particularly successful by promoting a '100 per cent donations policy', with nothing deducted from donations to cover fundraising or administration costs, which are instead covered through Gift Aid, profits from their charity shops and recycled clothing, and donations specified for administration. Second, Benthall and Bellion-Jourdan (2003) argue that, although they may be very committed, the staff of Muslim charities may lack specialist development experience and technical expertise, certainly when compared with their secular or non-Muslim counterparts. This in turn has been reflected in the type of activities the organizations undertake. Muslim FBOs from the UK were established more recently than non-Muslim development organizations such as Save the Children, which started in 1919, Oxfam, which was founded in 1942, or World Vision, which was established in 1950. For some of the larger Muslim FBOs at least, such as Islamic Relief, this explanation may no longer be valid as they have increasingly attracted very experienced and qualified staff, both Muslims and non-Muslims, and this is gradually translating into more complex programme activities and growing advocacy. Lastly, it is not well understood how Islamic teachings relate to a range of development issues and how faith can structure and guide work. This is surprising because, as the remainder of this chapter explores, Islamic teachings can provide guidance on more longer-term development projects, particularly those that seek to promote self-reliance among poor people, as well as advocating on matters related to social justice.

Empowerment through self-reliance

Islam considers it an obligation to earn a livelihood through one's own labour and strongly encourages helping people to become financially independent and self-sufficient. Indeed, the issue of self-reliance is extremely important. Islamic social teachings argue that working for a livelihood provides dignity and promotes self-reliance, whereas begging and relying on other people's assistance is humiliating. Although, as already highlighted, Islam obliges Muslims to provide for the poor and encourages charity, at the same time it discourages a culture of dependency as this is viewed as undermining one's dignity.

The *Qur'an* stresses the importance of work to earn one's own livelihood, and that the criteria for receiving worldly rewards, or one's livelihood, depend on one's efforts. Indeed, the *Qur'an* states that people's circumstances will not change unless they themselves take responsibility for changing their own conditions: 'Verily never will Allah change the condition of a people until they change what is in themselves' (*Qur'an*, 13: 11). It also states: 'Work and Allah will surely see your work and also His Messenger and the believers' (*Qur'an*, 9: 105).

Furthermore, there are several *ahadith* that stress the importance of self-reliance, self-sufficiency, and pride in one's own work, even if the work is menial, yields little, or involves hardship. In contrast, begging, passivity, and idleness are considered humiliating and are strongly discouraged (Bayat, 1992). Indeed, Islamic scholars agree that *zakat* cannot be given to those capable but unwilling to work. The following lengthy *hadith* illustrates the Islamic perspective clearly:

> A man from among the Muslims of Medina came to the Prophet Muhammad (PBUH) and asked for some nourishment. Although the Prophet Muhammad (PBUH) was not inclined to reject a request for assistance, at the same time he did not favour encouraging begging or dependence. He therefore asked the man, 'Don't you have anything in your house?' 'Yes,' replied the man. 'A piece of cloth, a part of which we wear and a part of which we spread on the floor sometimes, and a wooden bowl from which we drink water.' 'Bring them to me,' said the Prophet (PBUH). He then took the items and asked some of his companions, 'Who will buy these two articles?' 'I will,' said one man, 'for one dirham.' Another said, 'I will take them for two dirhams.' The Prophet (PBUH) sold the articles for two dirhams which he handed over to the man and said, 'With one dirham, buy food for your family and with the other buy an axe and bring it to me.' The man returned with the axe. The Prophet (PBUH) fixed a handle on it with his own hands and then instructed the man: 'Go and gather firewood and I do not want to see you for a fortnight.' The man went away, gathered firewood and sold it, and made a profit of 10 dirhams. With some of the money he bought food and with some he bought clothes. The Prophet (PBUH) then said, 'This is better for you than allowing begging to become a spot on your face on the Day of Judgment.' Begging is right for only three people: one who is in grinding poverty, one who is seriously in debt, or one who is responsible for compensation and finds it difficult to pay. (Abu Dawud, Book 9, *Hadith* 86)

In a similar vein, and stressing the dignity associated with work, there is another *hadith* that states: 'It is better for one of you to take a rope and cut the wood [from the forest] and carry it on his back and sell it [as a means of earning your living] rather than to ask a person for something which that person may give to you or not' (Bukhari, Book 34, *Hadith* 37). There is also a clear onus on self-reliance: 'No one has ever eaten better food than what he eats from the work done by his hands' (Bukhari, Book 34, *Hadith* 25). In fact, it is argued that 'Richness is not the abundance of wealth, rather it is self-sufficiency' (Bukhari and Muslim, Riyad as-Salihin, Book 1, *Hadith* 522).

Islamic teachings advocate that one should not depend on charity when he or she is able to earn enough subsistence for his or her family through their own efforts. The Prophet Muhammad (PBUH) said: 'Charity is not lawful for the rich nor for the physically fit' (Tirmidhi, Book 7, *Hadith* 36); 'Whoever has food for a day and a night, it is prohibited for him to beg' (Abu Dawud, Book 9, *Hadith* 74); and 'He who wishes to abstain from begging will be protected by Allah; and he who seeks self-sufficiency will be made self-sufficient by Allah' (Bukhari, Book 24, *Hadith* 72). Islam disapproves of begging in order that people can safeguard their dignity and develop self-reliance. However, if poor people are in dire need and forced to seek financial assistance then they are considered blameless. In fact, all able-bodied persons are exhorted to work to earn their living and no one who is physically and mentally able should become a liability on his or her family or the state through an unwillingness to work. Although the work that everyone is required to perform must be 'beneficial' and conform to *Shari'ah*, no work is considered inconsequential in terms of its rewards or punishments in this world and the next.

Importantly, though, while emphasizing the importance of self-sufficiency and not relying on charity, at the same time Islamic teachings encourage moderation in working: that is, generating enough to satisfy a person and his or her dependants' material needs. In contrast to the Protestant work ethic, Bayat (1992) argues that Islam does not encourage deprivation, asceticism, or hard work either as an end in itself or for accumulating wealth. In fact, it discourages an obsession with work and excessive toil, and instead encourages leisure and good health. To support his argument, the same author cites a *hadith*: 'There are two blessings which many people lose: [they are] health and free time for doing good' (Bukhari, Book 81, *Hadith* 1). Further illustrating the balance that should be sought between work and prayer, the famous Muslim theologian Abu Hamid Al-Ghazzali mentioned that the Prophet Jesus (PBUH) once saw a man who had completely devoted himself to worship. When he asked him how he got his daily bread, the man replied that his brother, who worked, provided him with food. Jesus (PBUH) then told him: 'That brother of yours is more religious than you are' (Karim, 1996). Al-Ghazzali also mentioned that the Prophet Muhammad's (PBUH) companion and second caliph, Umar ibn al-Khattab, stressed this point further by telling people: 'Never should anyone of you think that *dua* [supplication] for sustenance without work will avail him, for Heaven never rains gold or silver' (Karim, 1996).

Despite the emphasis in Islamic teachings on encouraging poor people to become self-sufficient, as Table 4.1 demonstrates, Muslim FBOs dedicate a relatively small proportion of their total expenditure on longer-term projects that promote sustainable livelihoods.[30] Human Appeal allocated just 1 per cent, Ummah Welfare Trust 1.5 per cent, and Islamic Relief 5.5 per cent of overall expenditure on sustainable livelihoods, while Muslim Aid assigned 8 per cent and Muslim Hands 14 per cent. In comparison, the corresponding figures for non-Muslim humanitarian aid and development organizations are higher: for example, the proportion for Save the Children was 15 per cent and for CAFOD

26 per cent. In contrast to fundraising strategies that reference Islamic teachings for orphan welfare, seasonal food distribution, and the provision of water and sanitation projects, Muslim FBOs employ few religious references to attract funding for sustainable livelihoods programmes. This may be because such projects comprise a relatively small part of their activities, or because they are less attractive to potential donors, or simply because the importance that Islamic teachings place on promoting economic self-reliance is not fully appreciated.

Encouraging microfinance

Promoting economic self-reliance through the provision of microfinance is particularly relevant in Islamic teachings. Muslims are encouraged to provide *qard hasan* to 'those in need'. *Qard hasan* is a cash loan that is repaid without interest, mark-up, or share in the venture for which the loan is used. 'Those in need' is generally understood to mean the more vulnerable sections of society, and it can be extended to include, for example, smallholder farmers or microentrepreneurs who are unable to receive finance from formal financial intermediaries such as commercial banks. There are several verses in the *Qur'an* that indicate that *qard hasan* loans are considered as if they were made to God or Allah, rather than to the loan recipients, to ease the pain for lenders of parting with their wealth. For example, 'Who is he that will give Allah *qard hasan*? For Allah will increase it manifold to his credit' (*Qur'an*, 57: 11); 'If you give Allah *qard hasan* ... He will grant you forgiveness' (*Qur'an*, 64: 17); and 'Establish regular prayer and give regular charity and give Allah *qard hasan*' (*Qur'an*, 73: 20).

While the borrower is obliged to return the loan, the lender is urged not to press the debtor if he or she is unable to repay the debt on time. In fact, the *Qur'an* states: 'If the debtor is in difficulty, grant him time till it is easy for him to repay' (*Qur'an*, 2: 280). Indeed, *qard hasan* is considered a 'benevolent loan', and this is generally interpreted to mean that if a borrower is unable to repay, the lender must accept the transaction as a charitable act. Sometimes a small administrative charge is permitted for *qard hasan* loans. Importantly, though, this charge cannot be made proportional to the amount or term of the loan, to prevent it from becoming equivalent to *riba* or interest. Underlining its importance, the Prophet Muhammad (PBUH) stated that the rewards provided by Allah for *qard hasan* are in fact greater than for *sadaqah*, even though the loan should be repaid. He is reported to have said:

> I saw on the gates of Heaven written 'the reward for *sadaqah* is 10 times and the reward for *qard hasan* is 18 times'. So, I asked the angel, how is it possible? The angel replied, 'Because the beggar who asked already had something, but a borrower did not ask for a loan unless he was in need.' (Ibn Majah, Volume 3, Book 15, *Hadith* 2431)

In fact, *qard hasan* is the only type of loan that is *Shari'ah*-compliant. Other financing arrangements employed in Islamic finance are in fact partnerships or sales contracts. There are many distinguished instances in Islamic history of partnerships and involvement in business and trade. For example, the first four caliphs and the famous Islamic jurist Imam Abu Hanifa were traders and most of the *Sahabah* or companions of the Prophet Muhammad (PBUH) worked as manual or craft labourers. Most prominently, though, the Prophet Muhammad (PBUH) himself was a successful merchant. He travelled widely on trade routes from the city of Mecca, which was a renowned market and centre for commerce at the time, to what is now Syria and Yemen with commercial caravans, most famously on behalf of Khadija bint Khwaylad, a wealthy and successful businesswoman, who would later become his wife. The Prophet Muhammad (PBUH) and his followers continued to trade during their exile in Medina and upon their return to Mecca. Unsurprisingly, therefore, there are numerous Islamic teachings and instructions in the areas of trade and business ethics – indeed, there are extensive collections of *ahadith* that deal exclusively with sales, trade and commercial transactions. More generally, Islamic social teachings support entrepreneurial activity, the profit motive, and economic competition (Clarke, 2011).

Despite its prominence in Islamic teachings, *Shari'ah*-compliant microfinance is not widespread among the activities of Muslim FBOs. Khan and Zeqiri (2017) describe a successful, but relatively small-scale, microfinance organization that Islamic Relief established in Kosovo that provides loans based on *qard hasan* and *murabaha* ('cost plus profit') financing. However, despite supporting microfinance programmes in nine other countries, some of which have been operational for more than 20 years, Islamic Relief has a total of just 16,037 active clients and an outstanding loans portfolio of £6.1 million. Although Islamic Relief is committed to 'strengthening our distinctive work in sustainable livelihoods (including Islamic microfinance)',[31] it has faced difficulties in attracting funding to support its microfinance operations.[32] As of the end of 2018, Muslim Aid had more clients, 27,362, but a smaller outstanding loans portfolio of £4.7 million.[33] While Muslim Hands promoted very small-scale Islamic microfinance projects in the past, Human Appeal and Ummah Welfare Trust do not encourage any such initiatives. Despite the challenges faced by Muslim FBOs, it is possible to develop successful, financially sustainable, and large-scale *qard hasan* microfinance institutions that are well-received by local populations. The most notable example is Akhuwat Islamic Microfinance from Pakistan, which in March 2020 had more than 800,000 active clients and an outstanding loans portfolio of approximately £90 million.[34] Drawing its inspiration from the concept of *mu'akhat* or brotherhood, a practice promoted by the Prophet Muhammad (PBUH) in the early days of Islam, the aim of the organization is to 'economically empower the poor through Qarz-e-Hasan [*qard hasan*]'.[35]

Advocacy on behalf of the poor

As mentioned earlier, of the leading Muslim FBOs only Islamic Relief reported allocating any of their budget to development advocacy. This has led Sparre and Juul Petersen (2007: 32) to describe the strategies used by Muslim

FBOs as 'implementation-oriented rather than advocacy-oriented', while Clarke (2007: 79) observes that faith-based development organizations in general are 'ready to advocate the charitable obligations of the faithful but less willing to press for political and social change'.

However, there is evidence that this approach is changing, beginning with the discourse of some of the leading Muslim FBOs. For example, Al-Khair Foundation aims to 'raise awareness of global issues',[36] while Muslim Aid claims that its advocacy includes 'engaging at policymaking forums at the United Nations, working with local governments in countries we operate in and influencing policies and parliamentarians in the UK Parliament as well as at the political party conferences.'[37] While it still comprises only a small proportion of its overall activities, Islamic Relief has also adopted a much stronger and more visible advocacy and campaigning role in recent years. This involves producing well-researched policy positions from an Islamic perspective to inform a range of development issues, such as protection for refugees, climate change, and violence against women and girls.[38] It also includes collaborating with other development organizations to lobby governments to raise awareness and change policies. It has supported, for example, the long-standing Jubilee Debt Campaign to cancel the debt of the world's most indebted developing countries, a more recent initiative demanding greater transparency of loans made to governments, as well as the annual global campaign against gender-based violence.

Another example of Islamic Relief's advocacy role relates to initiatives around HIV and AIDS. In November 2007, Islamic Relief organized five days of consultations on Islam and HIV/AIDS in South Africa with participants from more than 50 countries. Almost all those attending were people living with HIV, Islamic scholars and academics, and Muslim and non-Muslim development workers who were tackling the spread and impact of HIV/AIDS. The purpose of the discussions was to develop religiously acceptable approaches to the HIV pandemic that would help governments and development organizations effectively increase awareness of HIV and AIDS among individuals and communities, halt the spread of HIV, and support and care for those infected or impacted by HIV/AIDS. Among the objectives of the consultations was to push HIV/AIDS higher up the agenda of Muslim governments and communities through lobbying, advocacy work, and training, as well as to inspire and enable Muslim organizations to work more closely with marginalized groups. Juul Petersen (2015: 164) argues that Muslim FBOs, which already benefit from 'privileged access to working with Muslim communities', can utilize 'their religious identity as a tool to enhance development efforts'. Undoubtedly, Islamic Relief's position as a respected international FBO was key to attracting a wide range of participants for the consultations, including Islamic scholars willing to better understand a sensitive issue.[39]

There is support in Islamic social teachings for adopting a stronger position on advocacy. Specifically, there are several verses in the Qur'an that encourage believers to act as a voice for the poor and marginalized. For example:

'This was he that would not believe in Allah most high and would not encourage the feeding of the indigent' (*Qur'an*, 69: 33–4); and 'But you honour not the orphans! Nor do you encourage one another to feed the poor' (*Qur'an*, 89: 17–18). The *Qur'an* even equates the neglect of the poor with the neglect of religion: 'Have you seen him who rejects religion? That is the one who drives away the orphan and urges not the feeding of the poor' (*Qur'an*, 107: 1–3). These commands can be interpreted as asking believers to go beyond feeding the poor and providing charity, and to also encourage each other to help the poor. In this regard, and in contrast to their existing strategies, it has been argued that 'rather than aid deliverers they [Muslim FBOs] need to focus more on becoming change initiators'.[40]

More generally, Islam obliges Muslims to speak out on matters of social justice for the sake of the community. In fact, the concept of social justice is paramount in Islam. It includes three aspects: namely, a fair and equitable distribution of wealth; provision of the basic necessities of life to the poor and needy; and protection of the weak against economic exploitation by the powerful. Muslims are commanded to stand firm for justice at all costs: 'O ye who believe! Stand out firmly for justice, as witnesses to Allah, even as against yourselves, your parents, or your kin, and whether it be [against] rich or poor: for Allah can best protect both' (*Qur'an*, 4: 135). The importance of justice as a human value is emphasized in the following verse: 'Be just, that is closest to Godliness' (*Qur'an*, 5: 8).

Conclusion

Although quite diverse in the ways in which their faith identity is reflected in their development activities, the focus of Muslim FBOs has largely been on providing food and shelter, and satisfying the basic needs of poor and vulnerable people, particularly orphans. There is an emphasis on responding to natural hazards and assisting those fleeing conflict. In contrast, activities that encourage financial self-sufficiency through generating income and employment opportunities comprise only a small proportion of the endeavours of Muslim FBOs. Although the discourse of some of the larger and more established Muslim FBOs has evolved, particularly during the last decade, the focus of their programmes remains largely on providing emergency relief and satisfying basic needs. In fact, Muslim FBOs might generally be described as humanitarian relief agencies rather than longer-term development organizations.

As argued in this analysis, Islam encourages an approach that enables poor people to become financially self-sufficient. It reproaches begging and for those able to work, dependence on charity. This is an important consideration for development organizations working in Muslim communities, particularly Muslim FBOs that are largely reliant on religiously motivated *zakat* and *sadaqah* donations to support their operations. Islamic teachings can be interpreted as promoting sustainable livelihoods with a focus on developing small businesses and building capacity through activities that promote vocational training, technical assistance, marketing advice, business development services, and especially financial inclusion. At present, these activities comprise only a small proportion of the development programmes of Muslim FBOs.

Islam also encourages Muslims to be a 'voice of the poor'. In terms of development this can be translated into advocacy and campaigning on behalf of the poor on the many social and economic issues that most directly impact on their well-being, such as climate change, good governance, accountability, and unjust economic structures. Faith can and should be utilized to design the development strategies of Muslim FBOs. Indeed, once Muslim charities begin to more closely examine, interpret, and incorporate Islamic teachings into the way in which development projects are structured and implemented it might even be possible to begin discussing an 'Islamic approach to development'.

Notes

1. 'Faith-based' is generally used to describe organizations that have an affiliation with a religious body; a mission statement with explicit reference to religious values; financial support from religious sources; and a structure where staff selection or decision making is based on religious beliefs and values (Ferris, 2005). Following De Cordier (2009), Muslim faith-based organizations are described as non-governmental organizations that were founded by Muslims, receive most of their financial support from Muslims, and whose actions, to varying degrees, are inspired and legitimized by Islam.
2. The 17 member organizations are African Development Trust, African Relief Fund, Al-Imdaad Foundation UK, Al-Khair Foundation, Charity Right, Ethar Relief, Human Appeal, Human Care Syria, Human Relief Foundation, Islamic Help, Islamic Relief, Muslim Aid, Muslim Charity, Muslim Hands, Orphans in Need, Read Foundation, and the World Federation of Khoja Shia Ithna-Asheri Muslim Communities. See <https://www.muslimcharitiesforum.org.uk/our-member/> [accessed 25 March 2020].
3. Mostly these relate to accounts for 2019, although for some organizations it is 2018.
4. Personal communication with Chief Executive Officer, Muslim Charities Forum, 25 March 2019.
5. The singular is *hadith*.
6. This is a term of respect offered when referring to any prophet within the Islamic tradition.
7. Some Islamic charitable organizations, such as Islamic Relief, accept monetary donations as *waqf*, investing the money in, for example, property that is rented out and using the profits to fund their development programmes.
8. See <https://muslimhands.org.uk/about-us> [accessed 27 January 2019].
9. See <https://www.muslimaid.org/about-us/> [accessed 27 January 2019].

10. See <https://uwt.org/> [accessed 27 January 2019].
11. See, for example, <https://www.muslimaid.org/zakat-calculator/>; <https://www.islamic-relief.org.uk/about-us/what-we-do/zakat/zakat-calculator/> [both accessed 2 May 2019].
12. Institutional funding for Islamic Relief reached a high of almost 25 per cent in 2009 (Khan, 2012) with support from bodies such as DFID, but it has subsequently fallen. This does not include monetary equivalents of in-kind donations received from agencies such as the UN World Food Programme.
13. This is from Muslim Aid, although other Muslim FBOs have similar statements. See <https://www.muslimaid.org/what-we-do/> [accessed 18 June 2019].
14. See <https://muslimhands.org.uk/our-work> [accessed 18 June 2019].
15. See <https://www.islamic-relief.org/annual-reports/>.
16. See <http://apps.charitycommission.gov.uk/Accounts/Ends88/0001154288_AC_20171231_E_C.pdf>.
17. Ummah Welfare Trust (2019), p. 29.
18. See <https://www.muslimaid.org/about-us/finance/>.
19. See <http://apps.charitycommission.gov.uk/Accounts/Ends41/0001128341_AC_20180430_E_C.pdf>.
20. See <http://apps.charitycommission.gov.uk/Accounts/Ends08/0001126808_AC_20170731_E_C.pdf>.
21. See <https://muslimhands.org.uk/_ui/uploads/s3nyuw/MHAccounts2016.pdf>.
22. *Qurbani* means 'sacrifice' and refers to the ritual slaughter of animals. It can occur at any time of the year but is a requirement among Muslims during the religious festival *Eid ul-Adha*, commemorating the willingness of Abraham to sacrifice his son, Ismail, in the name of Allah.
23. In Islam an orphan is generally defined as a child who has lost his or her father, who is the family breadwinner.
24. Personal communication with Chief Operating Officer, Muslim Aid, 1 April 2019.
25. See <https://www.alkhair.org/mosques/> [accessed 4 April 2019].
26. *Da'wah* is literally translated from Arabic as 'making an invitation', although often it is understood as 'preaching Islam'. It has two dimensions: external and internal. External *da'wah* is to invite non-Muslims to Islam and teach them about Islamic beliefs and practices, while internal *da'wah* is to teach Muslims about aspects of Islam.
27. See <http://apps.charitycommission.gov.uk/Accounts/Ends18/0000202918_AC_20180331_E_C.pdf> [accessed 15 March 2019].
28. See <http://apps.charitycommission.gov.uk/Accounts/Ends90/0000213890_AC_20171231_E_C.pdf> [accessed 15 March 2019].
29. See <http://apps.charitycommission.gov.uk/Accounts/Ends84/0001160384_AC_20180331_E_C.pdf> [accessed 15 March 2019].
30. A livelihood comprises the capability, assets, and activities required for a means of living. It is deemed sustainable when it can cope with and recover from stresses and shocks and maintain or enhance its capability, assets, and activities both now and in the future, while not undermining the natural resource base.

31. See <https://www.islamic-relief.org/islamic-relief-global-strategy_2017-2021/> [accessed 25 March 2019].
32. Personal communication with Head of Islamic Microfinance Business Unit, Islamic Relief, 19 March 2019.
33. Personal communication with Director of International Programmes, Muslim Aid, 12 April 2019.
34. Personal communication with Chief Credit Officer, Akhuwat Islamic Microfinance, 25 March 2020.
35. Personal communication with Deputy Human Resources Manager, Akhuwat, 4 July 2019.
36. See <https://www.alkhair.org/about-us/> [accessed 21 July 2019].
37. See <https://www.muslimaid.org/what-we-do/global-advocacy/> [accessed 21 July 2019].
38. See <https://www.islamic-relief.org.uk/get-involved/campaigning/> [accessed 21 July 2019].
39. Personal communication with former Head of Policy and Research, Islamic Relief, 24 June 2019.
40. Personal communication with Chief Executive Officer, Muslim Charities Forum, 25 March 2019.

References

Bayat, A. (1992) 'The work ethic in Islam: a comparison with Protestantism', *The Islamic Quarterly* 36 (2): 5–27.
Benthall, J. and Bellion-Jourdan, J. (2003) *The Charitable Crescent: Politics of Aid in the Muslim World*, I.B. Tauris, London and New York.
Clarke, G. (2007) 'Agents of transformation? Donors, faith-based organisations and international development', *Third World Quarterly* 28 (1): 77–96.
Clarke, M. (2011) *Development and Religion: Theology and Practice*, Edward Elgar Publishing, Cheltenham.
De Cordier, B. (2009) 'Faith-based aid, globalisation and the humanitarian frontline: an analysis of Western-based Muslim aid organisations', *Disasters: The Journal of Disaster Studies, Policy and Management* 33 (4): 608–28.
Ferris, E. (2005) 'Faith-based and secular humanitarian organizations', *International Review of the Red Cross* 87 (858).
Human Appeal (2015) *Annual Report and Financial Statements 2015*, Human Appeal, Cheadle <https://www.humanappeal.org.uk/media/1513404/a4-annualreport-20153a16-web.pdf>.
Imtiaz, A. (2020) 'An examination of the inquiries conducted on British Muslim charities by the Charity Commission', *Forum* 2 (Winter 2019/20).
Islamic Relief (2019) *Islamic Relief Worldwide Annual Report 2018*, Islamic Relief Worldwide, Birmingham <https://www.islamic-relief.org/annual-reports/>.
Islamic Relief Worldwide (2018) *2017 Annual Report and Financial Statements*, Islamic Relief Worldwide, Birmingham <https://www.islamic-relief.org/annual-reports/>.
Itani, F. (2019) 'The way forward: reflections of MCF's Chief Executive', *Forum* 1 (Summer 2019).
Juul Petersen, M. (2015) *For Humanity or for the Umma? Aid and Islam in Transnational Muslim NGOs*, Hurst & Company, London.

Karim, F. (1996) *Imam Ghazzali's Ihya Ulum-Din: The Book of Religious Learnings*, Islamic Book Services, New Delhi.

Khan, A.A. (2012) 'Religious obligation or altruistic giving? Muslims and charitable donations', in M. Barnett and J. Gross Stein (eds), *Sacred Aid: Faith and Humanitarianism*, Oxford University Press, New York.

Khan, A.A. and Zeqiri, V. (2017) 'Pioneering Islamic microfinance in Kosovo: the experience of START', in M. Harper and A.A. Khan (eds), *Islamic Microfinance: Shari'ah compliant and sustainable?*, Practical Action Publishing, Rugby.

Khan, A.A., Ishaq, M.S., Afonso, J.S. and Akram, S. (2017) 'Is it possible to provide *qard hasan* and achieve financial self-sustainability? The experience of Akhuwat in Pakistan', in M. Harper and A.A. Khan (eds), *Islamic Microfinance: Shari'ah compliant and sustainable?*, Practical Action Publishing, Rugby.

Muslim Aid (2018) *Trustees Report and Financial Statements for the Year Ended 31 December 2017*, Muslim Aid, London <https://www.muslimaid.org/about-us/annual-report/>.

Muslim Hands (2018) *Annual Financial Report 2017*. Muslim Hands, Nottingham <https://muslimhands.org.uk/_ui/uploads/cq5s7c/MH%20Annual%20Accounts%202017.pdf>.

Singer, A. (2008) *Charity in Islamic Societies*, Cambridge University Press, Cambridge.

Sparre, S.L. and M. Juul Petersen (2007) *Islam and Civil Society: Case Studies from Jordan and Egypt*, Report 13, Danish Institute for International Studies, Copenhagen.

Ummah Welfare Trust (2019) *For the Ummah in Need: Annual Report 1440 (2019)*, Ummah Welfare Trust, Bolton <https://uwt.org/wp-content/uploads/2019/04/UWT-Annual-Report-2019-1440-RFS.pdf>.

About the author

Ajaz Ahmed Khan is Senior Microfinance Adviser with CARE International. He holds a PhD in Development Economics and has extensive experience of working in a diverse range of countries in Latin America, Eastern Europe, Asia, and Africa. He has written widely on microfinance and on Islamic microfinance in particular, as well as more generally on faith and development.

CHAPTER 5
Islamic perspectives on refugees, asylum, and forced migration

Sadia Najma Kidwai

Islam has a strong heritage of forced migrant protection, stemming from the original teachings of the Qur'an, as well as from historical examples taken from the lives of great prophets – from Abraham (Peace Be Upon Him), to Moses (PBUH), to the Prophet Muhammad (PBUH). This heritage includes strong – even stern – commands on the importance of seeking refuge if one is facing persecution, as well as on the duty of providing asylum to those who need it. It is a tradition that provides a robust and generous framework for the protection of and provision for forced migrants, enshrining rights such as the rights to dignity, non-refoulement, equal treatment, shelter, healthcare, family reunification, and protection of property. Yet this tradition is rarely understood or invoked in the modern context, despite Muslim countries currently hosting over 50 per cent of the world's forced migrants. There is a pressing need not only to nurture the theological discourse on the issue of forced migrant protection in Islam, but to translate these traditions into practical action. Such traditions could play a vital role in helping such countries assist forced migrants in a manner that respects the rights and dignity conferred on them by God.

Keywords: Islam, Muslim, refugees, rights, protection, displacement, forced migration

Introduction: forced migration in Islamic history

Forced migration has been a core element of the human experience throughout history. The Islamic tradition is rich with stories of forced migration and teachings on the importance of providing protection for those seeking refuge. Migration and escape from persecution have played a prominent role in the stories of many of Islam's great prophets – such as the Prophet Abraham's (Peace Be Upon Him[1]) migration to Canaan (*Qur'an*, 29: 26) and the Prophet Moses' (PBUH) migration to Midian (*Qur'an*, 28: 20–8). Forced migration played a particular role in the life of the Prophet Muhammad (PBUH) and his first companions. In 615 AD, approximately 100 early Muslims sought refuge with the Christian King Negus of Abyssinia to escape the brutal persecution of the ruling Qur'aysh tribe in Mecca (Ramadan, 2008: 59). This was followed by a larger migration to Medina in 622 AD, which the Prophet Muhammad

http://dx.doi.org/10.3362/9781788530613.005

(PBUH) joined (Rahaei, 2009: 4). As this chapter will discuss, Qur'anic narrations of these stories highlight the high status of both those who seek refuge from persecution and those who provide refuge.[2]

The International Organization for Migration (IOM) defines forced migration as:

> A migratory movement in which an element of coercion exists, including threats to life and livelihood, whether arising from natural or man-made causes (e.g. movements of refugees and internally displaced persons as well as people displaced by natural or environmental disasters, chemical or nuclear disasters, famine, or development projects).[3]

While there exists no exact linguistic equivalent of the term 'forced migrant' within Islamic legal traditions, the term *hijrah* (migration) and its derivatives are mentioned 27 times in the *Qur'an* (Munir, 2011: 4). Zaat notes that there are a further 650 *ahadith* (sayings of the Prophet Muhammad (PBUH)) on the topic of protection and assistance (2007: 6–7). The centrality of migration to the Islamic tradition is perhaps best evidenced by the Islamic calendar system, for the calendar does not start with the Prophet's birth or the commencement of revelation, nor even with the conquest of Mecca, but rather with the *hijrah* of the Prophet Muhammad (PBUH) and his companions to Medina ('Abd al-Rahim, 2008: 19).

Both Muslim scholars and leading international bodies (such as the Organisation of Islamic Cooperation (OIC), United Nations High Commissioner for Refugees (UNHCR), Ahmed Abou El-Wafa, and Abdul Rahman Latif of the US-based Yaqeen Institute) recognize the leading role that Islamic teachings can play in international forced migrant protection frameworks. Over the centuries, Islamic scholars built up a comprehensive body of ethical teachings and legal injunctions regarding the protection of forced migrants, based on Qur'anic teachings and examples from the *Sunnah* (practice) of the Prophet Muhammad (PBUH) and drawing on some of the cultural practices that became prominent across the Muslim world ('Abd al-Rahim, 2008: 15). A 2007 conference on asylum and Islam led by the UNHCR spoke of Islam's 'highly sophisticated tradition', with its 'fundamental humanitarian spirit' having strong parallels with existing international law (UNHCR, 2008: 64). The 2012 Ashgabat Declaration on Refugees in the Muslim World by the OIC stated: 'We recognize that over fourteen centuries ago, Islam laid down the bases for granting refuge, which is now deeply ingrained in Islamic faith, heritage and tradition.' Rahaei speaks of how respect for asylum seekers and those who provide refuge has a 'particular place in *Shari'ah*' and that 'Islam pays special attention to the suffering of forced migrants' (2009: 4).

The challenges of upholding Islamic traditions in the modern context

Unfortunately, such traditions are rarely invoked today. Following the collapse of the Islamic Ottoman state in 1924, many Muslim states (a term which, in this chapter, we use to refer to the 57 member states of the OIC[4] and/or countries with a Muslim-majority population), such as Turkey, Egypt, and Tunisia, underwent an immense process of secularization, with 'most Muslim governments [replacing] Islamic law with legal systems inspired by Western secular codes' (Esposito, 2010: 51). Scholars were excluded or played a marginal role in advising on matters of state (ibid.). As a result, Islamic scholarship has no longer been required to legislate on matters relating to Islamic protection frameworks, nor to adapt classical Islamic teachings to the changing circumstances of the modern world. Indeed, modern phenomenon such as increased restrictions on movement between states, or the growing prominence of the nation state as the primary gatekeeper and provider for citizens, which arguably has replaced the frameworks of community and individual obligations in which Islamic law evolved, may render some traditional rulings on protection irrelevant or impractical.

Perhaps as a consequence of this, Islamic Relief Worldwide's experiences have indicated that, while many Muslim states maintain strong cultures and traditions of hosting forced migrants, popular understanding and awareness of specific Islamic frameworks for the protection of forced migrants remain weak (FitzGibbon et al., 2014: 10). However, despite some apparent disjuncture between classical teachings and the modern context, reviving an awareness of such teachings among both host and migrant communities could play a powerful role in improving the condition of forced migrants globally, assisting in improving relations between host and migrant communities, as well as acting as a useful motivating factor for host states and communities.

Moreover, there is an urgent need for a comprehensive Islamic framework for the protection of forced migrants. As of 2017, three of the top five refugee-producing countries in the world were Muslim states (Syria, Afghanistan, and Somalia), with refugees from a fourth state (Myanmar) being predominantly Muslim. Similarly, of the top eight refugee-hosting countries in the world, a staggering seven were Muslim states (Turkey, Pakistan, Uganda, Lebanon, Iran, Bangladesh, and Sudan) (UNHCR, 2018a: 3). Beyond the sheer numbers, the 57 OIC states have become home to some of the largest, most protracted, and most complex forced migration situations in the world (OIC, 2006: 5). Indeed, as of 2017, Muslim states hosted more than 40 million refugees, internally displaced people (IDPs), asylum seekers, stateless people, and returnees – over 50 per cent of the persons who are of concern to UNHCR (UNHCR, 2018a: 64–7).

While the hospitality of such states should be commended, protection frameworks remain weak. Only 36 of the 57 OIC member states are signatories of the 1951 Refugee Convention (UNHCR, 2015).[5] Many states also lack effective domestic legislation on asylum, meaning that refugees and other forced migrants are forced to live in a legal vacuum (Munir, 2011: 19), leaving them without formal access to basic services such as housing, healthcare, education, or work, and therefore vulnerable to poverty and exploitation. Some such states criticize the 1951 Refugee Convention, concerned that it does not reflect the values and circumstances of non-European states.[6]

These concerns serve to emphasize the need for greater discussion around the rights of forced migrants in Islamic traditions, and for the development of a protection framework that is rooted in the values of both host states and forced migrant populations themselves. While progress has been made on this in recent years – 2012 saw the UNHCR and the OIC jointly organize the International Conference on Refugees in the Muslim World (the first ministerial-level meeting to deal specifically with this issue) – the international community still lacks a framework that clearly outlines the rights and duties of those who seek and provide asylum within Islamic traditions.

A comprehensive framework for forced migrant protection that is both rooted in Islamic values and applicable to modern challenges would have vital practical value. Developing such a framework would require further research and consultation with Islamic scholars, forced migration populations, and states and communities hosting forced migrants. As a starting point, this chapter seeks to outline the overarching principles and classical practices of forced migrant protection within Islamic traditions that may guide those working in forced migration protection today.

Who is a 'forced migrant'?

Islamic traditions do not offer a specific linguistic equivalent of a 'refugee', 'internally displaced person' or 'asylum seeker'. Unlike in international law, there is no legal distinction between the various categories of forced migrants (Zaat, 2007: 13), in part due to current legal definitions being dependent on a state-centric international system, whereas Islamic law evolved in contexts of community rule or empire. However, the *Qur'an* makes repeated reference to the link between persecution and forced migration, speaking of the 'oppressed' (*Qur'an*, 7: 137, 4: 97), 'those who have been driven unjustly from their homes' (*Qur'an*, 22: 40), and those 'driven out of their homeland' (*Qur'an*, 2: 246) – indicating that much of Islam's tradition relating to forced migrants deals with those escaping persecution or oppression.[7]

The form that such oppression may take is not always clarified. The *Qur'an* and *Sunnah* often refer to examples of religious persecution (as this was the persecution suffered by many of the prophets). Abou-El-Wafa argues that 'if a Muslim cannot pronounce his religion or perform his religious duties in a non-Muslim country, he shall be under an obligation to emigrate' (2009: 114–15). Ibn Arabi, however, broadens the definition of persecution, claiming that asylum is obligatory from states where there is injustice, intolerance, physical persecution, disease, and financial insecurity (Kirmani et al., 2008: 4). Drawing on Ibn Arabi's definition, we could say that any person who is obliged to leave a place due to the factors named above could be considered a forced migrant, including those suffering from extreme poverty or as a result of disasters.

Nonetheless, the first Muslims who migrated to Medina in 622 AD, despite being motivated by a desire to escape persecution, were simply named the *muhajirun* (the emigrants). Thus *hijrah* (migration) in contemporary legal terminology is the closest equivalent to territorial asylum – that is, the relocation of people from a place where they fear for their life, family, and protection, to a place where they avail themselves of protection and security (Abou-El-Wafa, 2009: 255).

The duty to seek asylum

This highlights a subtle yet fundamental difference between Islamic and international understandings of forced migrants' rights. Shahrani and Malkki both argue that current efforts by international organizations to portray forced migrants as symbols of 'shared humanity' and 'universal suffering' lead to forced migrants being perceived as passive, powerless, de-politicized figures who are denied a sense of history, culture, or nationality (Kirmani et al., 2008: 6–7).

Alternatively, Islamic teachings emphasize the fundamental dignity of mankind. The *Qur'an* states: 'We have honoured the children of Adam ... and favoured them specially above many of those We have created' (*Qur'an*, 17: 70). This honour given to mankind is unconditional and must be respected regardless of a person's gender, race, class, nationality, or legal status. Likewise, forced migrants must be treated with the dignity and honour that God has bestowed upon them.

In Islam, the seeking of asylum is rooted in the attributes of moral autonomy and free will – uniquely conferred by God on mankind ('Abd al-Rahim, 2008: 16). As such, within an Islamic framework we may speak of the 'duty' rather than the 'right' to seek asylum. The *Qur'an* states: 'When the angels take the souls of those who have wronged themselves, they ask them "What circumstances were you in?" They reply, "We were oppressed in this land," and the angels say, "But was God's Earth not spacious enough for you to migrate to some other place?"' (*Qur'an*, 4: 97).

Therefore, with the freedom bestowed upon mankind comes an obligation to preserve our human dignity by seeking refuge from oppression and persecution. The Islamic concept of a forced migrant does not merely imply a helpless victim of circumstance but rather one who has taken an active choice to preserve their life, according to the command of God. Such an understanding confers agency and dignity on forced migrants. The early Muslim migrants were defined as *muhajirun*, a definition that did not differentiate them from other categories of migrants and that emphasized their decision to emigrate, rather than their need for refuge.

The Qur'anic verse 4: 97 underlines the moral obligation to protect one's own life and seek refuge from oppression. The verse finishes by saying:

> These people will have Hell as their refuge, an evil destination. But not so the truly helpless men, women, and children who have no means in their power nor any way to leave – God may well pardon these, for He is most pardoning and most forgiving. Anyone who migrates for God's cause will find many a refuge and great plenty in the Earth. (*Qur'an*, 4: 97–9)

This verse refers to the specific context of the early Muslims' migration to Medina. Given the impossibility of practising Islam in Mecca, early Muslims were strongly encouraged to migrate to Medina from 622 AD (Ramadan, 2008: 76). The majority did so, obeying the encouragement of the Prophet (Lings, 1984: 113). However, Ad-Dahhak states that the stern warnings in this verse refer to a minority of hypocrites who did not migrate to Medina, but pretended to be weak in order to remain in Mecca and eventually chose to fight against the Muslims in the subsequent battle of Badr. Such people, he states, were committing injustice against themselves (Ibn Kathir, 2000).

Nonetheless, we can take from this verse the teaching that those who *truly* have the *means in their power* to escape persecution are morally obliged to do so. Failure to fulfil this duty is not only a denial of God's mercy – His spacious and plentiful Earth – but potentially a grave sin, in that such individuals may become complicit in the persecution committed against themselves (Agha, 2008: 32). In Islam, persecution is considered one of the gravest acts of injustice and is repeatedly cast as 'worse than killing' (*Qur'an*, 2: 191, 2: 217). While Islam encourages restraint and peaceful behaviour (*Qur'an*, 5: 32, 8: 61, 43: 89), the *Qur'an* calls on Muslims to 'uphold justice ... even if it is against yourselves' (*Qur'an*, 4: 135), while the Prophet Muhammad (PBUH) famously taught: 'Whosoever of you sees an evil, let him change it with his hand; and if he is not able to do so, then [let him change it] with his tongue; and if he is not able to do so, then with his heart – and that is the weakest of faith' (Nawawi, *Hadith* 34). This verse serves as a reminder to those suffering persecution that they are not helpless, that many of them have both the power and the agency to change their situation, and are therefore obligated to do so. While such a verse may appear stern, it underlines the vital importance of protecting oneself, and the dignity conferred on those who do so. Of course, such sternness is reserved only for those who are capable of migration – 'But not so the truly helpless ... who have no means in their power nor any way to leave.'

The *Qur'an* takes further steps to incentivize the persecuted to migrate by promising security and abundant reward with God. Referring to the first Muslims, the *Qur'an* states: 'Remember when you were few, victimized in the land ... but God sheltered you and strengthened you with his help, and provided you with good things' (*Qur'an*, 8: 26). The first emigrants are promised '[g]ardens graced with flowing streams [i.e. Heaven] ... a supreme triumph' (*Qur'an*, 9: 100). Those who emigrated in God's cause after being wronged are promised 'a good home in this world, but the reward of the Hereafter will be far greater' (*Qur'an*, 16: 41). The verse 'anyone who migrates for God's cause will find many a refuge and great plenty in the Earth' (*Qur'an*, 4: 99) implies that the persecuted are not only promised a safe refuge by God, if they seek it, but that they will also find 'a great plenty' – meaning provision and wealth (Ibn Kathir, 2000).

The duty to provide asylum

The verse above (*Qur'an*, 4: 99) also highlights that, while seeking asylum is a duty, being granted asylum is also a right. The verse implies that the persecuted have an obligation to find refuge, a right that has been conferred by God, and which their fellow humans have a duty to fulfil. This verse reminds Muslims that we are simply custodians of the Earth, not the owners, and thus do not have the right to deny territorial refuge to those to whom God has promised it. This right to asylum may be claimed by Muslims and non-Muslims alike from a Muslim community (Munir, 2011: 13). The *Qur'an* states: 'And if any one of the idolaters should seek your protection, grant it to him so that he may hear the word of God, then take him to a place safe for him' (*Qur'an*, 9: 6).

The Arabic word for protection used here is *istijara*. While it literally means 'protection', it also refers to an old Arab custom of honouring and protecting one's neighbour to the best of one's ability ('Abd al-Rahim, 2008: 20). Discussions around forced migrant protection also focus on the use of the word *aman* at the end of the verse, which could be translated as 'safe conduct' or an 'assurance of protection' (Munir, 2011: 6).

There are innumerable references in the *Qur'an* and *ahadith* (sayings of the Prophet Muhammad (PBUH)) to the duty of Muslims to provide asylum to those seeking refuge and to protect the persecuted. Within the Islamic framework, providing refuge to a forced migrant is not an act of charity, but rather an act of justice. Referring to the case of persecuted Muslims who migrated to Medina, the *Qur'an* says:

> As for those who believed but did not emigrate, you are not responsible for their protection until they have done so. But if they seek help from you against persecution, it is your duty to assist them, except against people with whom you have a treaty: God sees all that you do. (*Qur'an*, 8: 72)

Consequently, there is a clear religiously mandated requirement to provide protection and assistance to forced migrants (the nature of what this assistance and protection might look like is discussed below). This is reinforced by the aforementioned verses mandating Muslims to stand up for justice, and reminders that saving one life is the equivalent of saving all of mankind (*Qur'an*, 5: 32). Helping the oppressed is a core theme in Islamic teachings. The *Qur'an* speaks of how God wished to 'favour those who were oppressed in the land' (*Qur'an*, 28: 5), and calls on Muslims to fulfil the role of protectors and helpers to 'those oppressed men, women and children who cry out "Lord, rescue us from this town where people are oppressors!"' (*Qur'an*, 4: 75).

The Prophet Muhammad (PBUH) repeatedly commanded his followers to help the oppressed, with one famous narration capturing his directive to:

> Help your brother, whether he is an oppressor, or he is an oppressed one. People asked, 'O Allah's Messenger! It is all right to help him if he is oppressed, but how should we help him if he is an oppressor?'

The Prophet said, 'By preventing him from oppressing others.' (Bukhari, Book 46, *Hadith* 5).

The citizens of Medina who first offered refuge and help to the persecuted Muslims of Mecca are called 'the true believers' who 'will have forgiveness and generous provision' (*Qur'an*, 8: 74).

Who is responsible for providing asylum?

There is consensus among both classical and modern scholars that Muslims are obliged to provide asylum to those who seek it. Arnaout claims that it is not permitted for 'the asylum seeker to be refused access or admission to the territory of the country where he has requested refuge' (Zaat, 2007: 19).

However, there is a difference of opinion among Islamic scholars regarding whether this is a communal obligation (*fard kifaya*) or an individual obligation (*fard 'ayn*). Regardless, classical traditions indicate that individuals played a central role in providing protection to forced migrants, with some academics even claiming that 'refugee law in Islam is not an area in which the Muslim state and the non-Muslim state have much to do'; rather, it is citizens who are involved in this area of law (Munir, 2011: 2). Elmadmad argues that providing asylum is a duty of any person living in an Islamic country (2008: 54). While it may be challenging to see how that could be applied in the context of the modern refugee crisis, where refugee status can be determined only by governments or the UNHCR,[8] in principle it underlines the gravity of the individual responsibility of Muslims to protect forced migrants where it is in their power to do so.

Such asylum can be provided to a small group of men, women, and children (according to the means of the individual providing protection), either Muslim or non-Muslim, and is not dependent on the political, civil, social, cultural, religious, or economic characteristics of the person fleeing persecution (Zaat, 2007: 20). Even enemy combatants are entitled to receive protection, provided they prove their non-combatant status first (Abou-El-Wafa 2009: 22). Asylum can be given verbally or by gesture, by request or by invitation (Yacoob and Aiman, quoted in Zaat, 2007: 20), and does not even require asylum seekers to prove their persecuted status (Elmadmad, 2008: 54). While these practices may not always be possible to implement in the modern context, they again underline the individual obligation to protect and provide for forced migrants within Islamic teachings.

According to the leading Maliki[9] jurist Ibn Juzayy, once granted, this *aman*, whether given to a Muslim or a non-Muslim, would become binding on the imam and other citizens of the state, provided there were no harm in it – although it is not clear who would be responsible for judging the 'harm' (Munir, 2011: 7). Examples of this 'individual' refuge are often cited in the *seerah* (stories of the Prophet Muhammad's (PBUH) life). The Prophet Muhammad (PBUH) himself was granted protection first by his uncle Abu Talib, and later by al-Mot'am ibn 'Udayy, which prevented the Qur'aysh tribe from attacking him as they had attacked his unprotected followers (Abou-El-Wafa, 2009: 95). The Prophet Muhammad (PBUH) taught that 'Muslims are equal in respect of blood; the lowest of them is entitled to give protection on behalf of them, and the one residing far away may give protection on behalf of them' (Abu Dawud, Book 15, *Hadith* 275). Maliki, Shafi'i, and Hanbali jurists have interpreted this to mean that asylum can be granted by slaves as well as by free men (Munir, 2011: 7), and even by discerning children, according to some classical jurists ('Abd al-Rahim, 2008: 20). This teaching indicates that, whether asylum is given by an individual or the state, it must be respected by all within that society.

The right to grant more general asylum (e.g. for large groups of forced migrants, or protection agreements between states) would lie only with the imam or relevant state representative (Munir, 2011: 7). In Islamic history, anyone seeking refuge in *dar ul Islam* (the land of Islam) was granted asylum. If protection was granted, they became a *musta'min* or a protected person (OIC, 2006). There are only a handful of instances when an Islamic state may refuse asylum: first, if the migrant is a non-political criminal (particularly one who has committed offences in their country of origin and seeks refuge as a means to avoid punishment) (Abou-El-Wafa, 2009: 181–4); second, if the migrant is an enemy combatant who has not revoked their combatant status (Zaat, 2007: 20); and third, if hosting a migrant would contravene existing treaties with other states. An example of the latter could be the Hudaibiyah Treaty signed between the Prophet Muhammad (PBUH) and the Qur'aysh tribe of Mecca, which forbade the Muslim community in Medina from accepting any further Muslim refugees fleeing Mecca. When one such refugee attempted to seek asylum with the Prophet Muhammad (PBUH), the Prophet responded to him: 'Abu Baseer, we had given those people what you know [a treaty] and in our religion treachery is not good for us' (Abou-El-Wafa, 2009: 188).

The rights of forced migrants

The Islamic concepts of *aman* and *istijara* (asylum and protection) do not simply consist of allowing an asylum seeker entry into a country, city, or community. Rather, Islam provides a comprehensive framework for the *musta'min*'s protection and provision, or what an Arab parliamentarians' symposium called 'the rich traditions, customs and practices involved in Arab and Islamic values', which provide 'a firm underpinning for the integrated protection of refugees and respect for their human integrity' (Abou-El-Wafa, 2009: 52).

Once *aman* is granted, a *musta'min* should benefit from all the rights granted to nationals (Elmadmad, 2008: 54). Such a conceptual framework finds its foundations in the example of the Constitution of Medina, which promised equal protections for all citizens of Medina – be they migrants or indigenous, Muslims or non-Muslims (Ramadan, 2008: 88). Equally, a framework of forced migrant rights would need to reflect the five 'purposes' (or *maqasid*) of *Shari'ah* (Islamic law), which form the foundation of Islamic governance and citizens' rights: the protection of life, religion, intellect, wealth, and posterity (i.e. family) (Aminu-Kano, 2014). These principles provide a comprehensive framework within which we can understand the rights due to a *musta'min*, stemming from the right to protection, the right to non-refoulement, the right to have their physical needs met, the right to freedom of belief, the right to do business and have their wealth protected, the right to marry and raise children, and the right of family reunification (Munir, 2011: 14; 'Abd al-Rahim, 2008: 21; Abou-El-Wafa, 2009: 143). Such rights would be due to any *musta'min*, regardless of whether they were a refugee, an internally displaced person, or a stateless person (Zaat, 2007: 13).

The obligation to fulfil the rights of forced migrants finds its roots in the broader ethos of Islamic teachings on human rights (a comprehensive analysis of which can be found in Aminu-Kano, 2014). For Muslims, God is the source of human dignity and rights, leading to the notion that the fulfilment of the rights of others is an obligation upon all believers, for which individuals will feel the weight of divine accountability. Moreover, such obligations are a fulfilment of the rights of God over humankind, only manifested to us indirectly through our fellow man (ibid.: 6–7). Although modern protection frameworks tend to see government as the primary guardian of such rights, Islam emphasizes responsibility at all levels of society, from individuals and families to communities and wider civil society (ibid.). Thus, within an Islamic framework of rights, while the government must be the ultimate guarantor of protection and justice, it is only 'the guardian of he who has no guardian' (Abu Dawud, Book 12, *Hadith* 38).

As such, it is primarily the duty of the host community to ensure that a *musta'min* is not denied these rights. The *Qur'an* repeatedly calls on Muslims to 'give what is due to ... the wayfarer' (*Qur'an*, 30: 38, 17: 26). To do so should not be regarded as a burden, or as a source of resentment, but rather considered as a noble blessing conferred on people by God. The Prophet Muhammad (PBUH) reminds Muslims that:

> whoever fulfilled the needs of his brother, God will fulfil his needs; whoever brought his brother out of a discomfort, God will bring him out of the discomforts of the Day of Resurrection, and whoever screened [provided sanctuary to] a Muslim, God will screen [provide a sanctuary] to him on the Day of Resurrection. (Bukhari, Book 46, *Hadith* 3)

The right to protection

The first and most obvious right of a *musta'min* is the right to protection, for this is the fundamental purpose of seeking and providing refuge. This is implicit in the Qur'anic verse 9: 6, which calls on Muslims to grant protection (*istijara*) to those who seek it, while the juristic terminology of *aman* refers to an 'assurance of protection' (Munir, 2011: 6). The Prophet Muhammad (PBUH) taught his followers that

> the asylum [of protection] granted by any Muslim is to be secured [respected] by all the Muslims, even if it is granted by one of the lowest social status among them. And whoever betrays a Muslim in this respect incurs the curse of God, the angels and all the people. (Bukhari, Book 29, *Hadith* 4)

The protection of life is one of the key objectives of *Shari'ah*, and Islam provides firm teachings on the sanctity of life. God calls upon Muslims not only to refrain from murder, but also to actively strive to protect the lives of others – the *Qur'an* equates killing a person with '[killing] all mankind', while 'if any saves a life it is as if he saves the lives of all mankind'.

The right to non-refoulement (forced return to one's persecutor)

As part of this protection covenant it is forbidden to force a *musta'min* to return to their country of origin against their will. This is rooted in the prophetic teaching that 'a Muslim is a brother of another Muslim, so he should not oppress him, nor should he hand him over to an oppressor' (Bukhari, Book 46, *Hadith* 3). There is a consensus that this right extends to both Muslims and non-Muslims. Imam ash-Shaybani states that even if an enemy fighter came seeking *aman*, he should not be forced to return to his state if he feared being killed (Abou-El-Wafa, 2009: 56). To force him to do so would be considered treachery and a grave injustice, and jurists agree that Islamic states should continue their protection even if the refugee's state of origin threatens to wage war should the *musta'min* not be extradited (ibid.: 56).

Imam ash-Shaybani goes even further to state that, even 'if a person entered a Muslim state with *aman* and killed a Muslim intentionally or without intention, or committed robbery, or spied on the Muslims and sent it [the information] to the polytheists, or raped a Muslim or a non-Muslim woman [non-Muslim citizen of the Muslim state], or committed theft, then none of these amount to breach of his *aman*' (Munir, 2011: 10), but rather that *musta'min* would be subject to the laws of the state.

The sanctity of non-refoulement has been endorsed by prominent modern jurists such as Shaykh Faisal Mawlawi (in a *fatwa* – legal ruling – entitled 'The Rights of Refugees in Islam', cited in Zaat, 2007: 20) as well as by the OIC (OIC, 2006). Perhaps one of the most powerful examples of non-refoulement being practised in Islamic history is the story of Negus, the Abyssinian king with whom early Meccan Muslims sought refuge (before their eventual migration to Medina). When representatives of the Qur'aysh arrived, beseeching Negus to return the asylum seekers to Mecca in order to face justice for their treacherous behaviour, Negus responded:

> Nay, by God, they shall not be betrayed – a people that have sought my protection and made my country their abode and chosen me above

all others! Give them up I will not, until I have summoned them and questioned them concerning what these men say of them. If it be as they have said, then will I deliver them unto them, that they may restore them to their own people. But if not, then I will be their good protector, so long as they seek my protection. (Lings, 1984: 83–4)

After assessing the case, he said to the refugees: 'Go your ways, for ye are safe in my land. Not for mountains of gold would I harm a single man of you' (Lings, 1984).

The right to dignity, generosity, and a loving welcome

The Islamic protection framework emphasizes the importance of ensuring that *musta'min* are able to maintain their dignity. This stems from the inherent dignity due to all humans, as God stated that He has 'honoured the children of Adam ... favoured them specially above many of those We have created' (*Qur'an*, 17: 70). The Prophet Muhammad (PBUH) was 'deeply aware' of the hardship and destitution faced by the Meccan emigrants when they first arrived in Medina, for they had fled intolerable conditions and arrived bereft of property, belongings, and income (Agha, 2008: 36). To counter this, the Prophet famously declared the Meccan emigrants (the *Muhajirun*) and their hosts in Medina (the *Ansar*) brothers and sisters to one another. He established a unique system of protection wherein each *Ansar* family would take responsibility for one *Muhajir* family, sharing their wealth, food, home, and tribal protection with them. Such a system facilitated the integration of the *Muhajirs* into the society around them, providing them with a sense of belonging, as well as a source of spiritual assistance (Ramadan, 2008: 92). An example of community-based direct protection in the modern context could be the phenomenon of individuals hosting refugees in their own homes – especially popular across Europe (Wade, 2016) – or community-based sponsorship in Canada (see Box 5.1).

Box 5.1 Community-based protection in an urbanized world: the case of Muslim community sponsorship programmes in Canada

Islamic traditions often emphasize the integration of forced migrants into the communities (and even homes) of those who pledge to protect them – as opposed to being placed in camps, separate to host communities, as had been the dominant practice of states and UNHCR until recent years. It was only in 2014 that UNHCR introduced its policy on alternatives to camps, recognizing that when refugees are able to live and work among host communities, they 'have the possibility to live with greater dignity, independence and normality as members of the community' (UNHCR, 2014: 4).

In practice, 58 per cent of the world's refugees now live in urban areas (UNHCR, 2018a: 60). This can pose a challenge to humanitarian agencies – and even munici-palities – that may struggle to identify and meet the complex and diverse needs of new refugees in dense urban spaces. While local communities – and particularly local faith communities – have often historically been the first responders to the needs of forced migrants, there is now growing recognition in policy circles of the central role that local communities can play in caring for urban refugees (El Nakib and Ager, 2015: 5).

(Continued)

> **Box 5.1** Continued
>
> One contemporary example of community-based care is Canada's Community Sponsorship Scheme, which allows for community organizations to sponsor refugees to come to Canada. The scheme has seen a proliferation of Muslim community groups taking part – such as the Islamic Foundation of Toronto, the Muslim Association of Hamilton, Islamic Circle of North America (ICNA) Relief Canada, and Islamic Relief Canada. These community groups pledge to assume responsibility for the emotional and financial needs of incoming refugees,[10] many of whom are Muslims too. Islamic Relief staff in Canada have spoken of the central role that mosques play in orienting refugees in their new country, allowing them to socialize with the community and learn more about what services and facilities are available in the locality, while local Muslim community members volunteer their time to teach new refugees English or provide free health check-ups.[11] The Muslim Association of Brantford recruits volunteers to act as translators and mentors for new families, assisting new arrivals in navigating essential daily tasks such as banking or shopping for groceries.[12]

Abou-El-Wafa notes that, within Islamic history, 'it is established that refugees, Muslim or non-Muslim, were accorded a treatment that was no less, if not better, than that accorded to nationals' (2009: 245). While such generosity may be considered burdensome by many modern states, in the *Qur'an* God commends those who:

> show love for those who migrated to them for refuge and harbour no desire in their hearts for what has been given to [the migrants]. They give [the migrants] preference over themselves, even if [the hosts] too are poor: those who are saved from their own souls' greed are truly successful. (*Qur'an*, 59: 9)

In the commentary for the verse above, Ibn Kathir (2000) states that Anas, a companion of the Prophet Muhammad (PBUH), said:

> The Muhajirin said, 'O God's Messenger! We have never met people like those whom we emigrated to; comforting us in times of scarcity and giving to us with a good heart in times of abundance. They have sufficed for us and shared their wealth with us so much so that we feared that they might earn the whole reward instead of us.'

Thus, once assistance is given it should not be resented (Zaat, 2007: 19) – rather, forced migrants should be treated with consistent love and generosity.

The right to non-discrimination

As mentioned earlier, *musta'min* would be entitled to the same rights as citizens of the host state, regardless of whether they were an internally displaced person, a refugee, or a stateless person. However, it is also worth noting that, within the Islamic framework, forced migrants are entitled to receive *aman* regardless of religion, race, colour, or fortune (Shaykh Othman ibn Foudi, quoted in Abou-El-Wafa, 2009: 71). As a universal religion, Islam honours humans from all backgrounds – indeed, 'the diversity of [our] languages and colours' is 'truly' a sign from God (*Qur'an*, 30: 22), who 'made [us] into races and tribes so that [we] should recognize one another' (*Qur'an*, 49: 13). This sentiment is reflected in Article 1 of the Cairo Declaration on Human Rights in Islam, which states:

> All men are equal in terms of basic human dignity and basic obligations and responsibilities, without any discrimination on the grounds of race, colour, language, sex, religious belief, political affiliation, social status or other considerations. True faith is the guarantee for enhancing such dignity along the path to human perfection.

According to Imam Ash-Shaybani, a Muslim imam therefore has a duty to rescue, protect, and do justice to *any musta'min*, as long as they stay on Muslim territory (Abou-El-Wafa, 2009: 174).

The right to freedom of religion

This is often a point of contention and misunderstanding. The *Qur'an* clearly states that Muslims should grant protection to a non-Muslim 'so that he may hear the word of God' (*Qur'an*, 9: 6). This may be interpreted as conflicting with current sensibilities regarding proselytization towards vulnerable people. However, it must be made clear that *aman* is not conditional upon the faith of the recipient – as discussed earlier, both Muslims and non-Muslims are to be honoured under the covenant of *aman*, and afforded the full rights that they are due. The verse itself commands Muslims to take *musta'min* 'to a place safe for [them]', regardless of whether the *musta'min* has become Muslim or not. Professor Wahbah Zuhaili argues that it is compulsory for the state authority to protect non-Muslims who are in need of sanctuary (Manuty, 2008: 26).

There is a clear principle within Islam of freedom of religion – indeed, this is the essence of humanity, according to Islamic teachings. The *Qur'an* states that God created '*jinn* [spirits] and mankind only to worship Me' (*Qur'an*, 51: 56), but that such worship must be based on belief, reflection, and choice. Elsewhere, humankind is reminded that there is 'no compulsion in religion' (*Qur'an*, 2: 256), for 'Had your Lord willed, all the people on Earth would have believed. So can you compel people to believe?' (*Qur'an*, 10: 99). Throughout Islamic history, there are numerous examples of non-Muslims being granted *aman* by Muslim states. For example, following the collapse of the Kingdom of Granada in 1492, and the rising persecution and anti-Semitism perpetuated within Spain by Ferdinand and Isabella, large numbers of Iberian Jews took refuge in various parts of the Muslim world ('Abd al-Rahim, 2008: 22). Russian Jewish and Christian refugees were again welcomed into the Muslim world following Ivan the Terrible's imperial expansion in the sixteenth century, and again following the 1917 Bolshevik Revolution (ibid.: 22).

Therefore, to coerce any human being, whether by force, emotional blackmail, or bribery, into following Islam is fundamentally contrary to the commands of God. Rather, we should interpret verse 9: 6 in the *Qur'an* to mean that Muslims are encouraged to give asylum to non-Muslims as a way of *introducing* them to Islam, but non-Muslim asylum seekers should feel under no obligation to accept Islam (Elmadmad, 2008: 54).

The right to freedom of religion could also be interpreted in another way. In the context of the modern secular humanitarian framework, it is imperative to ensure that the spiritual and religious needs of forced migrants are recognized, supported, and fulfilled. Examples of how this could happen can be found in Box 5.2.

Box 5.2 The freedom to be faithful: the case of promoting spiritual resilience in Jordan and Lebanon

The humanitarian imperative to respect freedom of religion and oppose any form of proselytization has led to a highly secularized international development space. Yet to remove faith and spirituality from the discussion of international development is to deny the central role that faith plays in many societies and communities around the world, with 84 per cent of the global population identifying as belonging to a religious group (Grim and Hackett, 2012: 9). There is a growing recognition of the central role that faith and spirituality play in protecting and promoting resilience in displaced communities (Fiddian-Qasmiyeh and Ager, 2013: 31–6).

Islamic Relief's understanding of human development, for example, is one that recognizes the protection of faith as fundamental to human dignity (Aminu-Kano, 2014). Numerous studies have found that spirituality can provide redemption and healing through practising religious rituals and the provision of a supportive community; and it 'can allow displaced people to find a meaning to their suffering, a sense of belonging, protection, an inner strength and hope for their future' (Vinueza, 2017: 89).

El Nakib and Ager (2015) cite examples of Jordanian relief agency staff organizing *Qur'an* memorization sessions as a way to 'impart some sense of inner peace' among Syrian women who had experienced trauma (ibid.: 14). Similarly, Islamic Relief's annual food distribution to displaced communities during Ramadan allows Muslim families to continue participating in the ritual of fasting, if they so wish, facilitating a sense of normalcy, purpose, and belonging. For the communities Islamic Relief serves, even something as basic as being unable to afford new clothes or gifts for children to celebrate religious festivals such as Eid can have great ramifications for their emotional well-being. One Syrian mother in Lebanon remarked: 'Now we can't even afford to buy sweets. The children couldn't get new clothes this year which is heart-breaking. Since the war began in Syria, we haven't felt the spirit of Eid' (Islamic Relief Worldwide, 2012a). As part of Islamic Relief Lebanon's psycho-social programmes aimed at alleviating the trauma and scars of displaced Syrian children, staff organized an Eid fun day, featuring inflatable activity centres, singing and games, and ending with the distribution of gifts, food, and cards to the children, with overwhelmingly positive feedback from the participants (Islamic Relief Worldwide, 2012b).

Islamic Relief has long advocated for better recognition of the central role that faith and spirituality can play in psycho-social resilience. In 2018, Islamic Relief Worldwide partnered with the Lutheran World Federation, World Vision, and the International Federation of Red Cross and Red Crescent Societies, among others, to produce a document entitled 'A faith-sensitive approach in humanitarian response: guidance on mental health and psychosocial programming'. The guidance was developed with the intention of providing practical support to those involved in planning humanitarian programmes who wished to be more sensitive to the faith perspectives of the communities they served (Islamic Relief Worldwide and Lutheran World Federation, 2018).

The right to have their basic physical needs met

This is the right of any vulnerable citizen of a Muslim state and is similarly a right of forced migrants (Abou-El-Wafa, 2009: 143). The Islamic institutions of *zakat* (compulsory annual almsgiving) and *sadaqah* (voluntary charity) help form a rights-based understanding of provision for the vulnerable (Zaat, 2007: 23). The third pillar of Islam, *zakat*, calls on Muslims to offer a percentage of their annual savings as alms to assist eight categories of vulnerable people – one of which is 'travellers in need' (*Qur'an*, 9: 60). Such compulsory alms can be used to provide food, shelter, clothing, and transportation to travellers in need (al-Qaradawi, 1999: 429–37). It is the duty of the state, or relevant body, to collect such alms and ensure that they reach deserving recipients, such as forced migrants.

However, the *Qur'an* also exhorts Muslims to assist travellers in a voluntary capacity as well: 'the truly good are those who … give away some of their wealth, however much they cherish it … to the needy, travellers' (*Qur'an*, 2: 177); 'Whatever you give should be for parents, close relatives, orphans, the needy and travellers' (*Qur'an*, 2: 215). Examples of this can be found within original Islamic sources: as mentioned earlier, the citizens of Medina shared their possessions with the emigrants from Mecca, and when the Prophet Moses (PBUH) fled to Midian to escape the persecution of Egypt, he was taken in by an old man who reassured him 'Do not be afraid, you are safe now from people who do wrong' (*Qur'an*, 28: 25) and offered him shelter and employment.

The right to work

It is significant to note that the Prophet Muhammad (PBUH) encouraged the Meccan emigrants to utilize their experience in trade and commerce to build their own wealth, so as not to burden their hosts – demonstrating that it is also incumbent on the migrants to seek financial self-sufficiency and to ensure that they are not the perpetual recipients of charity (Agha, 2008: 38). Engendering an environment of genuine self-reliance, where forced migrants are provided with long-term support to utilize their own skills and experience, is a critical aspect of reaffirming a *musta'min*'s sense of dignity.

Box 5.3 Respecting rights, accepting responsibility: the case of Syrian refugees in Turkey

As of 2019, Turkey hosted the largest number of refugees worldwide for the sixth consecutive year – over 3.6 million people in total.[13] There are a number of elements of the government of Turkey's response that – though challenging at times – are notable for the way in which they diverge from common host-country responses to migration crises and the manner in which they largely align with Islamic principles on forced migrant protection:

1. A 'generous, open-door policy' (Ferris and Kirişci, 2015) since the conflict in Syria began has been praised by institutions such as UNHCR (UNHCR, 2013) and has seen Turkey host the largest refugee population in the world for over half a decade. While the open-door policy has been commendable and has resulted in an unmatched level of

---

(Continued)

Box 5.3 Continued

refugees being offered protection, in recent years Turkey appears to have reversed it. In 2018, Turkey completed construction of a 764-kilometre wall along the Turkish–Syrian border.[14] Along with claims from human rights groups that Turkish border guards now shoot and block Syrians seeking asylum (HRW, 2018), many now question the extent to which the 'open-door policy' is still honoured. However, in 2018 UNHCR did note that 'Turkey continues to demonstrate its capacity to receive and process admissions effectively' (UNHCR, 2018b: 4).

2. The country's non-camp approach sees 93 per cent of Syrians under temporary protection (SuTPs) settled in urban areas (UNHCR, 2018b: 4), where they are able to live independently, seek their own (formal or informal) work opportunities, and integrate with local communities.

3. A shared responsibility between governments and local communities has seen the government of Turkey spending an estimated US$30 billion on direct assistance to SuTPs (UNHCR, 2018b: 4), while a 2014 survey indicated that 31 per cent of Turkish respondents had made personal financial contributions in support of Syrian refugees – unlike many host countries, which depend on international development agencies and donors to fund and provide services for forced migrants (World Bank, 2015: 5).

4. Basic needs are met and rights protected through government services. SuTPs in Turkey are guaranteed access to healthcare, education, social services, electricity, water, communication services, and bank accounts, while psychosocial support and rehabilitation services are prioritized for children, women, and the elderly (World Bank, 2015: 5). The Emergency Social Safety Net was launched in 2016 as a means of providing multipurpose cash assistance for over 1 million of the most vulnerable refugees (UNHCR, 2018b: 5).

5. The right to work is protected through the introduction of legislation in 2016 that allows all SuTPs the right to apply for work permits and access formal employment. By the start of 2018, over 1,000 Syrian doctors and nurses had been trained in the Turkish health system, with over 400 working in refugee clinics around the country (UNHCR, 2018b: 4).

6. Some 40,000 SuTPs have been granted Turkish citizenship,[15] providing solutions to displacement.

Nonetheless, numerous challenges still remain in the Turkish context – strains on municipal infrastructure leading to poor WASH (water, sanitation, and hygiene) and shelter conditions, social tensions between refugees and host communities, the high number of Syrians (including children) who are forced to work in informal and exploitative jobs, the emotional strain of poverty and displacement on Syrian families, and language barriers are all urgent and deep-rooted challenges for the government of Turkey and the international community to address (UNHCR, 2018b: 6).

The right to have property and funds protected

Along with the right to gain employment and develop economic self-sufficiency, a *musta'min* also enjoys the right to have any property and wealth brought with them protected. These must not be confiscated against their will, for this would be a breach of the trust and honour of the *aman* pledge. However, this protection can (for practical reasons) extend only to the property brought with the asylum seeker, and not to that left behind in their country of origin. Imam an-Nawawi states that 'if a disbeliever enters under a covenant of *aman* … into a Muslim land, he shall enjoy security for the property, children and relatives in his company. However, he shall have no security for his property, children and relatives left behind in a non-Muslim land' (Abou-El-Wafa, 2009: 158).

The right to non-separation from family

Prophetic tradition makes non-separation obligatory for all Muslims (Abou-El-Wafa, 2009: 155). The *Shari'ah* and prophetic traditions stress the importance of family unity, which plays an essential role in people's moral and psychological needs (ibid.: 154), and it is the duty of the host state to keep families together and assist *musta'min* in being reunited with their own families. The Prophet Muhammad (PBUH) taught that 'whoever causes separation between a mother and her child, then God will separate him from his beloved on the Day of Judgment' (Tirmidhi, Book 21, *Hadith* 27).

The rights of vulnerable groups

Within Islamic *Shari'ah*, vulnerable categories of people are often afforded particular rights of provision and protection. Vulnerable people may include the disabled, the elderly, children (particularly orphans), and vulnerable categories of women, such as widows, divorced women, or mothers.

Aside from specific injunctions commanding individuals to care for their own parents, Islam repeatedly emphasizes the importance of communal care for the elderly, with the Prophet Muhammad (PBUH) stating that 'he is not one of us who does not show mercy to our young ones and respect our old ones' (Tirmidhi, Book 27, *Hadith* 27) and that 'if a young man honours an older person on account of his age, God appoints someone to show reverence to him in his old age' (Tirmidhi, Book 1, *Hadith* 359). The *Qur'an* repeatedly calls on Muslims to respect the dignity of the ill or disabled (*Qur'an*, 24: 61), even chastising the Prophet Muhammad (PBUH) himself for failing to do so (*Qur'an*, 80: 1–11). In this vein, the Caliph Umar ibn 'Abd al-Aziz conducted a census of people with disabilities, and appointed guides and servants to care for them (Equally Able Foundation, n.d.).

Provisions for vulnerable women are enshrined in the *Qur'an*, with widows being entitled to maintenance (*Qur'an*, 2: 234, 2: 240, 4: 12) and 'no expulsion from their homes' (*Qur'an*, 2: 240) for up to one year following their husband's death, while divorced women are entitled to 'such maintenance as is considered fair' (*Qur'an*, 2: 241). Mothers hold a particularly honoured status, and the Prophet Muhammad (PBUH) taught us that Paradise is to be found at the feet of a mother (Sunan an-Nasa'i, Book 25, *Hadith* 20). Equally, the *Qur'an* repeatedly commands Muslims to care for particularly vulnerable categories of children, such as orphans (*Qur'an*, 4: 36). However, the Islamic traditions provide a broader framework for children's rights, including the right to life, identity, family, freedom, upbringing, education and culture, rest and activity, health, justice, freedom, and so forth. The OIC has developed a Covenant on the Rights of the Child in Islam (OIC, 2004), which details further what children within an Islamic state should be entitled to. Article 21 of the Covenant states: 'States parties to this Covenant shall ensure, as much as possible, that refugee children, or those legally assimilated to this status, enjoy the rights provided for in this Covenant within their national legislation.'

Following the principle that a *musta'min* is entitled to the same rights as citizens of the host state, such forced migrants are entitled to receive that which is promised to vulnerable groups of the host state, and should be provided for out of *zakat* (being both needy and travellers in need) and *sadaqah*.

Solutions to displacement

There is a difference of opinion as to whether *aman* can be temporary or permanent. Munir claims that '*aman* is not limited in time and the departure of the protected or *musta'min* from *dar ul Islam* or the place of his/her residence will depend on the individual's decision' (Munir, 2011: 14). Abou-El-Wafa, however, claims that *aman* provides only temporary protection in Islam, stating that the migrant is recognized as a *musta'min* for up to one year. After this, a sustainable solution must be found (Abou-El-Wafa, 2009: 201), such as those outlined below.

Violation of aman

Abou-El-Wafa states that if a *musta'min* commits dangerous acts that particularly threaten the security of the state, then asylum should cease (Abou-El-Wafa, 2009: 223). However, he makes it clear that asylum should not be ceased suddenly – the *musta'min* must be given prior warning, a clear explanation for why his or her protection has ceased, and a reasonable period of time to make arrangements to relocate (ibid.: 224). Once the time period expires, he or she will be escorted to where he or she feels safe (*Qur'an*, 9: 6) and should not be assaulted or harmed in any way (ibid.: 203).

Integration into host communities

Aman may also end by the *musta'min* being formally integrated into the host community. This would entail the *musta'min* becoming a legal citizen of the state with the right to a long-term stay. According to classical tradition, both Muslim and non-Muslim *musta'min* would be entitled to citizenship within a Muslim state, thus ensuring their continued protection. Non-Muslim citizens of Islamic states (known as *zimmis or dhimmis* in classical Islamic terms) were traditionally entitled to the same rights and obligations as their fellow Muslim citizens. The only differences between the two were that Muslim citizens were obliged to fight to defend the territory in wartime, while *zimmis* were exempt; Muslims were required to pay *zakat* while *zimmis* were not; and in exchange for freedom from these two obligations, *zimmis* were required to contribute a small tax, or *jizya* (Abou-El-Wafa, 2009: 214). As *zimmis*, the non-Muslims' property would become inviolable. Imam Abu Yusuf wrote a letter to Haroun Ar-Rasheed stating:

> Prince of Believers, may God support you, you might have to show lenience to *zimmis* who enjoy the protection of your Prophet and cousin Muhammad (PBUH) and to see that they are not oppressed, injured, overtasked beyond their capacity or stripped of any of their property save for a right owed by them. (Abou-El-Wafa, 2009: 212)

On his deathbed, the second Caliph of Islam, Umar (PBUH), enjoined his successors to 'take care of *zimmis* under the protection of Prophet Muhammad (PBUH), to honour the covenant of *aman* granted to them, to fight in defence of them, and not to overtask them' (Abou-El-Wafa, 2009: 213).

Muslim forced migrants may equally choose to integrate into non-Muslim host communities. Muslims are encouraged to live within states that enable them to practise their faith fully and to adhere to the principles of the *Shari'ah*. Traditionally, this would have meant the *dar ul Islam*. While historically the *dar ul Islam* was clearly defined, in the modern context it has become less so. Shaykh Faysal Mawlawi points out that if *dar ul Islam* is where Islam is practised, then most Muslim countries can no longer be considered *dar ul Islam* (Abu-Sahlieh, 1996: 51). As such, the Islamic Fiqh Academy of the OIC has deemed that if *Shari'ah* is not practised in a Muslim's country of origin, then it would be permissible for them to seek citizenship in a non-Muslim state, with Hajj Abdullah Bah adding 'provided that such naturalisation would not lead to disruption or detraction from his religious duties' (Abou-El-Wafa, 2009: 217).

Voluntary repatriation

Alternatively, the *musta'min* may choose to end the asylum voluntarily and return to their country of origin. This may be the result of changing circumstances, for example if the reasons motivating asylum were to cease (Abou-El-Wafa, 2009: 226). For example, following the Hudaibiyah truce, the Prophet (PBUH) dispatched 'Amr ibn Umayyah ad-Dhimari to Negus, requesting him to send back the Muslims who had taken refuge with him (ibid.: 206). As mentioned earlier, however, it is incumbent on the host state to ensure that it is safe for the *musta'min* to return to their country of origin and to facilitate their safe passage (*Qur'an*, 9: 6).

Conclusion

Muslim countries such as Afghanistan, Pakistan, Iraq, Sudan, and Syria are among the greatest sources of forced migrants globally. Moreover, Muslim states and Muslim communities play a central role in hosting over 50 per cent of the world's forced migrants. Nonetheless, little remains of a forced migrant protection framework that spanned centuries of Islamic history. A total of 21 countries in the Muslim world have still not acceded to the international refugee instruments; only a few countries have developed comprehensive national policies for displaced people; many refugees are still denied basic rights and legislative protection in Muslim countries; sexual and gender-based violence is still a problem in IDP camps; educational provision for refugee children is insufficient, while unaccompanied and separated children lack protection; and there remains a fundamental lack of durable solutions, with refugees remaining on the fringe of society in fragile environments (OIC, 2006: 10–11).

As demonstrated, Islamic teachings – from the *Qur'an*, the life of the Prophet Muhammad (PBUH), and the actions of the early Muslims – provide a wealth of evidence to support a protection framework for forced migrants that is grounded in Islamic values. While legal rulings may have been developed on these issues in the past, such rulings may need to be re-evaluated so that they can be adapted to the modern context, particularly on issues relating to the obligations of states versus individuals or communities, and the unprec-edented scale of mass migration. In recent years, the OIC has made progress in developing an understanding of these general principles (OIC, 2006, 2012). However, more could be done to further develop theological understandings to enable the adaptation of classical teachings to the challenges of the modern context and to support protection practice. Such traditions could play a vital role in motivating host countries to respond to forced migrant crises in a manner that honours Islamic principles, while making clear to forced migrants the rights and dignity conferred on them by God.

Notes

1. Peace Be Upon Him (PBUH) is a term of respect offered when referring to any prophet within the Islamic tradition.
2. This chapter is a revised and updated version of Islamic Relief's report *The Rights of Forced Migrants in Islam* (Kidwai, 2014).
3. See <https://www.iom.int/key-migration-terms> [accessed January 2019].
4. See 'Membership', Organisation of Islamic Cooperation (OIC) <https://www.oic-oci.org/states/?lan=en> [accessed March 2019].
5. See also <https://www.oic-oci.org/>.
6. A summary of the main criticisms can be found in Zaat (2007: 4).
7. Quotes are taken from M.A.S. Abdel Haleem, *The Qur'an*, Oxford University Press, Oxford, 2005.
8. See <https://www.unhcr.org/refugee-status-determination.html>.
9. The term *Maliki* refers to one of the four major schools of thought within the Islamic juristic tradition: *Maliki, Shafi'i, Hanbali,* and *Hanafi*, named respectively after their founders (Imam Malik, Imam Ash-Shafi'i, Imam Ahmed ibn Hanbal, and Imam Abu Hanifah).
10. See 'Community sponsors: about the process' on the Government of Canada website at <https://www.canada.ca/en/immigration-refugees-citizenship/services/refugees/help-outside-canada/private-sponsorship-program/community-sponsors.html> [accessed February 2019].

11. Interview with A. Syed, 2017.
12. Details of the Muslim Association of Brantford's Syrian Refugee Resettlement Project are available at <http://www.brantfordmosque.ca/SyrianRefugeeResettlementProject/tabid/116/Default.aspx> [accessed February 2019].
13. See <https://data2.unhcr.org/en/situations/syria/location/113>.
14. 'Turkey finishes construction of 764-km security wall on Syria border', *Daily Sabah*, 9 June 2018 <https://www.dailysabah.com/war-on-terror/2018/06/09/turkey-finishes-construction-of-764-km-security-wall-on-syria-border>.
15. 'Syrian refugees find Turkey more welcoming than Western Europe', *The Economist*, 23 August 2018 <https://www.economist.com/europe/2018/08/23/syrian-refugees-find-turkey-more-welcoming-than-western-europe>.

References

'Abd al-Rahim, M. (2008) 'Asylum: A Moral and Legal Right in Islam', *Refugee Survey Quarterly* 27 (2): 15–23.

Abou-El-Wafa, A. (2009) *The Right to Asylum between Islamic Shari'ah and International Refugee Law: A Comparative Study*, UNHCR, Riyadh.

Abu-Sahlieh, S.A.A. (1996) 'The Islamic conception of migration', *International Migration Review* 30 (1): 37–57.

Agha, S.N. (2008) 'The ethics of asylum in early Muslim society', *Refugee Survey Quarterly* 27 (2): 30–40.

al-Qaradawi, Y. (1999) *Fiqh az-Zakat: A Comparative Study*, Dar Al Taqwa Ltd, London.

Aminu-Kano, M. (2014) *Human Development in Islam*, Islamic Relief Worldwide, Birmingham.

Elmadmad, K. (2008) 'Asylum in Islam and in Modern Refugee Law', *Refugee Survey Quarterly* 27 (2): 51–63.

El Nakib, S. and Ager, A. (2015) *Local Faith Community and Related Civil Society Engagement in Humanitarian Response with Syrian Refugees in Irbid, Jordan. Report to the Henry Luce Foundation*, Mailman School of Public Health, Columbia University, New York.

Equally Able Foundation (n.d.) *Disability in Islam: A Guide for Khutbas, Seminars and Workshops*, Equally Able Foundation, Chantilly VA <http://www.equallyable.org/wp-content/uploads/2015/10/15-EquallyAble-Under-standing-Disability-in-Islam-Guide-Lowres.pdf> [accessed 1 December 2018].

Esposito, J.L. (2010) 'Retreat from the secular path: the democracy–secularism debate in the Muslim world', *Quaderni di Relazioni Internazionali*, 12 April.

Ferris, E. and Kirişci, K. (2015) 'What Turkey's open-door policy means for Syrian refugees', Brookings Institute blog, 8 July <https://www.brookings.edu/blog/order-from-chaos/2015/07/08/what-turkeys-open-door-policy-means-for-syrian-refugees/> [accessed 11th April 2020].

Fiddian-Qasmiyeh, E. and Ager, A. (2013) 'Local faith communities and the promotion of resilience in humanitarian situations: a scoping study',

Working Paper Series 90, Refugee Studies Centre, University of Oxford, and Joint Learning Initiative on Local Faith Communities, Oxford.

FitzGibbon, A., Kidwai, S. and Moore, L.V. (2014) 'The role of religion in the formation of cross-community relationships', Forced Migration Review 48.

Grim, B.J. and Hackett, C. (2012) *The Global Religious Landscape: A Report on the Size and Distribution of the World's Major Religious Groups as of 2010*, Pew Research Center, Washington DC.

HRW (2018) 'Turkey/Syria: border guards shoot, block fleeing Syrians', Human Rights Watch (HRW), 3 February <https://www.hrw.org/news/2018/02/03/turkey/syria-border-guards-shoot-block-fleeing-syrians> [accessed 11th April 2020].

Ibn Kathir (2000) 'The prohibition of residing among the disbelievers while able to emigrate', commentary for *Qur'an*, 4: 97–9, in *Abridged Tafsir Ibn Kathir: Volumes 1–10 in the English Language with Arabic Verses*, Darussalam Publications, Riyadh <https://quran.worldofislam.info/tafsir/> [accessed March 2019].

Islamic Relief Worldwide (2012a) 'No Eid joy for Syrian children', Islamic Relief Worldwide, Birmingham.

Islamic Relief Worldwide (2012b) 'Belated Eid celebrations for Syrian children', Islamic Relief Worldwide, Birmingham.

Islamic Relief Worldwide and Lutheran World Federation (2018) *A Faith-sensitive Approach in Humanitarian Response: Guidance on Mental Health and Psychosocial Programming*, Islamic Relief Worldwide and Lutheran World Federation, Birmingham and Geneva.

Kidwai, S.N. (2014) *The Rights of Forced Migrants in Islam*, Islamic Relief Worldwide, Birmingham.

Kirmani, N., Khan, A.A. and Palmer, V. (2008) *Does Faith Matter?: An Examination of Islamic Relief's Work with Refugees and Internally Displaced Persons*, Islamic Relief Worldwide, Birmingham.

Lings, M. (1984) *Muhammad: His Life Based on the Earliest Sources*, The Islamic Texts Society, London.

Manuty, M.N. (2008) 'The protection of refugees in Islam: pluralism and inclusivity', *Refugee Survey Quarterly* 27 (2): 24–9.

Munir, M. (2011) 'Refugee Law in Islam', *Journal of Social Sciences* 4 (2): 1–18.

OIC (2004) 'Covenant on the rights of the child in Islam', Organisation of Islamic Cooperation (OIC), Jeddah.

OIC (2006) 'Enhancing refugee and IDP protection in the Muslim world', Working Document 1, Ministerial Conference on the Problems of Refugees in the Muslim World, Organisation of Islamic Cooperation (OIC), Jeddah.

OIC (2012) 'Ashgabat declaration of the International Ministerial Conference of the Organization of Islamic Cooperation on refugees in the Muslim world', Organisation of Islamic Cooperation (OIC), Jeddah.

Rahaei, S. (2009) 'The rights of refugee women and children in Islam', *Forced Migration Review*.

Ramadan, T. (2008) *The Messenger: The Meanings of the Life of Muhammad*, Penguin Books, London.

UNHCR (2008) 'Kuala Lumpur conclusions of the United Nations conference on asylum and Islam 2007', *Refugee Survey Quarterly* 27 (2): 64–5.

UNHCR (2013) 'UNHCR praises Turkey's leadership, seeks international support on refugees', United Nations High Commissioner for Refugees (UNHCR), 6 December <https://data2.unhcr.org/en/news/13024>.

UNHCR (2014) 'Policy on alternatives to camps', United Nations High Commissioner for Refugees (UNHCR) <https://www.refworld.org/docid/5423ded84.html> [accessed 12 May 2020].

UNHCR (2015) 'States parties to the 1951 Convention relating to the status of refugees and the 1967 Protocol', United Nations High Commissioner for Refugees (UNHCR), Geneva.

UNHCR (2018a) *Global Trends 2017*, United Nations High Commissioner for Refugees (UNHCR), Geneva.

UNHCR (2018b) *Regional Refugee and Resilience Plan 2018–2019 in Response to the Syria Crisis: Turkey*, United Nations High Commissioner for Refugees (UNHCR), Geneva.

Vinueza, M.A.A. (2017) 'The role of spirituality in building up the resilience of migrant children in Central America: bridging the gap between needs and responses', *International Journal of Children's Spirituality* 22 (1): 84–101.

Wade, A. (2016) 'Refugees and their European hosts – in pictures', *Guardian*, 7 September <https://www.theguardian.com/world/gallery/2016/sep/07/refugees-and-their-european-hosts-in-pictures-aubrey-wade-no-stranger-place>.

World Bank (2015) *Turkey's Response to the Syrian Refugee Crisis and the Road Ahead*, World Bank Group, Washington DC.

Zaat, K. (2007) 'The protection of forced migrants in Islamic law', New Issues in Refugee Research Paper 146, Policy Development and Evaluation Service, United Nations High Commissioner for Refugees, Geneva.

About the author

Sadia Najma Kidwai is a freelance policy and research consultant who specializes in forced migration. She is the author of Islamic Relief Worldwide's report *The Rights of Forced Migrants in Islam* and holds an MSc in Violence, Conflict, and Development. Sadia has previously conducted research on issues such as climate change, sexual and reproductive health, faith and development, and *zakat*.

CHAPTER 6
Gender and Islam

Shahin Ashraf and Najmo Abukar

Islam has a strong message on gender justice and the protection of the rights of women and children, stemming from the teachings in the Qur'an *and* ahadith. *Despite this, women's and children's rights have continuously been violated as a result of misconstrued understandings of religion rooted in a culture of systematic patriarchy. This has resulted in the development of harmful traditional practices (HTPs) such as female genital mutilation and early forced marriage, which have resulted in the marginalization of women and children. Gender justice is a key aspect for progressive development and poverty eradication. There is limited under-standing of gender justice and Islam. Faith-based organizations are uniquely positioned and well equipped to challenge HTPs and develop robust and modern frameworks that contest narratives that seek to use faith to reproduce patriarchal norms. Such a framework could play a vital role for the eradication of HTPs, the advancement of the economic empowerment of women, women's participation, and transformative leadership, as well as women's equal access to education. The framework would also be complementary to existing human rights laws as global initiatives on gender equality.*

Keywords: Islam, gender justice, *Maqasid* objectives, climate justice, female genital mutilation (FGM), early forced marriage (EFM), human rights, Muslim, development

Introduction

Over the past decade there has been increasing interest in mainstreaming gender issues in development and humanitarian programmes. Faith-based organizations (FBOs) can play a valuable role in using faith perspectives and principles to challenge harmful social and cultural practices that continue to marginalize women and girls and deprive them of their human rights. Women and girls are disproportionately affected by structural inequalities, for example by having less control over assets and resources that increase their vulner-abilities during times of natural hazard and conflict (Bradshaw and Fordham, 2013), although their vulnerabilities may differ in terms of their age, race, disability, nationality, and sexual orientation. Gender justice aims to end the inequalities between men and women, particularly in relation to the distri-bution of power, resources, and knowledge.

http://dx.doi.org/10.3362/9781788530613.006

The Islamic Declaration of Gender Justice seeks to contribute to this discourse by providing faith principles of justice and *Maqasid al-Shari'ah* objectives to underpin initiatives that challenge gender inequality (Islamic Relief, 2020). The following verse is one example of men and women being equal before God:

> Indeed, the Muslim men and Muslim women, the believing men and believing women, the obedient men and obedient women, the truthful men and truthful women, the patient men and patient women, the humble men and humble women, the charitable men and charitable women, the fasting men and fasting women ... for them Allah has prepared forgiveness and a great reward. (*Qur'an*, 33: 25)

There is a great need for FBOs and religious leaders to work in partnership and advocate for *adalah* (justice), equality, and fairness – principles that are already embedded in Islam. The Islamic perspective on development aims to create an environment that enables individuals to achieve full actualization of their spiritual, moral, and socio-economic well-being. In practice, using a faith-inspired approach to achieve Goal 5 (gender equality) of the Sustainable Development Goals (SDGs)[1] means working with FBOs, as well as humanitarian and development organizations, to remove structural issues at the root of gender inequality such as legal discrimination (particularly in relation to land ownership), decision making on marriage, sexual and reproductive rights, and the participation of women in leadership positions. In addition, at the centre of the faith-based approach to gender justice is the need to foster an attitude change at all levels, using an Islamic ethos and a human rights-based perspective.

Faith-inspired gender justice initiatives help provide a sustainable solution to gender inequality, particularly in situations where the *Qur'an*, the *ahadith* (sayings attributed to the Prophet Muhammad (Peace Be Upon Him)), and *Sunnah* (the body of traditional social and legal custom and practice of the Prophet and his companions) are misconstrued and influenced by culture and by political and socio-economic situations. The *Qur'an* and the teachings of the Prophet Muhammad (PBUH) provide a powerful case against gender inequality and are crucial in dispelling misconceptions that seek to perpetuate patriarchy and contribute to the suffering of women and girls. The following section defines the *Maqasid al-Shari'ah* (or *Maqasid*) framework and its complementary nature to existing humanitarian and gender justice principles.

Muslim-majority countries and human rights

Religion has all too often been blamed for gender inequality and the marginalization of other vulnerable groups in academic and political discourse. Muslim-majority countries have been consistently criticized for their deplorable human rights record, particularly in relation to women and girls.

For instance, most Muslim-majority countries are signed up to the Convention on the Elimination of All Forms of Discrimination Against Women (CEDAW), but most have reservations that seek to exclude or modify the legal effect of certain provisions in the treaty. Several countries (notably Saudi Arabia, Oman, and Pakistan) have also made blanket reservations stating that they are legally bound by the convention only as long as those provisions are in accordance with the provisions of Islamic *Shari'ah*. This perpetuates the narrative that Islam is incompatible with human rights, particularly those in relation to women. Dr Roja Fazaeli points out that questions around human rights and Islam are reduced to dichotomies of compatibility and incapability (Humphreys, 2016). Shifting blame to Islam or any other religion as a source of human rights violations is far too simplistic and naïve (ibid.). Those dichotomies do not take into consideration the nuances and differences between Muslim-majority countries, and they also assume that there is a distinct Islamic approach.

Dr Naiz Shah notes that there are three approaches in the debate around Islam and human rights. The first is voiced by those who advocate for strict compliance with international human rights law (Humphreys, 2016). The second relates to reformists who believe that Islamic human rights norms are compatible with international standards and that, where there is conflict or inconsistency, this can be reconciled through reinterpretation of religious scripture (ibid.). Thus, the second group perceive the *Qur'an* to be a 'living text' that can be reinterpreted to suit the contemporary needs of modern Muslim communities. The third group adopts a more conservative approach; they perceive the international human rights system to be hegemonic, a tool of the West, and thus a form of Western imperialism (ibid.). They do not ascribe to the notion that international human rights conventions are a 'yardstick for human dignity'; rather, they believe the Islamic legal ruling system to be superior to the international human rights system. Most Muslim-majority countries fall into this third category.

This approach certainly challenges the notion that human rights are universal; conversely, it raises questions about cultural and religious relativism. Treaty reservations are suggestive of a perceived incompatibility between the rights concerned and the cultural and religious beliefs of a particular state (Çalı and Montoya, 2017). As such, reservations about treaties reinforce the cultural and religious relativism argument while the withdrawal of such reservations or the decision to accede to a convention without any reservations reinforces the notion of universality (ibid.). Conventions such as CEDAW and the United Nations Convention on the Rights of the Child (UNCRC) that require states to actively take action to implement rights are often subject to more reservations than other treaties. For instance, there are currently over 440 reservations with regard to CEDAW, with over 60 per cent rooted in religious or cultural belief (ibid.). While Muslim-majority states are most likely to express religion-based reservations, they are not alone: such reservations have also been voiced by Catholic-majority states in Western Europe, Eastern

Europe, Latin America, and the Pacific, as well as by Jewish-majority, Hindu-majority, and Buddhist-majority countries in Asia and the Middle East.

Moreover, there are important historical underpinnings that would explain why Muslim-majority countries are hesitant about signing up to the existing normative international human rights framework without any reservations. During the Second World War, when major human rights conventions were being adopted, Asian and African countries (to which most Muslim countries belong) were notably absent from the discussion. Consequently, the cultural and religious experiences of Muslim-majority countries are not reflected in international human rights conventions, which creates a legitimacy deficit. Abdullahi An-Na'im alludes to this point, arguing that Muslim-majority countries are more likely to honour international human rights that have Islamic legitimacy (An-Na'im, 1990). Nevertheless, Muslim-majority countries have found it politically expedient to engage with the international human rights system. Thus, the fact that they sign up to conventions such as CEDAW is more a symbolic gesture than a commitment to improving women's rights. This is evident in the blanket reservations and the lack of follow-through with national legal reform (Humphreys, 2016).

Gouda and Potrafke (2016) state that *Shari'ah* law is incompatible with human rights as they pertain to gender equality, particularly in countries where Islam is a source of legislation. Nevertheless, there is still a possibility for harmonization of international human rights law and Islamic law (Baderin, 2005), although this will require good faith and the abandonment of prejudice (particularly Islamophobia) among Islamic law and international human rights law scholars. To dispel these prejudices, the following section explores how Islamic frameworks such as the *Maqasid* are compatible with existing international human rights conventions.

What is the *Maqasid* framework?

Islamic Relief is an international non-governmental organization that implements humanitarian relief and long-term development programmes in over 40 countries around the world. It is pushing for faith-informed gender justice in development and humanitarian contexts. Islamic Relief's integrated sustainable development approach is based on the *Maqasid*, a broad set of objectives used as guidance to achieve holistic human development. These include the protection of faith *(din)*, protection of life *(nafs)*, protection of lineage *(nasl)*, protection of intellect *(aqal)*, and protection of property *(mal)*. The framework reaffirms the equal value of humanity before God, irrespective of gender, by prioritizing and applying the *Maqasid* equally to all.

Maqasid are also the objectives and principles behind Islamic rulings (Auda, 2008). By leveraging this understanding and interpretation, interventions can be made that are relevant to Muslim contexts. The *Maqasid* can also be employed by Islamic jurists to derive new guidance around contemporary issues that have an impact on gender justice, and therefore they remain contextually relevant over time and in different circumstances.

Further, it is important to note that the framework is not a set of religious rulings but rather an ethical framework based on human dignity and the unitarian concept of *Tawhid* (holistic world view). Given that human dignity is at the heart of the framework it works in a complementary way with existing humanitarian principles. The framework's approach calls for integrated interventions that are sustainable and thus for a move away from the focus on short-term programming. The framework can provide an effective approach for gender justice programming and advocacy that is religiously and culturally sensitive to Muslim communities.

How do the *Maqasid* objectives intersect with gender justice?

The five *Maqasid* objectives (*din*, *nafs*, *nasl*, *aqal*, and *mal*) can be used as a toolkit to tackle gender inequality in a manner that is both rooted in Islamic values and applicable to modern challenges. All five objectives are currently codified in international human rights conventions, such as the Universal Declaration of Human Rights (UDHR), UNCRC, and CEDAW (UN General Assembly, 1979). Thus, the framework is complementary to existing international human rights law.

The first *Maqasid* objective is the protection of faith (*din*). The Islamic theological construct describes faith as an essential human need and dimension of well-being that can lead to the actualization of all other spiritual and material needs. Faith confers moral and ethical values while also helping to foster social solidarity, and it places responsibility on all members of society to tackle the adversity and vulnerability of women, girls, and other marginalized groups. Moreover, faith can be linked to protection through belief in one's accountability in the hereafter, thereby deterring a gender-based abuse of rights, violence, and injustice. In practice, this may include child protection and safeguarding issues. This is further reinforced by the *hadith* that states that 'the person who looks after an orphan and provides for them will be in Paradise' (Bukhari, Book 36, *Hadith* 1). This *hadith* demonstrates the importance attached to assisting those in vulnerable situations, whether that is due, for example, to age, gender, disability, or socio-economic status. In addition, the *hadith* attaches moral accountability, although child protection and safeguarding issues also encompass legal, cultural, and societal accountability.

The second objective is the protection of life (*nafs*). The objective here is the fulfilment of all human needs necessary to sustain the human body and to allow humanity to discharge their role as custodians (*khalifa*) of the Earth, by preserving dignity and good governance. The *Qur'an* (5: 32) states that 'whoever saves one life, it is as if they have saved humanity entirely'. This underlines the moral obligation to preserve life, which includes the fulfilment of human potential. Ensuring the physical and mental health of both women and men is essential for preventing suffering and for encouraging gender-just ideas and the fulfilment of human potential. Security, freedom from fear, and the protection of life are the most fundamental human needs, and with gender-based violence (GBV), maternal mortality, and conflict disproportionately affecting women and girls, fulfilling these needs is key to achieving gender justice. This objective is similar to Article 3 of the UDHR, which states that 'everyone has the right to life, liberty and security of person'. The protection of life in relation to gender justice is particularly important in times of conflict, when women's vulnerability to sexual and gender-based violence and threats to their sexual and reproductive health increase drastically due to limited access to healthcare (Namasivayam et al., 2017). One in five internally displaced or refugee women living in conditions of humanitarian crisis or armed conflict have experienced sexual violence (OCHA, 2019).

The third objective is the protection of the intellect (*aqal*). In this context, *aqal* also encompasses human freedom and removing barriers to human development. Preservation of the intellect is important for holistic well-being and can be achieved through gender-just equal education opportunities. Islamic scriptures encourage both men and women to seek knowledge. As such, Islamic institutions can play a pivotal role in providing educational, health, referral, and family services to both women and men. In addition, women should also play a key part on the boards of religious institutions such as mosques.

The Islamic practice of spiritual development aims to guide the intellect towards a just and balanced ideology, including gender justice. The Islamic right to freedom of thought and expression is vital for creating gender-just narratives, just as the right to education is important for ensuring that both women and men can achieve their full potential. This objective is also in line with the human right to education under Article 26 of the UDHR. The objective aligns with SDG 4, which aims to ensure inclusive and equitable quality education and promote lifelong learning opportunities for all. Like most SDGs, the success of SDG 4 depends on achieving gender justice and empowering all women and girls.[2] There is still a great disparity between the number of boys and girls in school; globally, there are currently 5.5 million more out-of-school girls than boys.[3] Children from poor families may be unable to attend school, as they are required to help out at home or support livelihood activities.

The first word revealed to the Prophet Muhammad (PBUH) was '*iqra*', which means 'read'. The revelation that follows continues to encourage humankind to seek out knowledge and to help others gain knowledge. Nevertheless, the quest for knowledge is difficult for certain groups due to lack of access. Harmful traditional practices (HTPs) such as female genital mutilation/cutting (FGM/C) (Islamic Relief, 2015b), early forced marriage (EFM) (Islamic Relief, 2017), and poor awareness about the importance of girls' education are particular obstacles faced by girls. Removing barriers involves addressing structural inequality by working to eliminate all legal, economic, and socio-cultural barriers to girls' education. In practice, this may include work to ensure that education facilities are gender-sensitive and provide safe, non-violent, inclusive, and effective learning environments. In addition, this may include developing facilities that cater to the needs of women and girls during their menstrual cycles to ensure that this does not become an access barrier to education.

To a certain degree, this objective also includes improving equal access to information and communication technology (ICT). Access to ICT is affected by a complex set of inequalities based on gender and geographical area (among other things), which often reflects the existing power relations within society (Intel, 2013).There is a noticeable gender gap in access to ICT that hinders women in their movement in public, political, social, and economic spheres. It also hinders women from mobilizing to challenge hegemonic mainstream misogynistic discourse and to provide a counternarrative. Consequently, the notion that underpins the rallying cry 'Leave No One Behind' is relevant in this context because it is the poor and marginalized groups (like women) who will be the last to benefit from ICT. To bridge the internet gender gap, holistic programmes and policies need to evolve that challenge the lack of awareness and ability, as well as the cultural norms that reinforce gender roles and power structures that block women's and girls' access to ICT. Addressing this gender gap can unleash the potential of women and girls by boosting their income potential and increasing their sense of empowerment and equity.

The fourth objective is posterity (*nasl*), which refers to the protection of future generations and the family as the basic unit of society and solidarity. This objective intersects with gender justice by protecting and building healthy families and by reinforcing positive gender norms and ideas that can be embedded in the home and transferred to the community. By promoting positive socio-cultural gender norms and practices the wider community can play an important role in achieving gender justice. The Islamic right to family life is based on just, equitable, and healthy relationships between genders, and the rights of the child include protection from gender injustice. This is particularly important for the reduction of maternal and child mortality rates as well as for improving access to sexual and reproductive health services for women and girls. To continue the progress of SDG 3 (good health and well-being), there needs to be support for the development of faith-based approaches for ensuring the menstrual, sexual, and reproductive health of women and girls, and for tackling harmful cultural ideas and practices. Several governments, most notably in Sweden and Canada, have adopted a feminist foreign policy and actively set aside budgets to implement these policies. For instance, Canada has pledged to spend 95 per cent of its Feminist International Assistance on mainstream gender equality, while Sweden spends nearly 90 per cent of its foreign policy budget on gender equality initiatives (Thompson and Clement, 2019). This objective also encompasses protection from domestic or intimate partner violence.

The final *Maqasid* objective is the protection of property (*mal*). *Mal* is the life blood of the community and must be in constant circulation, without hoarding.

This objective is closely linked to the Islamic principles of respect, equality, and balance. Investing in the education, training, and employment of both women and men can build a skilled population less vulnerable to poverty. In particular, women's rights can be protected from abuse through their control of wealth and resources. Abject poverty is both physically and spiritually harmful and undermines humanity's natural dignity, with women and girls the most vulnerable to poverty. The just distribution of wealth plays a vital role in ensuring that the rights of all people are met. *Zakat* (the purification of wealth through obligatory charity) can be used to ensure that women and girls have the resources to meet their essential needs while protecting them from exploitation, trafficking, and abuse. The Islamic right to work, acquire wealth, and own property must be protected and promoted equally for both women and men. This objective closely relates to Article 11 of CEDAW (the right to work) and SDG 8, which ensures that everyone has decent work and the potential for sustained economic growth. The significance of protecting and promoting economic rights and responsibilities in Islam is undeniable and is integral to achieving social justice, including gender justice. Accordingly, resources including *zakat* and *sadaqah* (charitable giving) must be mobilized to tackle socio-economic injustices, including extreme poverty and structural economic inequalities. In particular, the focus should be on how these injustices adversely affect women and girls and on creating better safeguards for those with increased vulnerability due to disability, conflict, displacement, human trafficking, and socio-cultural forms of discrimination. There must also be an increase in Islamic banking and microfinance options to support women's financial independence, security, and participation in work. There is significant work to be done to support and strengthen women's access to economic institutions.

General Islamic teachings on non-discrimination

Islamic Relief's understanding of religious texts informs its approach to working on gender issues. The principles at the core of this work are based on the *Qur'an* and the traditions of the Prophet Muhammad (PBUH). Fundamental principles such as dignity, justice, freedom, and equality are core teachings central to the full realization and fulfilment of God-given potential. These are the benchmarks for defining balanced relationships between genders and they bear similarities to international principles of justice, equality, and non-discrimination. This is a key example of the compatible nature of the Islamic approach to gender justice and existing international human rights principles. Following the same theology, Islamic Relief's work centres on preserving human dignity as an approach to human development. Many of these concepts are also reflected in some of Islamic Relief's values, such as sincerity, compassion, and social justice.

Revelation reveals that men and women were created from a single essence. The *Qur'an* (17: 80) states: 'We have bestowed dignity on the progeny of Adam.' The verse refers to the time of human creation when all mankind was created from a single soul and alludes to the notion that God created all human beings as equal, and thus there is no distinction among them. Furthermore, the *Qur'an* (16: 97) states: 'Whoever does righteousness, whether male or female, while he or she is a believer – cause him or her to live a good life, and We will surely give them their reward [in the hereafter] according to the best of what they used to do.' Thus, men and women are equal before God and distinction is made based only on our actions. The same message is reflected in Islamic Relief's Islamic Declaration of Gender Justice.

Islamic teachings reinforce the message that every human being has an inherent right to dignity and God-given rights by virtue of being human, irrespective of gender. These rights also come with responsibilities towards ensuring that those rights are not infringed. No human being has the right to deny the God-given and inalienable rights of humanity. Violations of human dignity and the abuse of reciprocal rights and responsibilities in the family, community, and society at large, and denial of the human right to security, protection, and dignity, can lead to acts of GBV, harmful gender-based practices, and the abuse of children's rights. The message is reinforced in both the *ahadith* and the *Qur'an*. The Prophet Muhammad (PBUH) stated: 'O people! I have forbidden oppression for myself, and I have made it forbidden amongst you, so do not oppress one another' (Muslim, Book 45, *Hadith* 70). The *Qur'an* (16: 90) also supports this, stating: 'Indeed, God orders justice and good conduct and giving to relatives and forbids immorality and bad conduct and oppression. God admonishes you that perhaps you will be reminded.'

Gender injustice is rooted in discriminatory and harmful attitudes that deny the human rights protected by Islam. Socio-cultural ideas, norms, and practices that violate the rights of others cannot be equated with religion or be used to justify discrimination against people based on gender. The *Qur'an* calls out and questions this discriminatory attitude, and speaks strongly against GBV, addressing the common practice (in pre-Islam Arabia) of burying girls alive because of the fear of poverty. As evidenced above, discrimination on grounds of gender has no place in Islam.

Moreover, Islam states that we have a God-given duty to overcome gender injustice globally, and this means overcoming the many other forms of discrimination linked to it. The disparities between all men and all women are not equal, and nor are those between all women or those between all men. Gender injustice is intersectional and is exacerbated by other inequalities such as those based on ethnicity, age, and disability, political, economic, and socio-cultural factors, and more. Gender injustice is a multifaceted issue that requires a multi-sector response and effective partnerships.

Patriarchy influences how sacred scriptures are selected and interpreted, and this tends to have a detrimental effect on the treatment of women and girls (Le Roux, 2019). In addition, GBV and sexual and reproductive issues are frequently taboo topics; in some cases there are even attempts to rationalize violence against women (Kaviti, 2017). The denial of women's rights has been more systematic in some Muslim-majority countries, with significant legal barriers to access basic rights such as the right to vote, own land, or file for divorce. In those contexts, there is also an intense politicization of religious texts, particularly when religion and/or religious texts are invoked in political discourse to rationalize the barriers surrounding human rights, particularly those relating to women and girls (Ivanescu, 2010). The abuse and manipulation of religion and religious texts are generally grounded in the quest for political power that denies the rights of women and girls and limits the expansion of their rights (Cader and Nimasivayam, 2017).

This presents an additional challenge for faith-based gender justice work. Nevertheless, challenging patriarchal structures that oppress the rights of women and girls is part of the prophetic example. The Prophet Muhammad (PBUH) did this by declaring the equal status and rights of women before God and in relation to men; encouraging the pursuit of knowledge for all human beings, irrespective of gender; respecting and valuing the participation of women in society and work; emphasizing the equal status and rights of spouses; and equating the violation of women's marital rights to a breach of the covenant with God. In his last sermon, the Prophet Muhammad (PBUH) makes specific reference to the treatment of women in Islam.[4] He commanded his followers to remember that all are created equal before God, stating that 'the best of you are those who are best to their women'. Evidently, the *Qur'an* and *ahadith* provide no justification for gender inequality or discrimination in any form.

The lack of consensus around gender and Islam appears to be one of misinterpretation of religious scripture. Interpretations of gender in Islam are often influenced by culture, politics, and different schools of thought (Pertek, 2012). While religion is misused as a tool to perpetuate patriarchy, the scriptures themselves are rooted in justice, equality, and fairness. Religious scriptures are largely interpreted by male scholars, and over time patriarchal rules have become embedded in societal customs and are seen as natural and unchangeable (Levitt and Ware, 2006). For this reason, it is important to have a more inclusive approach when engaging with religious leaders to ensure that women's needs are not being ignored. There is an overwhelming lack of Islamic female scholars and it is crucial to invest in the development of female Islamic scholarship and to increase community-facing opportunities for teaching. While this may upset the current patriarchal system that prioritizes male points of view, investing in female leaders will offer the added advantage of having unique access to women in the community (Le Roux, 2019). The participation of female scholars will amplify the voices of women, allowing for women's issues to be brought to the forefront on a community level while also increasing women's participation at leadership levels.

Implementing the *Maqasid* framework

Incorporating *Maqasid* teachings into the design and delivery of development projects will challenge the abuse of religion to violate the rights of women and girls. Engaging men and boys as partners in programmes targeting women and girls is an essential part of achieving gender justice. The situation of women and girls worldwide can be improved only if men and boys are engaged in and educated about the needs and rights of women and girls. There is evidence that projects that empower women and girls but that do not engage men and boys have the unintended consequence of increasing women's and girl's vulnerabilities, particularly in the short term (WHO, 2007). For instance, increased control over financial resources can alter dynamics and roles within the household, and this can increase reprisals in the form of GBV, psychological abuse, and community isolation. Women can also face added responsibilities as a result of being 'economically empowered', partly because their partners perceive them as moving from their traditionally assigned caregiver role to breadwinner. As a result, men view their own role as breadwinner as having been diminished. The more entrenched these ideas are, the bigger the backlash – and in some cases this can leave women in a much more vulnerable position. In many ways the *Maqasid* framework aligns with the SDGs and the 2030 Agenda (UN General Assembly, 2015). By its very nature, the framework challenges patriarchal norms and structural inequalities that deprive women and girls of their human rights. As such, implementing such a framework in traditionally patriarchal societies is likely to cause controversy. It is therefore crucial to recruit men and boys as allies to mitigate these unintended consequences. Implementing the *Maqasid* teachings in conjunction with the 'Do No Harm' principle will not only help to ensure a balance of power and resources, but it will also help mitigate these unintended consequences by considering the 'men versus women' dynamic, as we are all equal before God and have collective responsibilities to uphold.

Equal opportunities for women and men in decision making and leadership are also important for gender programming in development contexts. Using faith-inspired principles (such as justice, equality, and equity) as a guide, work must be done to ensure equal opportunities for females and males, including full recognition of respective social, economic, and political contributions to community and family life, as well as promoting equitable and active participation in decision making and leadership. The lack of women's participation in decision-making spaces is attributed to restrictive legislation, cultural practices, and institutional barriers (Ilesanmi, 2018). Participation needs to move beyond surface-level representation and encompass participation in economic and organizational decision making and political participation at all levels.

A consortium led by Tearfund on HTPs, with participation from Islamic Relief, stressed the importance of engaging faith leaders and FBOs (Le Roux and Bartelink, 2017), since they are uniquely positioned and have the power to influence and mobilize communities to change cultural norms and attitudes. Their position also allows them to command the respect and trust of local authorities, making them crucial stakeholders (UNDP, 2014). There is growing recognition of the role of faith-based actors and there are several initiatives to unlock their potential. The World Humanitarian Summit has initiatives (e.g. high-level special events that engage faith actors) to develop opportunities to increase the recognition given to the role of faith actors. Faith leaders have a very strong presence at grassroots level, often with vital knowledge and information that could expand the reach of interventions. Engaging faith leaders is not just a case of harnessing their influence for the greater good, it is also about challenging some of their beliefs and practices that contribute to HTPs. Training faith leaders on the *Maqasid* framework will help promote gender justice and eliminate HTPs. Engaging trained faith leaders will help ensure the sustainability of the project by maximizing impact and will also help provide added legitimacy in the eyes of the Muslim community. Civil society must make a conscious decision to engage and train female faith leaders in order to increase women's participation and transformative leadership.

Women and girls often have limited access to economic opportunities, and so expanding gender-just economic training and opportunities is paramount (Islamic Relief, 2015a). Implementing the *Maqasid* framework in this context would help resolve the imbalance in power and resources by addressing the structural and cultural barriers to women's economic empowerment. These barriers include discriminatory laws, particularly in relation to inheritance. Implementing the framework will include advocating for just and non-discriminatory inheritance laws and practices, including equal rights to land ownership and financial assets in line with Islamic ethical principles.

Feminist foreign policy and the Islamic Declaration of Gender Justice

There is a growing movement to implement feminist foreign policies (FFPs) at national and international levels. International FFPs focus on mainstreaming gender issues, with the most notable initiatives including the Beijing Declaration of 1995, which developed a platform for strategic action on several issues such as women and poverty and violence against women, all with the aim of improving the status of women.[5] UN Security Council Resolution 1325 also reinforced the participation of women in peace and security, affirming that 'peace and security efforts are more sustainable when women are equal partners in the prevention of violent conflict, the delivery of relief and recovery efforts and in the forging of lasting peace'.[6] The resolution centralizes women's participation in the four pillars of peace and security – namely, participation, prevention, protection, and relief and recovery – as part of wider peace and security initiatives.[7]

At a national level, several governments have adopted FFP as a policy or a strategic approach. These include Sweden, Canada, and France; the UK has also pledged to adopt an FFP. Sweden has been the strongest voice for gender equality, adopting a comprehensive and holistic FFP in 2014 that incorporates the 'four Rs' approach: this aims to centralize women's *rights*, backed by *resources*, to increase *representation*, and make gender equality a *reality*

(Thompson and Clement, 2019). Sweden spends approximately 90 per cent of its FFP budget on gender equality initiatives (ibid.).

Canada launched its Feminist International Assistance Policy (FIAP) in 2017 to solidify its commitment to women's rights and has set aside a budget to mainstream gender equality. The FIAP initiative is part of the country's broader economic and security goals and seeks to 'eliminate poverty and build a peaceful and prosperous world' (Government of Canada, 2017). Canada spends 70 per cent of its FIAP spending on gender equality and has pledged to increase this to 95 per cent by 2022 (ibid.). Canada's priority areas include human dignity, which encompasses education and health; women's economic empowerment, including access to and control over resources; and climate action and women's participation. There are several organizations, including Islamic Relief, Tearfund, and Oxfam, that actively work in these priority areas. For instance, Islamic Relief and Oxfam have several projects on increasing women's economic empowerment and their participation in decision-making spaces, such as Islamic Relief's Islamic Declaration of Gender Justice.

While these foreign policies undoubtedly contribute to improving women's position in society it is also important to remain aware of different interests embedded in these policies as well as their applicability in development contexts. The FFP minimizes the intersectional forms of discrimination and marginalization, including age, race, disability, and socio-economic status. Moreover, the Western feminist approach of these policies ignores crucial historical underpinnings, such as the legacy of colonialism (Rosamond, 2013), and there is a concern that FFP is another postcolonial norm of countries of the global North. The consequence of this is that they reproduce a patriarchal culture that continues to marginalize women and children and people of colour. Further consideration needs to be given to the ways in which past and present policies contribute to these challenges. In some cases, these concerns are well founded, given that wider feminist discourse does not consider the voices or interests of women in the developing world; this contributes to paternalism and the 'othering' of women in the developing world (ibid.).

The issue of intersectionality is particularly evident in the policies on and response to domestic violence, particularly in relation to migrant and Muslim women. Migrant women experience victimization in relation to their immigration status, where the perpetrator uses the threat of deportation to control their victim. Muslim women still face significant barriers in accessing domestic violence services (such as shelters) and those that do often report being unable to properly practise their faith or cultural traditions in those environments (Kulwicki et al., 2010). This occurs against a backdrop where Islam is viewed as a being 'violent and oppressive towards women', and thus, by extension, Muslim women are viewed as being submissive and oppressed (Ghafournia, 2017). This perception may hinder some Muslim women from accessing support services for fear of discrimination. The lack of protective rights-based intersectional policies has created the conditions for the systematic exploitation of migrant and Muslim women (Henderson, 2019). This complex interplay between religious identity and immigration status is something that is not clearly understood by organizations and governments responding to domestic abuse.

Faith and change in practice

The examples below show the transition from a theological understanding of gender and Islam to practical examples that change people's lives.

Box 6.1 Young changemaker Salimata Togoloa refuses to accept FGM and child marriage in Mali

My name is Salimata Togoloa and I am 17 years old, currently attending school in grade 12. I grew up in Daoudabougou, which is one of the poorest areas of Bamako. When my parents passed away, my siblings and I struggled to maintain a livelihood. Thanks to the sponsorship of the Islamic Relief Mali orphan programme, our lives have regained some stability.

I am grateful to the Islamic Relief Channels of Hope project staff, as they have been such a strong influence in my life. Through their training programmes, I have been made aware of our rights as children and women and am convinced of their cause. I have learned about the importance of child protection and our teachers have shown us how our religion preaches only well-being, compassion, and non-violence. Since then, I have followed this as a guide to conduct awareness-training sessions in my community.

Prior to these workshops, I was unaware of my rights as a young woman. Worse yet, I did not know that FGM is a harmful practice, as I had previously considered it as something dictated by our holy book, the *Qur'an*. Now I know this is not the case; it is a dangerous cultural practice with many damaging consequences. It is so common in our society that it has become normalized. Because of this training from Islamic Relief, I feel like I have become another girl; I now know how different children's rights really are. I feel like I am enlightened, and I owe so much to the Channels of Hope project. By multiplying such training in our communities, we can eradicate these practices and instil change.

I will transmit this knowledge wherever I can, so that we can stop jeopardizing children's health, progress, and future through these harmful and avoidable practices. I was recently elected the president of the children's club at school, and I endeavour to sensitize my friends, parents, and community about child rights and the detrimental consequences that FGM entails.

I have conducted seven awareness sessions to sensitize teachers on the importance of girls' education and to promote the end of physical violence against children at school. Additionally, I have conducted three awareness sessions with parents in our community to raise awareness around the devastating effects of FGM on girls' lives.

This wasn't always easy. One case stands out to me the most; in a session I delivered for FGM practitioners and parents, I was rejected point-blank, as they saw me as being Westernized, acculturated, and disrespectful. Despite this setback, I held onto my determination to be a catalyst of behaviour change. In the long run, I succeeded in convincing them via my repeated awareness sessions. Today, five FGM practitioners have become change agents with me and are helping to sensitize others to abandon FGM. This is a huge achievement as this has considerably reduced the practice of FGM in our surrounding community.

(Continued)

Box 6.1 Continued

The parents who were initially reluctant to keep girls at school in favour of early marriage have begun to stop the practice, and many are helping to sensitize other parents to keep their girls at school. So far, I have convinced 50 parents to do so.

By replicating the knowledge I received with the Islamic Relief training, I have engaged over 100 family chiefs, 150 mothers, and 50 schoolteachers on upholding the dignity of all children, girls, and women by ensuring their rights.

After having seen the huge impact of this project on our community, I ask Islamic Relief to keep implementing such a project so that everybody can be a channel of hope for children's bright futures. It is true that culture and tradition have much sway in our communities, but as witnessed in the progress of this project in just one year, I believe that together we can end FGM and all types of violence against women and children.

Box 6.2 Fighting for women's and children's access to education in the Philippines

Anissa Taha Arab is now the director of an organization in Cotabato City in the Philippines. She grew up as one of nine children and was the only one to complete education. An understanding of how Islam encouraged women to be educated was fundamental to her story. She grew up during the martial law years under President Marcos in the 1970s and 1980s. As the situation declined in Mindanao, her father did not want her to go to school out of fear of what would happen to her on the way. The ongoing conflict meant that her family soon became internally displaced people, moving from place to place, and she had to stop her studies for 10 years. Her father wanted her to marry at 14, to someone she did not know. Anissa argued that Islam gave her the right to be educated; he relented, and she graduated. Her parents were very proud, and she was driven by the fact that she believes that women are equal to men – and that this is what others need to know. Women have the right to be educated, just like men. This drive inspires her to help other girls and she works in partnership with Islamic Relief Philippines to advocate for women's and children's rights.

Box 6.3 Engaging faith leaders in Pakistan

In Pakistan, a study of three provinces revealed that 75 per cent of women have experienced physical violence and 66 per cent have experienced sexual violence (Rutgers, 2013). The Rutgers study also found that Pakistani men face strong social, cultural, and traditional societal pressure to conform and to 'act like men': for example, their role is as provider and protector of the family and the one who makes all the decisions. As a result of unemployment and economic pressure, they are not always able to meet all these expectations. This results in frustration, which in turn may lead to violence.

In the same area, Islamic Relief Pakistan (IRP) involved public-sector staff in its stakeholder engagement. IRP found that it was tribal and community leaders who settle most cases informally. It is therefore essential to understand the local context to recognize and utilize entry points for legal and other help.

In trying to involve women and children in a male-dominated community, IRP liaised with decision makers, who in this context were male religious leaders. They found that even organizations working on GBV and child protection issues in conservative communities would not talk openly unless there were *fatwas* (religious edicts) supporting their statements.

IRP engaged with prominent faith leaders such as Maulvi Muhammad Anwar. He stated: 'Islamic Relief has revolutionized my way of thinking and encouraged me to play an active role as a faith leader to bring positive change in my community and support the rights of the most vulnerable members of the community – women and children.'

Conclusion

An Islamic faith-inspired approach to gender justice plays an important role in dispelling the systematic use of religion to marginalize women and girls. This includes HTPs that continue to inhibit the development of women and girls. The *Maqasid* framework – along with other Islamic principles of justice, equality, and balance – reinforces women's rights to faith, life, property, intellect, and posterity. Nevertheless, there are few examples of these teachings being implemented in development projects. As demonstrated, Islamic teachings from the *Qur'an* and *Sunnah* provide evidence to support gender justice. These teachings are aligned with international legal frameworks on human rights such as CEDAW, as well as global commitments such as the SDGs, FFPs, and Islamic Declaration of Gender Justice. Moreover, training and engaging both male and female faith leaders in applying the *Maqasid* framework to challenge HTPs would significantly increase the eradication of these practices.

HTPs, along with structural inequality, are at the root of gender inequality, which manifests itself as different forms of GBV such as domestic violence, sexual violence, FGM/C, and EFM. Vulnerable groups, particularly women and girls, suffer from forms of cultural, structural, and direct violence that are interrelated and mutually reinforcing. Direct violence refers to physical violence and behaviours that threaten life: for example, killings and sexual violence. Structural violence covers the systematic barriers that hinder certain groups from accessing opportunities, goods, and services necessary to meet basic needs. It includes laws that enforce marginalization and that limit access to education (Galtung, 1990). Cultural violence relates to social norms that seek to normalize direct and structural violence (ibid.). In order to address gender inequality in a sustainable manner, interventions should seek to break this cycle to disrupt social norms that normalize direct violence while also working to address systematic barriers at a societal level. The *Maqasid* framework would be a particularly useful tool in breaking this cycle because its objectives encompass issues pertaining to structural and direct violence such as the protection of life, intellect, and property.

Dispelling misconstrued understandings of Islamic scriptures that perpetuate gender injustice is an issue that requires global partnerships, particularly with Islamic scholars and Islamic organizations. We must also recognize that these misconstrued understandings of Islamic scriptures have become so ingrained in some societies that they now form part of a shared identity. Muslim-majority countries also play a role in perpetuating these misconstrued understandings in their quest for political leverage on the global stage. Their engagement with international human rights systems have been symbolic, providing little to no protection for women's rights.

To challenge these misconceptions we must use a faith-informed integrated approach with tailored interventions to tackle harmful cultural practices (such as FGM/C and EFM) and promote gender justice in all projects.

In order for this to come to fruition there needs to be investment in the development of female Islamic scholarship that contributes to faith literacy and addresses social issues affecting Muslim women and men through faith-based approaches.

Notes

1. The SDGs are a set of 17 goals that form a blueprint to achieve a better and more sustainable future for all.
2. SDG 5, 2030 Agenda (UN General Assembly, 2015).
3. See <https://data.unicef.org/topic/gender/gender-disparities-in-education/> [accessed 12 May 2020].
4. See <https://d1.islamhouse.com/data/en/ih_articles/single2/en_Prophet_Muhammad_Last_Sermon.pdf>.
5. See <https://www.un.org/en/events/pastevents/pdfs/Beijing_Declaration_and_Platform_for_Action.pdf>.
6. See <https://www.refworld.org/docid/3b00f4672e.html> [accessed 2 September 2019].
7. See <https://www.usip.org/gender_peacebuilding/about_UNSCR_1325> [accessed 29 August 2019].

References

An-Na'im, A. (1990) 'Human rights in the Muslim world: socio-political conditions and scriptural imperatives – a preliminary inquiry', *Harvard Human Rights Journal* 3: 13–52.

Auda, J. (2008) 'Maqasid Al-Shariah: an introductory guide', International Institute of Islamic Thought, Herndon VA <https://www.jasserauda.net/new/pdf/maqasid_guide-Feb_2008.pdf>.

Baderin, M.A. (2005) *International Human Rights and Islamic Law*, Oxford University Press, New York.

Bradshaw, S. and Fordham, M. (2013) *'Women, girls and disasters: a review for DFID'*, Department for International Development (DFID), London <https://assets.publishing.service.gov.uk/government/uploads/system/uploads/attachment_data/file/844489/withdrawn-women-girls-disasters.pdf>.

Cader, A. and Namasivayam, M. (2017) 'Intersections: the politicisation of religion and sexual and reproductive health and rights', *Asian-Pacific Resource and Research Centre for Women* 23 (1) <https://arrow.org.my/wp-content/uploads/2017/05/AFC-23_1_2017-WEB.pdf>.

Çalı, B. and Montoya, M (2017) *The March of Universality? Religion-based Reservations to the Core UN Treaties and What They Tell Us about Human Rights and Universality in the 21st century*, Universal Rights Group, Versoix, Switzerland <https://www.universal-rights.org/urg-policy-reports/march-universality-religion-based-reservations-core-un-human-rights-treaties-tell-us-human-rights-religion-universality-21st-century/> [accessed 12 May 2020].

Galtung, J. (1990) 'Cultural violence', *Journal of Peace Research* 27 (3): 291–305.

Ghafournia, N. (2017) 'Muslim women and domestic violence: developing a framework for social work practice', *Journal of Religion and Spirituality in Social Work: Social Thought* 36 (1–2): 146–63.

Gouda, M. and Potrafke, N. (2016) 'Gender equality in Muslim-majority countries', *Economic Systems* 40 (4): 683–98.

Government of Canada (2017) *Canada's Feminist International Assistance Policy*, Global Affairs Canada, Ottawa <https://www.international.gc.ca/world-monde/assets/pdfs/iap2-eng.pdf?_ga=2.63745451.566082633.1574601417-1414009118.1574601417>.

Henderson, S. (2019) 'State-sanctioned structural violence: women migrant domestic workers in the Philippines and Sri Lanka', *Violence Against Women* <https://journals.sagepub.com/doi/10.1177/1077801219880969>.

Humphreys, J. (2016) 'Unthinkable: is Islam compatible with human rights law?' <https://www.dublincityinterfaithforum.org/news/story/1075/unthinkable-is-islam-compatible-with-human-rights-law> [accessed 7 December 2019].

Ilesanmi, O. (2018) 'Women's visibility in decision making processes in Africa: progress, challenges, and way forward', *Frontiers in Sociology* 3.

Intel (2013) *Women and the Web: Bridging the Internet Gap and Creating New Global Opportunities in Low and Middle-income Countries*, Intel, Santa Clara CA <https://www.intel.com/content/dam/www/public/us/en/documents/pdf/women-and-the-web.pdf>.

Islamic Relief (2015a) *'Gender justice policy'*, Islamic Relief Worldwide, Birmingham.

Islamic Relief (2015b) *'One cut too many: Islamic Relief on female genital mutilation/cutting'*, Islamic Relief Worldwide, Birmingham <https://www.islamic-relief.org/publications/>.

Islamic Relief (2017) *'Don't force me! A policy brief on early forced marriage'*, Islamic Relief Worldwide, Birmingham <https://www.islamic-relief.org/publications/>.

Islamic Relief (2020) *Islamic Gender Justice Declaration*, Islamic Relief, Birmingham.

Ivanescu, C. (2010) 'Politicised religion and the religionisation of politics', *Culture and Religion* 11 (4): 309–25 <https://doi.org/10.1080/14755610.2010.527611>.

Kaviti, L. (2017) 'Impact of the Tamar communication strategy on sexual gender-based violence in Eastern Africa', *International Journal of Humanities and Cultural Studies* 2 (3).

Kulwicki, A., Aswad, B., Carmona, T. and Ballout, S. (2010) 'Barriers in the utilization of domestic violence services among Arab immigrant women: perceptions of professionals, service providers and community leaders', *Journal of Family Violence* 25 (8): 727–35.

Le Roux, E. (2019) *Religion, Development, and GBV: Suggestions for a Strategic Research Agenda*, Joint Learning Initiative on Faith and Local Communities, Washington DC.

Le Roux, E. and Bartelink, B.E. (2017) *No More 'Harmful Traditional Practices': Working Effectively with Faith Leaders. Synthesis Report of the UK-Government Funded Project: 'Working Effectively with Faith Leaders to Challenge Harmful Traditional Practices'*, Tearfund, Teddington.

Levitt, H. and Ware, K. (2006) 'Religious leaders' perspectives on marriage, divorce, and intimate partner violence', *Psychology of Women Quarterly* 30 (2): 212–22.

Namasivayam, A., Arcos González, P., Castro Delgado, R. and Chi, P.C. (2017) 'The effect of armed conflict on the utilization of maternal health services in Uganda: a population-based study', *PLoS Currents* 9.

OCHA (2019) 'Gender-based violence: a closer look at the numbers', United Nations Office for the Coordination of Humanitarian Affairs (OCHA), 21 May <https://www.unocha.org/story/gender-based-violence-closer-look-numbers> [accessed 6 December 2019].

Pertek, S. (2012) 'Gender justice in programme delivery of Muslim faith-based development organisations: towards gender-sensitive faith-based framework', MSc thesis, Development Planning Unit, University College London.

Rosamond, A.B. (2013) 'Protection beyond borders: gender cosmopolitanism and co-constitutive obligation', *Global Society* 27 (3): 319–36.

Rutgers (2013) *Domestic Violence against Women: Prevalence and Men's Perception in PGRN Districts of Pakistan*, Rutgers WPF, Utrecht.

Thompson, L. and Clement, R. (2019) *Defining Feminist Foreign Policy*, International Center for Research on Women, Washington DC.

UNDP (2014) 'UNDP guidelines on engaging with faith-based organizations and religious leaders', United Nations Development Programme (UNDP), New York <http://www.undp.org/content/dam/undp/documents/partners/2014_UNDP_Guidelines-on-Engaging-with-FBOs-and-Religious-Leaders_EN.pdf> [accessed 12 May 2020].

UN General Assembly (1979) *Convention on the Elimination of All Forms of Discrimination Against Women*, Treaty Series Volume 1249, p. 13, United Nations (UN), 18 December <https://www.ohchr.org/en/professionalinterest/pages/cedaw.aspx>.

UN General Assembly (2015) *Transforming Our World: The 2030 Agenda for Sustainable Development*, United Nations (UN), New York.

WHO (2007) *Engaging Men and Boys in Changing Gender-based Inequity in Health: Evidence from Programme Interventions*, World Health Organization (WHO), Geneva.

About the authors

Shahin Ashraf is Head of Global Advocacy for Islamic Relief. She has over 25 years of experience and specializes in faith, development, and gender advocacy. Shahin has held senior positions with several global humanitarian, women's rights, and civil society organizations. She developed Islamic Relief's Climate Change Advocacy framework and leads on many of its global discussions relating to Islam and climate change.

Najmo Abukar is Research and Advocacy Officer at Islamic Relief. She has a master's degree in Humanitarian Action and Conflict from Uppsala University in Sweden.

CHAPTER 7

Deconstructing Islamic perspectives on sexual and gender-based violence, toward a faith-inclusive approach

Sandra Iman Pertek

The potential of faith perspectives to combat violence against women and girls has been overshadowed by misunderstanding religion as a contributing factor to sexual and gender-based violence (SGBV). In fact, religion can be a protective factor against SGBV. This chapter develops the argument that religion can be a resource to prevent SGBV and that faith-inspired interventions can be effective strategies to challenge societal discriminatory norms and violence. I examine Islamic perspectives on SGBV and how a faith-sensitive SGBV intervention of Islamic Relief Ethiopia employs faith to combat SGBV in a humanitarian context. I argue that local faith communities, including faith leaders, can seek to end SGBV. Humanitarian infrastructure should recognize religious resources as capacities of local faith communities and integrate their perspectives into programming to increase the effectiveness of SGBV programmes in faith communities.

Keywords: sexual and gender-based violence (SGBV), violence against women and girls, domestic violence, spousal violence, intimate partner violence, early and forced marriage, female genital mutilation and cutting (FGM/C), religion, faith, Islam

Introduction

Sexual and gender-based violence (SGBV) is a global phenomenon undermining dignity and human rights across all regions and backgrounds. Official data show that one in three women and one in five men worldwide experience some type of SGBV.[1] UNHCR (2011: 6) defines SGBV as:

> any harmful act that is perpetrated against one person's will and that is based on socially ascribed (gender) differences between males and females. It includes acts that inflict physical, mental, or sexual harm or suffering, threats of such acts, coercion and other deprivations of liberty, whether occurring in public or in private life.

However, SGBV survivors attach subjective meanings to their experiences as violence can be expressed differently in diverse cultures.

http://dx.doi.org/10.3362/9781788530613.007

Even though SGBV exists in all religions and across all contexts (Crisp, 2012), it is often associated with patriarchal cultures and religions are blamed for condoning or inciting violence against women (Carlson, 2005). The prevalence of SGBV spreads across various geographical regions. According to the World Health Organization (WHO), the lifetime prevalence of physical and/or sexual intimate partner violence among women who have ever had a partner is highest in South-East Asia, the Eastern Mediterranean, and Africa, at 37.7 per cent, 37 per cent, and 36 per cent respectively, compared with 29.8 per cent in the Americas and 25.4 per cent in Europe (WHO, 2013). The lifetime prevalence of non-partner sexual violence is highest in Africa (11.9 per cent), followed by the Americas (10.7 per cent). However there are no official SGBV data disaggregated by religion and therefore claims that faith communities may have higher SGBV prevalence are not necessarily true and require further research.

Patriarchy permeates religions, allowing the superior position of men over women which can manifest in abuse of power and violence. Despite increasing policy commitments to explore the potential of faith-based actors[2] to tackle SGBV the efforts of development actors to utilize religious precepts of justice and equality to seek an end to SGBV are still rare. As the social constructions of religion can both condone and combat SGBV it is essential to have a better understanding of contextual factors and an improved faith literacy for more constructive engagement with faith perspectives and faith actors, and to recognize that both the risk and protective factors associated with religion are vital for SGBV programme design. There is not only a distinction between religious teachings and patriarchal cultural interpretations of religious teachings, but also a distinction between religious behaviour and cultural behaviour.

The purpose of this chapter is to contribute to a better understanding and application of Muslim faith perspectives in SGBV programming in the humanitarian and development sector. First, I review faith perspectives on SGBV. Second, I consider the ways in which a faith-sensitive SGBV intervention in a humanitarian setting employs religion to combat SGBV. I specifically explore how religious beliefs and religious practices can tackle SGBV in faith communities by examining a case study of Islamic Relief's pilot SGBV project in the Somali region of Ethiopia. I conduct my analysis based on existing knowledge and my own experience of adapting faith approaches in development contexts. The analysis draws upon the distinction between religious teachings and patriarchal cultural interpretations. I end with recommendations to practitioners and policymakers to engage faith perspectives in SGBV programmes targeted at faith communities.

SGBV and religion in humanitarian and development contexts

The intersection of SGBV and religion in humanitarian and development contexts is central. SGBV is often a cause and a consequence of oppression and violation of human rights. SGBV increases in conflict and humanitarian crises due to multiple factors such as reduced and fragmented local security, weakened legal enforcement, and general disruption in social relations and social norms, including gender dynamics. The consequences of SGBV are long-lasting and undermine survivors' and victims' dignity. Violence jeopardizes physical, mental, and reproductive health, and can have effects including trauma and post-traumatic stress disorder, physical injuries, depression and anxiety, to name just a few. In addition, SGBV perpetuates poverty, divides communities, and hinders survivors' opportunities for personal growth.

The root causes of SGBV vary across contexts and individual cases. They include stigma, lack of social acceptance, substance abuse, and some harmful traditional practices. Power imbalances between females and males are commonly recognized as underlying causes of violence against women and girls. In addition, deprivation, unemployment, and lack of opportunity can result in a masculinity crisis that is often manifested in increased levels of violence.[3] Gender power dynamics intersect with other forms of oppression such as racism and ageism, often exacerbating people's experiences of violence with multiple effects.

Muslim perspectives as a framework to combat SGBV

SGBV in Islam is severely misunderstood in both Muslim and non-Muslim circles. The fundamental faith principles of justice and non-violence are often overshadowed by patriarchy and the harmful traditional practices of some communities. A growing faith-oriented engagement with the root causes of SGBV, such as societal and cultural norms, which are often conflated with religion, helps separate the religious precepts from cultural influences. Such efforts must recognize that patriarchy permeates most cultures and that socially constructed interpretations of religious text often twist religions in ways that can be used to justify oppression. Subsequently, socially constructed understandings of religious practices have often been blamed for condoning SGBV, and especially violence against women and girls. In the following sections I examine Islamic faith principles and teachings that faith communities can use to challenge SGBV, as well as some contestations of these concepts.

Overarching Qur'anic principles and SGBV

Despite the vast diversity of Islamic thought and how multicultural the global Muslim population is there are some central tenants of Islam that are universal for all Muslims. One of these principles is to uphold justice, as commanded numerous times in the *Qur'an* (for example, in verses 4: 135, 5: 8, 49: 9, and 16: 90).[4] Equality of women and men in front of God, while contested by various groups, is well articulated throughout both the *Qur'an* and the *Sunnah*,[5] the primary sources of Islam (Ashraf, 2005; see, for example, *Qur'an*, 4: 1, 2: 228, 4: 32). The inherent dignity of all human beings, women and men alike, as enshrined in religious sources requires us to preserve human dignity and take all possible measures to abstain from any actions that undermine it. The *Qur'an* also requires humanity to protect oppressed groups, including survivors of violence. The tradition of the Prophet Muhammad (Peace Be Upon Him) urges faith communities to prevent wrongdoing: 'Whosoever of you sees an evil, let him change it with his hand; and if he is not able to do so, then [let him change it] with his tongue; and if he is not able to do so, then with his heart and that is the weakest of faith.'[6]

When one considers these overarching principles it is unambiguous that any violence against either women or men must be prevented and stopped. I look at three types of violence: domestic violence, early and forced marriage (EFM), and female genital mutilation and cutting (FGM/C). In conducting this analysis I acknowledge the variety of contested opinions and religious viewpoints on SGBV issues, as reflected in the diversity of Muslim faith communities. Therefore, the following discussion is by no means exhaustive; rather, it is an introduction to key complexities.

Demystifying myths: an Islamic perspective on SGBV

While there are no official data demonstrating that religious beliefs are among the key drivers behind SGBV incidents and the official statistics do not indicate higher rates of SGBV among Muslim nations, qualitative evidence suggests that religious misconceptions and patriarchal interpretations are sometimes used by abusers to justify violence or by survivors to make sense of their experiences (McKerl, 2009: 264; Alkahteeb, n.d.). Some studies have found that religion is a source of strength, resilience, and protection among vulnerable groups. For example, a study by Ghafournia (2017) found that a majority of abused Muslim immigrant women interviewed in Australia believed that their religion protects them from violence and promotes equality with men. Accounts of these women included: 'My religion says equal rights of women and men, but people of my country do not follow that rule. They say men are always up and women are down';[7] and 'I just know that I feel what people are doing in the name of Islam is different from what God or His prophet really want and say ... Now they use whatever is beneficial for them.'[8] Most of the abused women interviewed in Ghafournia's study differentiated between Islamic values and cultural beliefs and said that social expectations delayed their decision to seek help. A minority of interviewed women equated culture with religion and blamed both as barriers to seeking help (ibid.).

Intersection of domestic violence and Islam

Islamic sources and prophetic examples are unambivalent in encouraging love, kindness, and peace in the family. For example, one of the Qur'anic verses states: 'And among His signs is this: that He created for you mates from among yourselves, that you may dwell in tranquillity with them, and He has put love and mercy between your [hearts]' (*Qur'an*, 30: 21). The tradition of the Prophet Muhammad (PBUH) as a non-violent and supportive husband and father shows no tolerance for violence. In one of his sayings, he explained: 'The best of you is the best to his family, and I am the best to my family.' Yet, religious scriptures, influenced by culture, have been blamed for man's violence against women, particularly intimate-partner violence (IPV), within the framework of reciprocal marital responsibilities.

Some religious texts have been interpreted in ambiguous ways. The most contentious verse of the *Qur'an* referred to in the discussion on domestic violence is verse 34 in Chapter 4 (called *al-nisa*, or 'women'). Among various English translations, Abdel Haleem's translation of this verse reads:

> Husbands should take good care of their wives, with [the bounties] God has given to some more than others and with what they spend out of their own money. Righteous wives are devout and guard what God would have them guard in their husbands' absence. If you fear high-handedness from your wives, remind them [of the teachings of God], then ignore them when you go to bed, then hit them. If they obey you, you have no right to act against them: God is most high and great. (*Qur'an*, 4: 34)

This excerpt describes the way in which a husband should behave in cases of spousal disobedience and lewdness. The third step, after advising them and forsaking them in bed, relates to *idribuhunna* in Arabic. This has several interpretations in English, including 'striking'. Some interpretations seem to contradict each other, as well as the overarching religious principles and prophetic guidance on love and mercy in marital relationships. Many translate the verse as lightly hitting and striking, whereas others refer to separating, departing, travelling, ignoring, abandoning, and blocking ears, to name a few (see Hasan, 2013).

Many Islamic scholars agree that there is no excuse in religious sources to resort to domestic violence (Hasan, 2013; IICPSR and UNFPA, 2016), but still a diversity of opinion exists in Muslim faith communities. In an effort to conceptualize varied views on domestic violence in Muslim communities, Ammar (2007) developed a typology of domestic violence in Islam with four approaches: 1) interpreting Qur'anic verse 4: 34 as permission to beat and discipline one's wife; 2) permitting light/symbolic wife beating with strict conditions and as a last resort to reconcile, after the two preceding steps of reprimanding a spouse and refusing to share a bed with her; 3) interpreting the verse as an exception to the general principles of Islamic sources and indicating that beating is permissible but not desirable; and 4) interpreting the Arabic word *idribuhunna* (traditionally translated as 'lightly hitting' and compared with a tap with a toothbrush) as something other than hitting and showing a list of alternative meanings of the Arabic word in English. Religious interpretations should be critically read from the perspective of practices promoted by the Prophet Muhammad (PBUH), who never violated his family members.

Nonetheless, some abusers sometimes refer to religious interpretations to justify behaviour that is rooted in patriarchy, which often replaces religious values. Ghafournia highlights: 'It was not the patriarchal precepts of religion but the patriarchal interpretation that facilitated the abuse' (2017: 159).

Patriarchal cultures and religious constructs often influence the acceptability of domestic violence by both spouses and have a profound and detrimental impact on survivors of violence. Often, abused women who are religious endure their predicament with the idea that 'this life is not important', awaiting a better life and reward in Heaven for their endurance. Abusive husbands sometimes use IPV to contest and reinforce power dynamics in their relationship, misusing religion to legitimize their behaviour (Carlson, 2005). Such techniques can lead survivors to isolation, self-blame, emotional abuse, coercion, intimidation, and fear (ibid.; Alkahteeb, n.d.). Therefore, in the spirit of the central faith principles, such as social justice and human dignity, the logical interpretation of the Qur'anic verse 4: 34 is as a condemnation of spousal violence.

Early and forced marriage

Around the globe, women, men, girls, and boys of various social backgrounds are married without their consent and often before the age of 18. This phenomenon, described by the term 'forced marriage' and 'early marriage', is experienced by individuals of all ages and religions. It involves a range of negative consequences, including early pregnancies of girls aged 15 to 19 and increased risk of death in child delivery, fistulas, sexually transmitted diseases, including HIV and AIDS, and increased risk of experiencing family violence, as well as social isolation and restricted social mobility.

In Muslim tradition, several conditions must be met to validate a marriage contract. One of them is the consent of both individuals intending to enter marital union, as well as a mutual physical attraction. The *Qur'an* prohibits forced marriage: 'It is not lawful for you to inherit women by force' (4: 19). Also, in a *hadith*[9] recorded by Abu Huraira and validated by a scholar named Muslim, the Prophet stated explicitly that a woman should not be married until her consent is obtained.[10] Paying a dowry by a husband to his wife is another major prerequisite (*Qur'an*, 4: 4, 4: 24–5, 5: 5). Other conditions refer to the intellectual capacity of a groom and bride to present sound judgement in making responsible decisions, such as managing one's finances and understanding the responsibilities that marriage entails.

Nonetheless, some beliefs and contextual factors, such as poverty and displacement, perpetuate the acceptance of early and forced marriage, or impel families to adapt early marriage as a coping or protection strategy for their survival in crisis situations. Beliefs can sometimes relate, for instance, to varied historical accounts concerning the age of Ayesha, the Prophet Muhammad's (PBUH) wife. According to the primary sources of Islam, all marriages must be conducted with the consent of mature individuals who have the legal, mental, intellectual, and physical capacity to consent. Thus, early marriage, or child marriage, is by default not allowed in Muslim tradition, as minors entering the marital union lack the capacity to consent, and so the marriage is void (Islamic Relief Worldwide, 2018).

One of the motives that Islamic communities deploy to advocate against forced marriage is the principle of *maslahah mursalah*, which relates to unrestricted public interest. Considering the negative effects that early and forced marriage and pregnancy have on adolescent girls, it is explicit that *maslahah mursalah* obliges Muslims to protect against these practices. Therefore, many Muslim-majority countries have adopted 18 as the minimum age for marriage. Some international development organizations, such as Islamic Relief Worldwide, have also developed policies that advocate for 18 as the minimum age for marriage (Pertek and Abdulaziz, 2018). Such legal and advocacy efforts consider the particular difficulties that girls face in development settings if they are married as minors, including dropping out of school, the perpetuation of poverty, and a range of mental, emotional, physical, and reproductive health effects.

Female genital mutilation/cutting

Around the world, 2 million women and girls are at risk of female genital mutilation or cutting (FGM/C) annually, mainly in Africa and the Middle East, but also in Indonesia and elsewhere (UNICEF, 2013). The WHO defines FGM/C as 'all procedures that involve partial or total removal of the external female genitalia, or other injury to the female genital organs for non-medical reasons' (WHO, 2018). Four types of FGM/C are commonly recognized, namely:

1. partial or total removal of the clitoris;
2. partial or total removal of the clitoris and the labia minora;
3. narrowing of the vaginal orifice; and
4. all other harmful procedures to the female genitalia, e.g. pricking or piercing (Abdulcadir et al., 2016).

FGM/C occurs in faith communities of various affiliations; it is not only Muslim communities that refer to FGM/C as a religious practice. This incorrect belief that it is a Muslim issue is rooted in the misconstrued link between FGM/C and Islam, even though FGM/C is not mentioned in the *Qur'an*. Muslim communities that identify FGM/C with religion refer to contested *ahadith* that are mostly weak or inauthentic. Asmani and Abdi (2008) undertook great efforts to delink FGM/C from Islam by analysing, discussing, and demystifying Islamic sources and several *ahadith* that were used to justify FGM/C practices.

Essentially, harm caused by FGM/C contradicts the principal objectives of *Shari'ah*, which are to protect life and safeguard humanity. This assertion provides a strong basis for Islamic scholars and faith communities to advocate against FGM/C as it poses serious health risks for women and girls, as well as hindering married women's right to marital pleasure (Islamic Relief

Worldwide, 2016). Furthermore, Islamic teachings negate FGM/C as a practice that can pose a risk of death: for instance, 'The killing of one soul without just cause is like killing the whole of humanity' (*Qur'an*, 5: 32). A growing number of religious leaders publicly condemn FGM/C, as the harm and suffering caused by this practice become more widely recognized. This is supported by the principle of Islamic law that a permissible practice (*mubaah*) can become prohibited (*haram*) when its harmful effect is proven. The International Islamic Center for Population Studies and Research at Al-Azhar University and the United Nations Population Fund (IICPSR and UNFPA, 2016) developed critical guidelines on SGBV from an Islamic perspective that challenged misconceptions and provided Islamic stances on various SGBV types.

I now explore the interaction between SGBV and Islam in practice by examining the intervention of Islamic Relief Ethiopia (IRE), a faith-based organization (FBO) and part of Islamic Relief Worldwide.[11]

A faith-based approach to SGBV programming

FBOs are often local service providers, offering support services for SGBV survivors, including education, health services, emergency shelter, protection spaces, psychosocial support, spiritual care, counselling, and livelihood support. Some FBOs engage faith leaders and local faith communities in preventing and responding to SGBV. An example of a faith-based approach to tackle SGBV is IRE's project entitled 'Combating Gender-based Violence of Women and Girls in the Dekasuftu Woreda of Liben Zone', within the Somali regional state of Ethiopia. The key aims of the project were to increase the safety of women and girls, decrease SGBV tolerance among communities, and promote adequate access to health services for people subjected to SGBV by integrating a health component in the project (Surti and Pertek, 2018). This pilot intervention was part of a wider organizational shift within Islamic Relief, aiming to integrate gender perspectives into humanitarian and development work and seeking to end SGBV, in accordance with Islamic Relief's overarching Gender Justice Policy (Pertek, 2015). The project supported one of the policy commitments to tackle SGBV by engaging faith leaders to help dismantle religious misconceptions fuelling violence against women and girls. Islamic Relief's strategy for eradicating SGBV involves 'including religion as part of the solution and tailoring interventions to the specific needs and sensitivities of the community' (Islamic Relief Worldwide, 2016: 3). The project adapted a pilot SGBV methodology to test a faith-sensitive approach to combating SGBV.

Community conversation

During project implementation IRE adopted a 'community conversation' (CC) approach to the prevention of SGBV and fully embedded its activities in communities, building on their capacities and knowledge. CC is a participatory

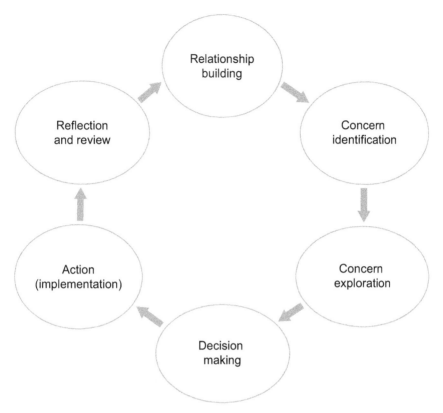

Figure 7.1 The 'community conversation' process
Source: IRE (2016a).

and transformational methodology from the 1970s that aims to challenge and change people's attitudes and behaviours and to instil more equitable and dignity-protecting practices. CC is a continuous process of building relationships, identifying and exploring concerns, taking joint community decisions, and acting and reflecting on outcomes (see Figure 7.1). Community members gather, discuss, and reflect on important social issues affecting their lives, drawing on their own principles and beliefs, including religious ideas. Religion is an integral part of the displaced Somali communities' identity, inseparable from their culture, and so an Islamic perspective was inevitably central to all discussions. By utilizing the inherent resources of faith communities, the project catalysed collective empowerment.

IRE implemented the project in a phased process to ensure community ownership and acceptance. Several project activities were implemented in sequence (see Figure 7.2).

At the outset, faith leaders from project locations were invited to a training session in the capital, Addis Ababa, which was dedicated to women's issues, children's rights, family issues, and Islam. Subsequently, IRE, together

Figure 7.2 Process of IRE's project activities
Source: Surti and Pertek (2018).

with trained religious leaders, mobilized community volunteers. In total, 16 workshops were organized to equip them to deal with enquiries from communities regarding the relevance of some religious teachings and their interpretation in reference to specific social and health issues, such as FGM/C, marriage by inheritance, and domestic violence, from both an Islamic and an Ethiopian constitutional perspective. Second, religious and community leaders utilized a sequence of behavioural change communication methods to sensitize communities on the most prevalent SGBV issues in their villages during female and male community conversations, as well as during mixed sessions. Also, several community-owned activities, including women's and men's discussion groups, school clubs, and sermons on women's rights and SGBV issues at congregational prayers were held to address SGBV in the Dekasuftu district.

Faith leaders acted as focal points of reference at times of confusion and disagreement on SGBV issues, particularly with regard to highly sensitive topics such as wife beating and FGM/C. As an authority, they provided rulings regarding harmful practices that were wrongly believed to be rooted in religious teachings. They were also a source of solace and guidance regarding forgiveness for wrongdoing. In cases where local communities did not believe a faith leader from a neighbouring village, testimony and guidance were sought and obtained from a trusted local faith leader. Faith leaders from the same locality played an essential role in the community's reflection and in changing their thinking on the acceptability of some harmful practices, since local faith leaders had an authority and influence on the perceptions and attitudes of their communities. Religious leaders also offered sermons during

Friday prayers regarding women's status, SGBV, and girls' education, reaching out to 800 congregation members. Local authorities participated in some parts of the project and offered their support for its implementation.

Various psychosocial support activities were conducted in four villages, each known as a *kebele*,[12] to challenge different forms of SGBV. *Kebele* officials, elders, and other community members belonging to the men- and women-only discussion groups performed drama, poetry, and cultural songs against SGBV and promoting women's status. For instance, in the Gunway *kebele*, traditional birth attendants enacted a drama to raise awareness of the harm of FGM/C. Other volunteers read poetry with the message of the wrongness of FGM/C in front of the community, highlighting the dangers of this practice. Conversely, in the Sora *kebele*, different methods of teaching and awareness, such as songs and poetry, were used to educate the community about the detrimental effect of rape on survivors and the society at large, and on how to handle incidents of sexual violence. The communities reported that they enjoyed the psycho-social activities and recommended expanding awareness-raising activities to all communities in Dekasuftu *woreda*.[13] They promised to share the activities and stories with the neighbouring community. Interestingly, men took an equal part in the process of sensitization and were instrumental in delivering anti-violence messages.

The impact of faith-based intervention

The project's monthly reports and final evaluation reports recorded qualitative evidence of project impact (Le Roux and Bartelink, 2017). Dozens of positive and open group, and community conversations stimulated local engagement, ownership, and reflection on various SGBV issues. The project resulted in dismantling some religious misconceptions driving FGM/C, domestic violence, marriage by inheritance, barriers to girls' education, and misuse of dowry (Surti and Pertek, 2018). In total, 199 women and 200 men from 16 *kebeles* attended regular monthly meetings in a safe and friendly space for eight months, while over 38,000 people benefited from the project indirectly (IRE, 2017). Some women and girls started seeking justice from community leaders and reporting abuse to the police (ibid.). I now discuss in more detail the changes relating to several SGBV issues that occurred during project implementation.

Domestic violence

One of the most contentious and debated issues was domestic violence. The majority of male group members believed that beating a woman is right and necessary; only a minority of males opposed such views (IRE, 2016b). In men-only groups in the Bundakaran, Takahagar, Gunway, Qurabul, and Sora *kebeles*, the facilitators asked questions such as: 'Is sexual violence/ rape culturally or religiously acceptable in our community?'; 'If a rape case has occurred in our *kebele*, how do we manage it?' Such questions incited lengthy discussions in each group, revealing a range of diverse cultural beliefs and traditions that allowed domestic violence. Some views infantilized and undermined women's capacities. For instance:

> Woman should [be] beaten because they are like children and therefore need to be punished [physically] when they make mistakes ... sometimes women need to be beaten even when they are depressed to stimulate them ... beating is the solution for women to discipline them. Otherwise, the women undermine the husbands up to the point that it will be difficult to identify who is the husband or the wife. (Male representative, aged 32, Sero *kebele*)

Those who believed that physical violence (beating women) is right argued, for example, that a husband should beat his wife from the beginning of the marriage union by beating her with a stick three times: the first time when she enters the house to ascertain whether she is possessed by an evil spirit. A woman's submission and acceptance of violence symbolizes her purity, whereas her refusal and escape reveal that she is cursed. If she escapes, a woman should be tied to a tree and undergo a ritual with dark smoke to cleanse her.

On the other hand, community members opposing domestic violence argued that women have equal rights to men and are equally, if not more, important in the family. Such beliefs mainly stemmed from the appreciation of women's reproductive role and their caring responsibilities. This group of men perceived perpetrators as criminals deserving adequate measures in legal justice.

Religious leaders referred men's groups to religious sources and explained that it is imperative to follow their religion, rather than a culture of abuse. They highlighted, in both group discussions and Friday sermons, that rape is completely unacceptable from both a religious and a cultural perspective. Religious leaders clarified that physical violence against women (spousal violence/IPV) is wrong by referencing the *Qur'an* and the *ahadith*. They referred to the prophetic example and recalled how the Prophet Muhammad (PBUH) encouraged others to treat people kindly and to honour one's wife. Local leaders recalled the saying of the Prophet: 'The best of you are those who are the best to their wives, and I am the best of you to my wives.' As a result, all group members agreed and accepted that spousal violence is wrong and has no place in Islam or under any law. They also promised to abide by this and pass on the message to others.

In the women's groups, even though most women were against domestic violence, sometimes their attitudes also perpetuated violence. For example, one woman disclosed:

> [I] believe being beaten by [my] husband is right and acceptable ... if [my] husband did not beat [me] when [I] make a mistake it implies that there is something wrong with marriage or [my] husband doesn't love [me]. (Female representative, aged 27, Kudabul *kebele*, quoted in IRE, 2016b)

Religious leaders also explained to the women's groups that physical violence against them is wrong and unacceptable from an Islamic perspective. Consequently, all woman agreed that physical violence should not be accepted and they were determined to combat misbeliefs and the acceptance of domestic violence. Dismantling some of the patriarchal interpretations of religious sources helped tackle religious misconceptions perpetuating abuse. Although IRE observed that physical violence against women decreased towards the end of the project's implementation (IRE, 2017), educating women and working on changing gender norms and mindsets is a long-term process. It requires continued commitments, engaging communities, regularly challenging myths, and confronting stigma.

FGM/C

FGM/C is a deeply ingrained practice in Somali culture. There was a strong perception among community members that FGM/C is part of their culture and girls who are not genitally mutilated would be unmarriable. FGM/C was believed to help control girls and prevent them from unacceptable and unsafe sex (IRE, 2016e). Female representatives in group discussions unanimously agreed that FGM/C is part of their tradition, with comments such as: 'FGM/C is our culture; it is difficult to change or stop [it]'; 'If we stop FGM/C, who [will] marr[y] our girls?'; 'I am 57 years old and we were Muslim long century ago; I have never heard before [that] FGM/C is harmful. Why today [has it] become harmful?' (women from various *kebeles* in Dekasuftu *woreda*, quoted in IRE, 2016e).

Men who used to believe that FGM/C was correct reflected that they were ignorant in front of God when they became aware of its harmful effects and heard the *ahadith* opposing FGM/C. They questioned why previous religious leaders had not told them that FGM/C is forbidden. They also blamed women for conducting FGM/C and were determined to persuade them to stop it. They requested further support from IRE on spreading more awareness of this issue.

The reports show that the project made a difference among FGM/C practitioners, even during its relatively short duration. Faith leaders joined discussions and explained the meaning of misunderstood religious sources, declaring that 'FGM/C is not based on Muslim religion' (IRE, 2016e) and that it is a sinful act because of the harm it causes. Female representatives, including FGM/C practitioners, cried and repented their wrongdoing, promising to work on stopping FGM/C and changing the rest of their communities. In addition, discussions with women revealed that using the same blade for FGM/C spreads different diseases, as well as having other harmful effects. The participants requested additional training for mothers' groups to ensure a behavioural change away from FGM/C and expressed their wish to gather women from all *kebeles* for a conference to discuss this issue further (ibid.).

In practical terms, community champions recorded a gradual shift from type 3 and type 4 FGM/C to type 1 (as some communities view type 1 as the mildest

Figure 7.3 A community conversation with women, an imam, and volunteers

form of FGM/C) or to the complete abandonment of the practice by FGM/C practitioners. Further work is required to help communities stop this practice completely, including economic solutions to create an alternative source of income for the practitioners who used to make a living from FGM/C.

Dowry

A violation of one's dowry can be classified as economic violence against women. The discussions on women's rights to inheritance and property encouraged some women to claim promised but not received dowry (*mahr*) from their spouses. One woman revealed:

> Previously before the intervention if a marriage gift [*mahr*] is given to a woman during her marriage lifetime we used to perceive it as a divorce (or sign of it). After the intervention we have learned that marriage gift [*mahr*] and divorce are not related; and we start to request or accept our *mahr* at any time. (Female group representative, Sero *kebele*, quoted in IRE, 2016c)

The discussion on the misunderstood role of dowry and the intervention of a religious leader to help dismantle the misconceptions helped several women claim their belated dowry. Others expressed their eagerness to demand their dowry as religiously prescribed. For example, a woman from the Tagthager *kebele* claimed a camel after 16 years of marriage.

Marriage by inheritance

A considerable proportion of women believed that religion supports 'marriage by inheritance' and that this is a religious obligation on a widow. Such beliefs were culturally supported in this context. For example, one woman explained:

> If in case a woman marries someone else she will lose everything: her children and the property. In addition, the new husband will be punished, traditionally called '*gogol laab*', and pay a compensation of 10 camels or an equivalent price to the deceased family. (Female respondent, quoted in IRE, 2016d)

Further sensitization is required to dismantle such beliefs.
Religious leaders also helped in dispelling 'marriage by inheritance', an example of socio-cultural violence practised against widowed women who are forced to marry their deceased husband's brother. In the Bondaqaran *kebele*, a woman said: '[I] believe marriage by inheritance is obligation by religion, and therefore [women] have no choice but to accept it.' Others supported the idea of obligation: 'If we refuse the inheritance marriage we will lose our children, the property and a chance to marry [anyone] again' (IRE, 2016d).

Education of women and girls

Girl's and women's education was also discussed during regular community conversations as violating one's right to education and training can constitute socio-cultural and economic violence. There were proponents and opponents of girls' education for various reasons. One argument against it was the fear that girls would become corrupted and ill-mannered if they went to school, for instance in the Bundakaran *kebele*. In community conversations, they learned about the importance of educating girls and about the Islamic obligation to seek knowledge. As a result, 78 additional girls from different households were enrolled in school.

A shift in attitudes and perceptions had immediate results on the attendance of girls in education in other *kebeles* as well. For example, a teaching assistant helped 35 girls to return to school by visiting households and talking to parents about the importance of their girls' education. Gender school clubs, which provide extracurricular activities, helped two girls to return to school by convincing their parents to allow girls to study. Even women themselves started demanding adult literacy programmes from the local authority.

Reflections on the case study

The pilot faith-based SGBV intervention by IRE started to challenge Muslim faith communities' personal and collective misconceptions about SGBV, particularly about violence against women and girls. IRE's project reports state that the communities initially believed that some types of SGBV are permitted by their religion, but after engaging with faith perspectives in community conversations together with religious leaders they realized that violence has no grounds in religion. Such a realization helped them change their mindset and commit to move away from harmful practices, promising a potential transformation in social norms in the long term.

The IRE case study shows that faith communities follow varied religious interpretations and that navigating through them can help communities build on their own capacity to understand that SGBV has no place in religion. The process of self-realization and changing mindsets is best supported by revealing evidence of the harmful effects of violent practices on individuals and communities. The rational and spiritual aspects of understanding the harm of SGBV can drive change in communities and turn them away from harmful traditional practices, as in the case of FGM/C practitioners in Dekasuftu. The project developed a context-specific approach and methods to combat SGBV that build on the community's assets and its spiritual and social capital.

Religious leaders involved in this project were vital in condemning SGBV by providing sound religious evidence that SGBV practices are sinful and by promoting a holistic and comprehensive explanation that there is no justification for violence against women and girls in Islam. Faith leaders were found to be particularly aware of potentially sensitive issues in their communities and helped find the most acceptable ways to address abuse in the community. Trained faith leaders played a pivotal role in challenging a community's discriminatory attitudes towards women and girls. They worked in tandem with community volunteers to clarify people's misconceptions about religious teachings and violence against women by correcting their understanding of scriptural sources and they promoted non-violence from the legal and Muslim faith perspective in gender relations. Selected community volunteers became champions against SGBV as they drove transformation in social norms and social acceptance of abuse. Such champions need to be recognized in their communities and their capacities should be harnessed so that they can be empowered to achieve their mission in the long term. The case study shows the role that faith leaders can play in the prevention of SGBV by working with sacred texts and using them as a powerful tool to challenge oppressive structures and harmful practices.

The evidence from this novel intervention provided the basis for further organizational SGBV-orientated initiatives in the Islamic Relief federation, such as the 'Honour Her' campaign from 2018. The project also inspired and informed another SGBV project in another location of Ethiopia. Finally, this pilot provided the impetus for Islamic Relief Worldwide to collaborate on other SGBV programmes, such as a Muslim version of Channels of Hope for Gender in partnership with World Vision in 2017 (Le Roux and Bartelink, 2017), and to develop an Islamic Declaration of Gender Justice, an advocacy initiative aiming to mobilize other actors in pursuit of gender equality in Muslim communities.

Conclusions

This chapter has discussed SGBV – in particular, domestic violence, early and forced marriage, and FGM/C – from a Muslim faith perspective and has provided a case study demonstrating that faith-based intervention can effectively challenge societal norms and the acceptance of violence against women and girls. A review of faith perspectives on SGBV provides useful resources to debunk SGBV practices in faith communities and to restore the human dignity of survivors. Learning from initiatives such as IRE's SGBV pilot project can help us find innovative and tailored interventions to prevent violence and discrimination in faith communities. The considerations in this chapter can help humanitarian and development agencies better understand, engage with, and adapt faith-inspired solutions to prevent and respond to SGBV more effectively and sensitively, particularly in faith communities.

Globally, more than eight in ten people identify with a religious group (Pew, 2012). Therefore it is imperative for governments, donors, academics, and humanitarian and development agencies to critically engage with religious beliefs and practices, and to recognize their impact not only as problems but as solutions to cultural misconceptions and patriarchal interpretations. The perception that religion encourages oppression and cannot be employed to combat SGBV should be challenged in order to utilize the inherent resources of communities and individuals in ways that resonate with their spiritual, emotional, and social worlds. Discriminatory attitudes towards faith communities by practitioners and organizations can be harmful for humanitarian and development practices and policy.

An effective SGBV intervention requires recognition of, and a response to, the contextual drivers of SGBV – the risks as well as the protective factors in communities. Responses should build on the existing resources and capacities of affected communities and individuals, while addressing risks determined by their social location. For instance, effective intervention also requires the social and spiritual capital of faith communities to be recognized and integrated in programme design. Otherwise, non-faith-inclusive SGBV interventions that have been found useful elsewhere may bring more harm than benefit in faith-specific contexts.

Although I referred here to just one practical example of a faith-based intervention, numerous other faith-inspired initiatives and frameworks seek to address SGBV in faith communities and to clarify religious misconceptions.[14] The most traditional strategy is to recall the prophetic example of justice and non-violence and to tackle cultural norms by disconnecting them from religion (Bartelink et al., 2017). Other meaningful efforts relate to legal change. Islamic feminists, Muslim women, and progressive Islamic scholars are challenging the patriarchal cultural patterns and traditionalist interpretations that produce and legitimize violence against women through independent analysis of religious sources (*ijtihad*) and interpretation of the *Qur'an* (*tafsir*) (Minganti, 2015: 96). These alternative voices have the potential to challenge SGBV in faith communities although they require recognition and support from other humanitarian and development actors.

Social change and ending SGBV in faith communities can be possible with further effort, resources, and coordination and with greater scale-up. So far, capacity building of faith communities and sensitization based on faith values have received considerable attention and have inspired further action in local communities such as local campaigning during 16 days of activism against violence against women and girls that takes place every year between 25 November and 10 December. This is part of an international campaign by the UN and is promoted by many organizations, including since 2015, Islamic Relief. Similarly, faith-inspired approaches have been deployed in other faith settings, for example by Christian organizations, such as in Tearfund's 'Transforming Masculinity' methodology (La Trobe et al., 2017) and CAFOD's toolkit for Catholic communities on gender equality (CAFOD, 2018). A faith movement called Side by Side has emerged, bringing together predominantly Christian FBOs to take on a collaborative approach to addressing SGBV while unlocking Christian faith values to end injustice and restore dignity across communities. Such efforts and others, have strong inter-faith links as well as a will to synergize faith values in SGBV prevention and response.

Conversely, the challenges of a faith approach to SGBV should not be underestimated. The complexities related to working with faith-based actors require an evaluation of adequate strategies. These strategies should build on strengths, mitigate risks, 'do no harm', and maximize opportunities that arise from well-planned and informed engagement with faith-based actors and religion. More needs to be done, not only to mainstream faith sensitivity in SGBV interventions but also to strategically develop faith-inclusive interventions to assist the survivors of violence and respond to their holistic needs. More research is needed to create robust evidence of the effectiveness of faith-inspired and faith-inclusive SGBV interventions in the long term.

Notes

1. See <http://www.unwomen.org/en/digital-library/multimedia/2015/11/infographicviolence-against-women> [accessed 10 May 2018].
2. Faith actors in this chapter include faith-based organizations (FBOs), faith leaders, religious institutions, and local faith communities. Religious actors and faith actors are used interchangeably.
3. For example, the inability to fulfil a man's breadwinning gender role in displacement situations often manifests in frustration, anger, and increased male violence against women (Harvey et al., 2013).
4. All English Qur'anic citations are from Haleem (2005).
5. *Sunnah* is known as the tradition of the Prophet Muhammad (PBUH), a record of his sayings and behaviours.
6. Narrated by Muslim, classed as *saheeh*; *Hadith* 34 in *40 Hadith Nawawi*.
7. Amal, aged 35, Syria, quoted in Ghafournia (2017: 155).

8. Zeinab, 26, Iraq, quoted in ibid.
9. Narrations of the sayings of the Prophet Muhammad (PBUH).
10. 'Abu Huraira (Allah be pleased with him) reported Allah's Messenger (may peace be upon him) as having said: "A woman without a husband (or divorced or a widow) must not be married until she is consulted, and a virgin must not be married until her permission is sought." They asked the Prophet of Allah (may peace be upon him): "How her (virgin's) consent can be solicited?" He (the Holy Prophet) said: "That she keeps silence"' (Muslim, Book 16, *Hadith* 75). Classed as *saheeh* by Muslim.
11. The author would like to thank IRE and Islamic Relief Worldwide for access to project reports and photographs.
12. A *kebele* is the smallest administrative unit of Ethiopia, similar to a ward or a neighbourhood.
13. A *woreda* is an administrative district in Ethiopia.
14. For instance, Safe Havens Interfaith Partnership Against Domestic Violence (<https://www.interfaithpartners.org>) uses a wealth of resources to support religious leaders in responding to violence by making a mosque a safe place with referral pathways for survivors and to educate children and communities. Also, Heart Women and Girls in the US (<https://www.heartwomenandgirls.org>) provides toolboxes, guidelines, and educational resources on sexual assault in the Muslim community to increase community awareness about the issue and facilitate access to support for survivors.

References

Abdulcadir, J., Catania, L., Hindin, M.J., et al. (2016) 'Female genital mutilation: a visual reference and learning tool for health care professionals', *Obstetrics and Gynecology* 128 (5): 958–63 <https://doi.org/10.1097/AOG.0000000000001686>.

Alkahteeb, S. (n.d.) 'Muslim wheel of domestic violence', Project Sakinah <http://projectsakinah.org/Family-Violence/Understanding-Abuse/The-Muslim-Wheel-of-Domestic-Violence>.

Ammar, N.H. (2007) 'Wife battery in Islam: a comprehensive understanding of interpretations', *Violence Against Women* 13 (5): 516–26 <https://doi.org/10.1177/1077801207300658>.

Ashraf, V.A.M. (2005) *Islam and Gender Justice*, Kalpaz Publications, Delhi.

Asmani, I.L. and Abdi, M.S. (2008) *Delinking Female Genital Mutilation/Cutting from Islam*, Population Council, Washington DC <https://www.unfpa.org/sites/default/files/pub-pdf/De-linking%20FGM%20from%20Islam%20final%20report.pdf> [accessed 20 September 2018].

Bartelink, B., Le Roux, E. and Palm, S. (2017) 'Sleeping giants: mobilising faith leaders as agents of change', Policy Brief, Joint Learning Initiative on Faith and Local Communities, Washington DC <https://jliflc.com/resources/sleeping-giants-mobilising-faith-leaders-agents-change/> [accessed 18 May 2018].

CAFOD (2018) *Believe in Change: A Toolkit for the Catholic Community to Promote Gender Equality*, Catholic Agency for Overseas Development (CAFOD), London.

Carlson, S. (2005) 'Contesting and reinforcing patriarchy: an analysis of domestic violence in the Dzaleka refugee camp', RSC Working Paper 23, University of Oxford, Oxford <https://www.rsc.ox.ac.uk/files/files-1/wp23-contesting-reinforcing-patriarchy-2005.pdf> [accessed 10 May 2018].

Crisp, B.R. (2012) 'The spiritual implications of sexual abuse: not an issue only for religious women', *Feminist Theology* 20 (2): 133–45.

Ghafournia, N. (2017) 'Muslim women and domestic violence: developing a framework for social work practice', *Journal of Religion and Spirituality in Social Work: Social Thought* 36 (1–2): 146–63 <https://doi.org/10.1080/1542 6432.2017.1313150>.

Haleem, A. (2005) *The Quran*, Oxford World Classics, Oxford University Press, New York.

Harvey, C., Garwood, R. and El-Masri, R. (2013) *Shifting Sands: Changing Gender Roles among Refugees in Lebanon*, Oxfam International, Oxford <https://policy-practice.oxfam.org.uk/publications/shifting-sands-changing-gender-roles-among-refugees-in-lebanon-300408> [accessed 18 May 2018].

Hasan, A. (2013) *The End to Hitting Women: The Qur'ānic Concept of Darb ('Hitting'). Islamic Perspective of Spousal Reprimand, Domestic Violence and Intimate Partner Violence (IPV)*, Imāms Against Domestic Abuse (IADA) and Islamic Sharī'ah Council (ISCR), London <https://muslimmatters.org/wp-content/uploads/The-End-to-Hitting-Wome-2-2.pdf> [accessed 1 October 2018].

IICPSR and UNFPA (2016) *Islamic Perspectives on Gender-Based Violence*, International Islamic Center for Population Studies and Research at Al-Azhar University (IICPSR) and United Nations Population Fund (UNFPA), Cairo <https://egypt.unfpa.org/en/publications/islamic-perspectives-gender-based-violence> [accessed 12 September 2018].

IRE (2016a) *Community Conversation Guidelines for Awareness Creation of Gender-based Violence in Dheka-suftu Woreda: Working Manual*, Islamic Relief Ethiopia (IRE), Addis Ababa.

IRE (2016b) *Combating Gender-based Violence of Women and Girls in Dekasuftu Woreda Somali Regional State of Ethiopia: Monthly Project Report September 2016*, Islamic Relief Ethiopia (IRE), Addis Ababa.

IRE (2016c) *Combating Gender-based Violence of Women and Girls in Dekasuftu Woreda Somali Regional State of Ethiopia: Monthly Project Report October 2016*, Islamic Relief Ethiopia (IRE), Addis Ababa.

IRE (2016d) *Combating Gender-based Violence of Women and Girls in Dekasuftu Woreda Somali Regional State of Ethiopia: Monthly Project Report November 2016*, Islamic Relief Ethiopia (IRE), Addis Ababa.

IRE (2016e) *Combating Gender-based Violence of Women and Girls in Dekasuftu Woreda Somali Regional State of Ethiopia: Monthly Project Report December 2016*, Islamic Relief Ethiopia (IRE), Addis Ababa.

IRE (2017) *Combating Gender-based Violence of Women and Girls in Dekasuftu Woreda Somali Regional State of Ethiopia: Final Project Report*, Islamic Relief Ethiopia (IRE), Addis Ababa.

Islamic Relief Worldwide (2016) 'One cut too many: policy briefing on female genital mutilation and cutting', Islamic Relief Worldwide, Birmingham <https://www.islamic-relief.org/wp-content/uploads/2018/03/FGM-CSW62.pdf> [accessed 20 September 2018].

Islamic Relief Worldwide (2018) *An Islamic Human Rights Perspective on Early and Forced Marriage*, Islamic Relief Worldwide, Birmingham <https://www.islamic-relief.org/wp-content/uploads/2018/03/EFM-HUMAN-RIGHTS-CSW62.pdf> [accessed 20 September 2018].

La Trobe, S., Gardner, L. and Deepan, P. (2017) *Exploring the Linkages of Gender, Masculinities and Faith a Qualitative Research Report on Sexual and Gender-based Violence in Liberia*, Tearfund UK, Teddington <https://learn.tearfund.org/~/media/files/tilz/sgbv/2017-tearfund-_exploring-the-linkages-of-gender-masculinities-and-faith-en.pdf?la=en> [accessed 14 February 2019].

Le Roux, E. and Bartelink, B.E. (2017) *Case Study with Islamic Relief Worldwide as Part of the UK Government-funded 'Working Effectively with Faith Leaders to Challenge Harmful Traditional Practices'*, Research Report, Joint Learning Initiative on Faith and Local Communities <https://jliflc.com/wp/wp-content/uploads/2017/11/CS3_-Islamic-Relief-1.pdf>.

McKerl, A. (2009) 'Gender, multiculturalism, and violence: developing intersectional methodologies from a Muslim understanding, PhD thesis, University of Aberdeen.

Minganti, P.K. (2015) 'Muslim women managing women's shelters: Somaya, the Muslimwoman and religion as resource', *NORA: Nordic Journal of Feminist and Gender Research* 23 (2): 93–108 <https://doi.org/10.1080/0803 8740.2014.935744>.

Pertek, S.I. (2015) *Gender Justice Policy*, Islamic Relief Worldwide, Birmingham <http://www.islamic-relief.org/wp-content/uploads/2016/05/Gender-policy.pdf> [accessed 15 May 2018].

Pertek, S.I. and Abdulaziz, S. (2018) 'Don't force me: a policy brief on early and forced marriage', Islamic Relief Worldwide, Birmingham <http://www.islamic-relief.org/wp-content/uploads/2018/03/FORCED-MARRIAGE-CSW62.pdf> [accessed 16 April 2018].

Pew (2012) 'The global religious landscape', Pew Research Center <http://www.pewforum.org/2012/12/18/global-religious-landscape-exec/> [accessed 12 May 2018].

Surti, A. and Pertek, S.I. (2018) *Lessons Learnt from Somali Regional State of Ethiopia: Combating Gender-based Violence against Women and Girls in Dekasuftu Woreda. Faith Inspired Action to End SGBV*, Islamic Relief Worldwide, Birmingham <http://www.islamic-relief.org/wp-content/uploads/2018/03/GBV-ETHIOPIA-CSW62.pdf> [accessed 7 June 2018].

UNHCR (2011) *Action against Sexual and Gender-Based Violence: An Updated Strategy*, United Nations High Commissioner for Refugees (UNHCR), Geneva <https://cms.emergency.unhcr.org/documents/11982/51689/UNHCR %2C+Action+Against+ Sexual+and+Gender-based+Violence.+An+Updated+ Strategy%2C+2011/4f9d2a1c-280e-4ac8-a832-1a789de63d46> [accessed 7 June 2018].

UNICEF (2013) *Female Genital Mutilation/Cutting: A Statistical Overview and Exploration of the Dynamics of Change*, United Nations Children's Fund (UNICEF), New York <https://www.unicef.org/cbsc/files/UNICEF_FGM_report _July_2013_Hi_res.pdf> [accessed 1 October 2018].

WHO (2013) *Global and Regional Estimates of Violence against Women: Prevalence and Health Effects of Intimate Partner Violence and Non-partner Sexual Violence*, World Health Organization (WHO), Geneva.

WHO (2018) 'Female genital mutilation', World Health Organization (WHO), Geneva<http://www.who.int/news-room/fact-sheets/detail/female-genital-mutilation> [accessed 20 September 2018].

About the author

Sandra Iman Pertek is a doctoral researcher at the University of Birmingham and a director of EQUISTY. As a gender and gender-based violence specialist, she worked as a consultant for several international organizations in Africa, the Middle East, and the UK. Previously, she served as Senior Policy Adviser on Gender and Gender Technical Lead at Islamic Relief Worldwide, spearheading gender mainstreaming strategy in policy and programmes. She is a member of several networks relating to gender, religion, and development. She holds an MSc in Social Development Practice from University College London and a BA in European Studies from the University of Warsaw.

CHAPTER 8

Child protection and safeguarding in an Islamic context: understanding the critical role faith plays in supporting protective mechanisms in humanitarian action

Neelam Fida

Now more than ever there is a need to have a multifaceted approach to child protection with faith leaders and communities playing a key role in informing safeguarding and protective systems and mechanisms. A number of tools exist within the humanitarian sector that protect children from all forms of abuse, violence, and exploitation but they do not engage all communities in the same way. This chapter demonstrates how Islamic principles and humanitarian standards complement each other and speak against harmful practices. It also illustrates how innovative approaches have developed the capacity of faith leaders and the impact this has had on local hard-to-reach communities in sensitive contexts.

Keywords: child protection, *Maqasid al-Shari'ah*, child rights, early and forced marriage, child abuse, harmful practices, equality, Islam, Muslim, safeguarding, humanitarian action

Introduction

In many countries, particularly in the global South, religion plays a critical role in supporting the moral, spiritual, and practical development of families' and caregivers' ability to protect and safeguard children from all forms of violence, abuse, and exploitation. There are also situations in which faith communities are complicit in perpetrating violence against children. Globally, it is estimated that up to 1 billion children aged between 2 and 17 have experienced physical, sexual, or emotional violence or neglect in the past year (Hillis et al., 2016). It is further estimated that 250 million (6 in 10) children are punished by physical means, and that every seven minutes, somewhere in the world, an adolescent is killed by an act of violence. In 2015 alone violence took the lives of around 82,000 adolescents worldwide (UNICEF, 2017). There are more than 50 million displaced children in need of protection, of whom 28 million have been displaced due to war and extreme poverty.

http://dx.doi.org/10.3362/9781788530613.008

The number of children suffering as a result of the crisis in Syria and Iraq alone has reached 14 million (UNICEF USA, 2019).

These figures are staggering and demonstrate the plight of the most disadvantaged and vulnerable in society, a situation that is further exacerbated in times of humanitarian crisis. In addition, limited access to resources, to capacity and to capabilities of faith leaders, and communities as first responders becomes a compounding factor. However there are multi-institutional structures and systems in place that aim to protect the well-being and safety of children and their families. In accordance with Islamic law and jurisprudence there is a legal system that governs the safety and protection of human life known as *Maqasid al-Shari'ah*, or the goals and objectives of Islamic law. An understanding of this is critical to appreciating the role and position Islam takes in relation to child protection and safeguarding. The term '*maqasid*' refers to a purpose, goal, objective, or principle (Ashur, 2006: ii), and the *Maqasid* of Islamic law provides the principles behind Islamic rulings (von Jhering, 2001). Al Qarafi (d. 1285 AH or 1868 CE) linked *Maslahah* and *Maqasid* via a 'fundamental rule': 'A purpose [*Maqasid*] is not valid unless it leads to the fulfilment of good [*Maslahah*] or the avoidance of some mischief [*Mafsadah*]' (Auda, 2008). Therefore, a *Maqasid* is there for the 'interest of humanity'. *Shari'ah* in all its parts aims to secure benefits and assist in the protection and safeguarding of people against harm, corruption, and evil.

Muslim jurists have further classified *Maqasid* into three categories: 1) the essentials or necessities (*daruriyyat*); 2) the needs (*hajiyyat*); and 3) the contemporary or luxuries (*tahsiniyat*).[1] There are five necessities – faith, life, progeny, intellect, and property (al-Ghazali, 2018) – that are considered instrumental in the development and well-being of human life. If measures are not in place to protect these necessities and the environment, human life is at risk of harm, which is why the Prophet Muhammad (Peace Be Upon Him) forbade harm being caused in any shape or form against all living beings. The *Qur'an* (2: 60) is clear: 'And do not commit abuse on the Earth, spreading corruption.' Among the protection of all things, high status is given to the preservation of 'offspring'. Islamic rulings regulate the promotion and excellence of education and kindness towards children (Auda, 2008). Islam also acknowledges the vulnerability of children, which is why there is a strong emphasis on the family structure and the responsibility of parents and caregivers to nurture and protect children. The *Qur'an* describes children as 'the coolness of our eyes' (*Qur'an*, 25: 74), and children are also considered a gift from Allah. Parents and families are therefore expected to provide children with love, care, and safety, with responsibility entrusted to them until the Day of Judgement.

Islamic teachings underline the role of family for children's care and protection as the first and most basic social unit a child is exposed too. This makes it critical for mothers as the primary caregivers to understand the risks attached to harmful behaviour, attitudes, and practices. The Prophet Muhammad (PBUH) said: 'Each of you is a shepherd and each of you is responsible for his flock' (Abu Dawud, Book 20, *Hadith* 1). The Prophet also said: 'Indeed Allah will question everyone who is responsible about his charge' (Tirmidhi, Book 23, *Hadith* 37). Due to the importance of the parent–child relationship there is a clear description of the rights and obligations that apply to both parents and children. This means that a parent or caregiver has an obligation (or duty) towards a child by providing a protective, empowering, and caring environment in which they can grow, learn, and develop.

Child protection framework

Shari'ah explains how one of the fundamental objectives of *Maqasid*, especially regarding children, is fostering a safe, compassionate, and nurturing environment through the preservation of institutional and community mechanisms, with legislation enforcing safeguards. That said, many countries and communities exposed to humanitarian crises do not have safe access to such mechanisms but are instead supported by international and humanitarian standards that are implemented in times of emergency. The United Nations Convention on the Rights of the Child (UNCRC) is a legally binding international agreement setting out 54 articles that cover the civil, political, economic, social, and cultural rights of every child, regardless of their race, religion, or ability.[3] All UN member states except for the United States of America have ratified the Convention. These articles explain how governments, international non-governmental organizations (INGOs), communities, and adults can work together to make sure that all children can enjoy all their rights.

A similar commitment to uphold child protection principles was formally accepted by the Organisation of Islamic Cooperation (OIC) through the adoption in 2005 of the Covenant on the Rights of the Child in Islam (CRCI).[4] This follows several major Islamic human rights events that paved the way: the Dhaka Declaration of Human Rights in Islam in 1983, the Cairo Declaration on Human Rights in Islam in 1990, and the Declaration on the Rights and Care of Children in Islam in 1994. The CRCI is considered an inclusive framework for the protection and safeguarding of children's rights, mainly, but not exclusively, by Muslim countries. The UNCRC defines a child as being under the age of 18 unless domestic laws set a lower age for adulthood, but according to Islamic principles, a child is any human being who, according to the law applicable to him or her, has not attained puberty or maturity (CRCI). With no specific age assigned to describe who is a child the covenant is left open to interpretation, which varies depending on context, cultural practices, and understanding. When a female child embraces puberty early she is at potential risk of child marriage. This ambiguity around age is why faith leaders – and, in particular, female faith leaders – need to be empowered with the capacity and tools to refer back to scripture and the *Maqasid al-Shari'ah* in order to dispel some of the misunderstanding and practices that expose children to risk. The *Qur'an* also puts practical measures in place to ensure the care and protection of people and children with disabilities:

> And test the orphans [in their abilities] until they reach marriageable age. Then if you perceive in them sound judgement, release their property to them. And do not consume it excessively and quickly, [anticipating] that they will grow up. And whoever [when acting as guardian] is self-sufficient should refrain [from taking a fee]; and whoever is poor – let him take according to what is acceptable. Then when you release their property to them, bring witnesses upon them. And sufficient is Allah as accountant. (*Qur'an*, 4: 6)

Not only does Allah emphasize the protection of rights, but if someone is unable to manage their affairs and lacks mental or physical capacity, they should be supported and not taken advantage of or manipulated for personal gain.

In times of crisis or emergencies, the rights of children – particularly those with disabilities – are at risk of violation. Child protection in emergencies (CPiE) refers to all efforts to prevent and to respond to all forms of abuse and violence against children in the aftermath of a disaster. CPiE prioritizes the fulfilment of certain rights for children in emergencies: namely, those rights that protect children against mistreatment and ensure their survival and well-being (UNICEF, 2015). However, there has been growing concern about and scepticism towards the UNCRC principles in the Islamic context (UNICEF, 2012; Ali et al., 2005). INGOs have reported difficulties in implementing child protection programming due to their limited awareness and understanding of Islamic systems of governance and their influence, localized customs, and Islamic jurisprudence (O'Leary and Squire, 2012; Squire and Hope, 2013; Miles, 1996; UNICEF, 2012). This is exacerbated when INGOs are non-Islamic or 'Western-based' institutions that are less likely to be embedded within the local community's culture and are suspected of delivering aid with a covert political, social, religious, and/or economic agenda (Holtzhausen, 2011; O'Leary and Squire, 2012; Rajabi-Ardeshiri, 2009).

Muslims account for approximately 24 per cent of the world's population (Lipka, 2017), making it the second largest religion in the world. Spread over five continents and diverse in culture and practice, Islam comes with its own complexities on issues of child protection. For example, in some parts of the world, female genital mutilation or cutting (FGM/C) is justified by a minority of faith leaders, whereas the majority reject it outright and consider it a pre-Islamic tribal practice. There is an understanding that religious interpretation and application vary from context to context, which may play a destructive role in the lives of children. However it is important to understand in such situations that culture and tradition exert a stronger influence than religious understanding. This thinking is much more prevalent in contexts where tribal and informal settings are established and knowledge of scripture is limited, which allows harmful behaviour – particularly towards women and girls – to exist. There is a need for more evidence-based research on faith engagement to guide and support governments and INGOs to work collaboratively and holistically with communities, understanding the different paradigms influencing behaviour and attitudes while having a deeper awareness of their needs. The following section explores the importance of understanding the role Islam plays in safeguarding and protecting children within humanitarian action. How does Islamic guidance support and strengthen existing protective mechanisms? And what can be done to encourage humanitarian actors and faith communities to promote a peaceful and inclusive society for children?

Contrasting humanitarian instruments with Islamic principles

The Islamic concept of human rights is based on the principle of a just God or Allah providing a foundation to achieve the overall goal of justice. Human rights in Islam are an integral part of the overall Islamic order and an obligation upon all. The *Maqasid al-Shari'ah* declares that all people are equal in terms of human values, and all individuals are equal regardless of their race, ethnicity, or ability. Similarly the UNCRC, which was adopted in 1989 and entered into force in 1990, binds all members – including the 49 Muslim-majority states – to a commitment to children.[5]

The UNCRC and CRCI emphasize a non-discriminatory approach towards children. Under Article 12 of the convention, the opinions of children should be taken into consideration when making decisions that affect them, as their opinions are often overlooked. A body of independent experts monitors implementation of the UNCRC by member states. The CRCI has some important provisions, such as the rights to identity, education, healthcare, and an adequate standard of living, and in some cases its provisions go beyond international standards (for example, the right to free and compulsory secondary education, the right to personal freedom under principles of *Shari'ah*, and the right to parental guidance). States are required to provide provisions to ensure the survival and development of a child and for his or her protection from violence, abuse, and sexual exploitation. It is incumbent on states to support parents, guardians, and carers in creating a protective and loving environment for children that fulfils their rights.

Convergence and divergence on rights

Looking at the UNCRC and CRCI articles there are areas where overlap is evident but also some clear differences when approaching child protection in Muslim communities. The UNCRC articles are child-centred, focusing on strengthening the family by promoting and supporting the rights of children. In contrast, the CRCI is family-centred, mainly concentrating on protection and delegating responsibility to the state and parents to ensure that safeguards are in place that go beyond the legal instruments safeguarding children, encouraging the development of a good character on the basis of Islamic teachings.

As already highlighted, the protection of life, progeny, and intellect are three of the fundamental objectives of *Maqasid al-Shari'ah* that are necessary to create a nurturing environment, good health, and the right to better life choices facilitated through education. There is further guidance on the care of pregnant women, encouraging them to rest and focus on their well-being and that of the foetus. It is important to state that a pregnant woman is protected against religious obligations that may put her or her foetus at risk, such as fasting during the month of Ramadan. The Prophet Muhammad (PBUH) 'granted a concession to pregnant women who fear for themselves, allowing them not to fast, and to nursing mothers who fear for their infants' (Sunan Ibn Majah, Book 7, *Hadith* 1737). The role of a mother in the very early stages of a child's development is critical. There is an Urdu saying – 'The mother is the first school of a child' – that illustrates that the mother not only is a source of nourishment for the child but also creates a nurturing and loving environment to enable the child to develop their basic skills and abilities in their early years. Yet many women and girls are restricted from accessing their basic rights.

The Prophet Muhammad (PBUH) said: 'It is sufficient sin for a man that he neglects him whom he maintains' (Abu Dawud, Book 9, *Hadith* 137). This saying of the Prophet (PBUH) emphasizes that any person who neglects those in their care is held to account. There are some who are unable to provide sufficiently due to social, economic, or political reasons but who do what they can within their limited means; this is not considered intentional abuse. This is why there is an obligation on national and local governments and society as a whole to respond to the needs of families through rigorous assessments and reviews of existing systems, both formal and informal.

Children's right to education

Among the principles outlined in the UNCRC and CRCI, providing children with safe and free access to education is an important one. This is embodied in the UNCRC's Article 2 on non-discrimination'; Article 3 on the best interests of the child; Article 6 on the right to life, survival, and development; and Article 12 on the right to express views and have them taken into account (respect for the views of the child). The UN estimates that 1 billion children live in conflict-affected areas, of whom 250 million are under the age of five. One of the challenges in emergencies is children's education: 303 million 5–17-year-olds are out of school worldwide, with 58 million primary school aged children and 20 million secondary school aged children currently out of school due to conflict (UNICEF, 2018).

Education is an important driver of social development and a contributor to transformational changes in behaviour and attitudes, helping lift econom-ically and socially marginalized families out of poverty. One of the core principles of *Shari'ah* is the protection of intellect. The *Qur'an* and *Sunnah* emphasize the importance of education as a right of every child – a right to be honoured by parents, community, society, and the state, all of which play a crucial role, as demonstrated in the Social Ecological Model (UNICEF, 2009).[6] In fact, the first revelation to the Prophet Muhammad (PBUH) was: 'Read in the name of thy Lord who created; [He] created the human being from a blood clot. Read in the name of thy Lord who taught by the pen: [He] taught the human being what he did not know' (*Qur'an*, 96: 1–5). In other verses, the *Qur'an* says: 'Ask them: are those equal to those who do not know?' (*Qur'an*, 39: 9); and 'Allah will raise to high ranks those of you who believe and are endowed with knowledge' (*Qur'an*, 58: 11). Barumand further argues that 'some of the most important teaching and instruction methods that are confirmed by the *Qur'an* and Islamic traditions are lecture, question and answer, discussion, drama, role playing, imitation, discovery, story-telling, and self-instruction' (Alavi, 2008).

The Arabic word *ilm* (knowledge) encompasses all necessary worldly knowledge in all areas, while learning, recreation, and leisure are all considered important elements of education. It is reported that the Prophet Muhammad (PBUH) asked a group of his companions to learn foreign languages (Abu 'Abdullah Muhammad, 1968: 358). The *Qur'an* says: 'There are many signs on Earth for those of sure faith, and also in your own selves. Do you not see?' (*Qur'an*, 51: 20–1). In addition, the Prophet (PBUH) is reported to have said, 'Teach your children swimming, archery and horse-riding' (Ala'ddin, 1981: 443), stressing the importance of creating a loving and nurturing environment. However, currently, one in four of the world's out-of-school children live in crisis-affected countries, with girls two and half times more likely to be out of school than boys (UNICEF, 2019). Intersectional factors such as disability, ethnicity, insecurity, and school-related gender-based violence, combined with harmful stereotypes about their value mean that girls face the most risk of exclusion.

Children's right to equal treatment

With conflict and crisis comes the abuse of the right to equity for children. In principle, there is commonality between the UNCRC and CRCI, but in practice there are discrepancies that are further strained in times of difficulty. Differing gender preferences are prevalent in contexts where poverty is a contributing factor and such preferences are deeply embedded practice in some cultures (Fikree and Pasha, 2004); not only does this deprive people of their dignity but it traps them in a cycle of poverty. Although Muslims may feel that many of the social and emotional differences between genders relate to our natural predisposition as humans (*Fitrah*), we can see that these roles are not all universal. Within the Muslim world, gender relations and roles differ significantly and of course within the wider community even more variance can be observed. Islam lays down basic rights and obligations within the family dynamic and community, but within this broad framework considerable diversity in culture and gender roles is considered legitimate. In some communities the rights of women, girls, and other groups are not always respected, which leads to even greater cultural and gender disparities. In some traditional Muslim communities the male child is considered to be the one who continues the name of the family and is expected to support and provide for parents in their old age. Where resources are limited and girls are seen as a burden, they are forced to leave school without completing primary or secondary education since preference is given to the male child. This is compounded by some religious educational systems that further restrict access for girls.

It is important to make a distinction between cultural norms that create barriers and the teachings of Islam that support equity: 'People, be mindful of your Allah, who created you from a single soul, and from it created its mate, and from the pair of them spread countless men and women far and wide' (Qur'an, 4: 1). This verse shows the same equality and dignity for both males and females. The Maqasid framework emphatically discourages discrimination between men and women, and especially between male and female children.

The Qur'an abolished female infanticide, one of the cruellest practices in pre-Islamic Arabia. It warns parents: 'Do not kill your children in fear of poverty; we will provide for you and for them' (Qur'an, 6: 151); also, 'When the baby girl buried alive is asked, for what sin she was killed' (Qur'an, 81: 8–9). Nevertheless, there are still some communities that consider females to be a burden or a bad omen – the opposite to the way in which a male child is treated. However the Prophet Muhammad (PBUH) said: 'Whoever has three daughters, or three sisters, or two daughters, or two sisters and he keeps good company with them and fears Allah regarding them, then Paradise is for him' (Tirmidhi, Book 27, Hadith 22). He also said: 'Whoever raises two girls till they attain maturity, he and I will come on the Day of Resurrection like this' [the Messenger of Allah joined his fingers to illustrate this] (Riyad as-Salihin, Book 1, Hadith 267). These examples from the Prophet Muhammad (PBUH) contradict the reality of inequality and unjust treatment of female children and any lack of opportunity for their growth, intellectual development, or well-being. This is why it is so critical to engage faith leaders in affirming the authentic teachings of the Prophet (PBUH).

Children with disabilities face particular challenges during humanitarian crises (Thomas, 2018), while another contentious issue is the inclusion of children of all abilities. A person from Burundi stated: 'Persons with disabilities are specifically vulnerable to physical, sexual, and emotional abuse, requiring additional protection. Lack of access to latrines and bathing areas increases the risk of abuse' (Handicap International, 2015). This is just one example of the challenges faced by people with disabilities. Discrimination and stigma arise not as a result of the intrinsic nature of children's disability, but rather as a consequence of a lack of understanding and knowledge about its causes and implications, fear of difference, fear of contagion or contamination, or negative religious or cultural views of disability. This is further compounded by poverty, social isolation, humanitarian emergencies, lack of services, gender and lack of support, and a hostile and inaccessible environment. The exclusion and invisibility of disabled children serves to render them uniquely vulnerable, denying them respect for their dignity, their individuality, and even their right to life itself (UNICEF, 2013). Islamic teachings consider all children a gift from God and therefore they should all be treated and respected equally, without discrimination. The Prophet Muhammad (PBUH) said: 'Anyone who does not show mercy to our children nor acknowledge the right of our old people is not one of us' (Al-Adab Al-Mufrad, Book 18, *Hadith* 353). Allah loves those who treat children with mercy, love, and care, and informs parents and caregivers to fulfil their responsibility to provide a nurturing environment. Unfortunately, children with disabilities are excluded from society and sometimes neglected by families because of their condition. Islam prohibits the humiliation of the sick, disabled, and those with special needs. The *Qur'an* says:

> Believers, no one group of men should jeer at another, who may after all be better than them; no one group of women should jeer at another, who may after all be better than them; do not speak ill of one another; do not use offensive nicknames for one another. How bad it is to be called a mischief-maker after accepting faith! (*Qur'an*, 49: 11)

Protecting children from all forms of abuse, violence, and exploitation

The World Health Organization (WHO) defines child abuse as follows:

> Child maltreatment is the abuse and neglect that occurs to children under 18 years of age. It includes all types of physical and/or emotional ill-treatment, sexual abuse, neglect, negligence and commercial or other exploitation, which results in actual or potential harm to the child's health, survival, development or dignity in the context of a relationship of responsibility, trust or power. Exposure to intimate partner violence is also sometimes included as a form of child maltreatment. (WHO, 2016).

Perpetrators of abuse and violence are often people within the family, or known to the family and although universal frameworks including the *Maqasid al-Shari'ah* enforce safeguards, some attitudes and behaviours run contrary to such frameworks. Corporal punishment is the most common form of violence children experience, usually within the home: worldwide, 300 million (three in four) children aged two to four experience violent discipline by their caregivers on a regular basis (UNICEF, 2017). Parents or caregivers do not always intend to cause harm or injury to children; in some situations their actions stem from anger, frustration, or a lack of understanding of the impact of violence on the child. Corporal punishment of children predisposes them to aggression, delinquency, and conjugal violence later in life (Durrant and

Ensom, 2012), as well as anxiety disorders, substance abuse, externalization problems (MacMillan et al., 1999), thoughts of suicide, and a disconnection from faith. Among the most intensive and frequent sources of stress that children may suffer early in life are multiple types of abuse, neglect, violence between parents or caregivers, other kinds of serious household dysfunction (such as alcohol and substance abuse), and violence among peers and within the community. Together, these are known as adverse childhood experiences (WHO, 2018).

The Prophet Muhammad (PBUH) is reported to have said: 'The one who does not show mercy will not be shown mercy [by Allah]' (Al-Adab Al-Mufrad, Book 5, *Hadith* 95). It is reported that a Bedouin was surprised to see that the Prophet Muhammad (PBUH) kissed his grandsons, Al-Hasan and Al-Husain. 'Do you kiss your children?' He said: 'Yes.' They then said: 'By Allah, but we do not kiss our children.' Thereupon Allah's Messenger (PBUH) said: 'Then what can I do if Allah has deprived you of mercy?' (Muslim, Book 43, *Hadith* 85). The *Qur'an* states: 'Believers, there are enemies to you among your spouses and your offspring, so beware of them. But if you forgive and overlook their offences and pardon them, then surely Allah is Most Forgiving, Most Compassionate' (*Qur'an*, 64: 14). The Prophet Muhammad's (PBUH) traditions advocate against aggressive behaviour, particularly towards children. 'None of you truly believes until he loves for his brother,' or, he said, 'for his neighbour, what he loves for himself' (Sunan Ibn Majah, Book 1, *Hadith* 69).

According to Bowlby's attachment theory:

> from several core ideas of early life experiences, we can discern valuable insights into parenting practices. Sensitive and responsive care from parents is vital for the optimal growth and development of each child. Children who are rarely spoken to, who are left to cry themselves out, who have little opportunity to explore their environment, or who experience frequent anger or boredom cannot fully develop their potential and stable personalities, despite their normal genetic endowment. (Barbour, 1970)

This demonstrates the need to nurture a caring and loving space for children in which they can develop, where the primary source of bonding and development is the parent or caregiver.

Despite parents or caregivers understanding their role and responsibilities, and despite the existence of robust child protection systems, abuse does exist, causing tremendous damage to the ability of children to flourish and succeed. Physical violence, emotional or sexual abuse, and neglect can potentially foster delinquent behaviour. One of the most renowned Islamic scholars, Imam al-Ghazali, narrates that a person once complained about the disobedience of his son to 'Abdullah ibn Mubarak, who then asked him, 'Did you curse him?' The man replied that he did. Upon hearing this, Ibn Mubarak said, 'You yourself are to blame for this' (Fazl-Ul-Karim, 1993). Under the *Maqasid al-Shari'ah*, cursing is a condemnable act and no one should be cursed, especially not one's own child. The Prophet Muhammad (PBUH), on seeing a mistake, would only advise the child in the politest of ways and never used any form of abuse, either physical or verbal. Anas ibn Malik, a companion of the Prophet Muhammad (PBUH), reported: 'I served the Prophet for 10 years. He never said Uff and never blamed me by saying: "Why did you do so or why did you not do so?" And the Messenger of Allah had the best character among all of the people' (Tirmidhi, Book 27, *Hadith* 121). He further asserts that whenever he was slow to follow the Prophet's requests or did something other than what he had been ordered to do, he would never be blamed or chided. According to the teachings of the Prophet Muhammad (PBUH), parents should never curse or abuse their children. Instead, they should always make *du'a* (supplication) for them, as God responds to supplications for their children. The Prophet (PBUH) is reported as having said: 'Three supplications are surely answered: the supplication of someone who is oppressed, the supplication of someone on a journey, and the supplication of parents for their children' (Al-Adab Al-Mufrad, Book 1, *Hadith* 32).

Tackling child abuse linked to faith and culture

Traditional cultural practices reflect values, religious rituals, and beliefs held by members of a community over a number of generations. Different social groups from around the world have specific cultural practices and beliefs, some of which benefit communities and enrich them while others expose people to harm, especially women and girls. These harmful practices include, but are not limited to, FGM/C), early and forced marriage (EFM), the preference for sons, female infanticide, and dowry prices. Despite the impact of these harmful practices and the fact that they violate human rights, such practices exist because insufficient work has been done from a faith perspective and in a holistic manner with those practising such behaviour, which affects children in a profound way.

According to the WHO, FGM/C is defined as 'all procedures which involve partial or total removal of the external female genitalia or other injury to the female genital organs whether for cultural or any other non-therapeutic reasons' (WHO, 1997). Worldwide prevalence of FGM/C is estimated to be about 130 million, with an additional 2 million girls and women undergoing the procedure every year (UNICEF, 2014a). The practice is prevalent in over 26 African countries and among a few minority groups in Asia and the Middle East (Lockhat, 2004). In many communities – mainly Muslim but not exclusively so – FGM/C is attributed at least partly to religion, with some holding the view that Islam requires FGM/C as an obligation. However, FGM/C predates Islam, it is not mentioned in the *Qur'an*, and the Prophet Muhammad (PBUH) did not advocate for it. It is also a relatively unknown practice in large parts of the Muslim world (Islamic Relief Worldwide, 2017a). It should be noted that there is no debate among religious scholars on male circumcision, which is *Sunnah* – action done by the Prophet Muhammad (PBUH).

Similarly, EFM is another practice inflicted on many young girls globally (UNICEF, 2014b) and is closely linked to traditions or customary behaviours that are prevalent in many Muslim societies. Forced marriage is any marriage in which at least one spouse has not given their free consent, either with regard to the timing of the marriage or the choice of partner (UNFPA, 2012), regardless of age or ability. Research conducted by UNICEF illustrates that globally 'more than 700 million women alive today were married before their 18th birthday. More than 1 in 3 girls (about 250 million) entered into union before age 15' (UNICEF, 2014b). Child marriage is defined as the marriage of a girl or boy before the age of 18 and refers to both formal and informal unions in which children under the age of 18 live with a partner as if married (ibid.). Around the world, most countries have set 18 as the minimum age for marriage,[7] but at least 50 countries allow girls below the age of 16 to marry with parental consent.[8] Furthermore, in 54 countries, girls are permitted to marry up to three years younger than boys (Lahaie et al., 2013). Muslims are entrusted to follow the rules of the land, whether they live in Muslim or non-Muslim countries, and this includes adhering to the minimum legal age for marriage (Islamic Relief Worldwide, 2016). Marriage in Islam is written in a covenant between two individuals (*Shafqat*),[9] and as such it is recommended that it should be between two consenting adults who are able to understand the responsibilities and intricacies of such an agreement.

In some schools of thought however, silence is considered acceptance, while in other situations a male relative (*wali*) – usually the father – speaks on behalf of the bride. His role is to obtain her free consent and negotiate the conditions of marriage. If the *wali* fails in his role or is unjust this may result in EFM occurring. The *Qur'an* gives women a number of marital rights, including a clear prohibition against forced marriage as well as the right to be treated with kindness: 'O ye who believe! Ye are forbidden to inherit women against their will. Nor should ye treat them with harshness ... live with them on a footing of kindness and equity' (*Qur'an*, 4: 19). The Prophet Muhammad (PBUH) is reported to have annulled the marriage of Khansa'a bint-e-Khizaam when she complained to him that her father had forced her into a marriage without her will. One can therefore draw the inference from this reference that EFM has no legal validity in Islam. The *Qur'an* states: 'It is not lawful for you to inherit women by force. Nor may you treat them harshly so that you can make off with part of what you have given them, unless they commit an act of flagrant indecency. Live together with them correctly and courteously' (*Qur'an*, 4: 19).

Using data from various countries in Asia and Africa, several studies reveal that child marriage is associated with poor levels of health, education, labour force participation, mortality, and participation in household decision making (Jensen and Thornton, 2003; Nguyen and Wodon, 2015; UNICEF, 2014b).

Box 8.1 An integrated approach to gender-based violence and child protection

Islamic Relief Worldwide (IRW) carried out a project in Mali, Pakistan, and Niger using an integrated approach to address child protection and gender-based violence (GBV). This approach helped address issues of harmful practices, abuse, discrimination, and inequality more effectively (Almugahed et al, 2017). Using such an approach allowed for institutional expertise to be developed in order to strengthen outcomes for women and children, particularly girls. The project used existing social networks by identifying community champions, who were the 'movers and shakers' of their communities. Through analysis, key child protection and GBV concerns were identified, such as FGM/C, child marriage, domestic violence, sexual violence, exploitation, and child labour. The approach engaged male as well as female members of the community as it sought to involve agents wherever appropriate. IRW trained staff, community champions, and agents to lead community mobilization efforts and to develop advocacy messages that were relevant to the GBV and child protection concerns of their communities. As Muslim-majority countries, faith leaders were happy to use their platform to deliver sermons and community engagement sessions to help build trust, influence communities, and support behaviour and attitudinal change in this initiative. Although IRW had well-established and trusted links with communities, the voice and support of faith leaders further added credibility to the work being done.

Key to this initiative, which also sought to strengthen existing referral pathways, was survivors becoming confident and comfortable in accessing support. Local stakeholders were targeted through awareness-raising workshops and advocacy sessions. The approach also developed Community Hope Action Teams (CHATs), through which GBV and child protection champions organized community events, shared prevention messages, and discussed their response activities. Key findings of this project included the exclusion of people with disabilities, a lack of tailored approaches, faith leaders' limited technical knowledge, a lack of safe referral mechanisms for survivors, and the need to involve community and faith leaders, especially when addressing sensitive issues. Maulvi[10] Mohammed Anwar stated: 'Islamic Relief has revolutionized my way of thinking and encouraged me to play an active role as a faith leader to bring positive change in my community and support the rights of the most vulnerable members of the community – women and children.'

Building on innovative approaches to address child protection needs, IRW in partnership with World Vision – an international Christian child-focused faith-based organization – developed a Muslim adaption of Channels of Hope Child Protection (CoH CP). Channels of Hope employs a programme methodology that motivates and builds the capacity of faith communities to address violence, abuse, and exploitation of vulnerable communities and families and to advocate for their rights. It further allows communities to become better protectors and ultimately to strengthen local protection and referral systems and mechanisms. CoH CP relies on scripture-based guiding principles and scientific/technical information to build on the desires of faith leaders and community activists to guide them to be better within their own families and to look to develop informal mechanisms where none exist in order to create protective environments for women and children. This active approach responds to the most vulnerable women, children, and families. Currently, IRW is running CoH CP projects in Pakistan, Mali, and Lebanon with the aim of expanding to an additional eight countries.

There are some situations where religious teachings are tangled with culture and there are difficulties with scriptural and theological interpretations that fuel harmful attitudes and practices towards women and children, and so the initiative faced some questions from faith leaders participating in the initial phase. Faith leaders were resistant to an unknown methodology speaking against practices handed down from one generation to the next. There were concerns about the underlying drivers pushing forward the agenda and

(Continued)

Box 8.1 Continued

apprehension about how this approach would influence children and potentially turn them against their faith leaders. These concerns and others were addressed through extensive consultation with faith leaders involved in the development of faith-sensitive materials, and also by creating an enabling environment in which their concerns could truly be heard. What the project certainly did not aim to do was to challenge individuals' belief, a frequent concern raised; rather, its intention was to provide an alternative perspective and understanding through a faith-sensitive approach. As a result of CoH CP, faith leaders and community champions are now promoting faith-guided child protection principles through advocacy messages, sermons, new-found technical knowledge, and the capacity to effectively engage in the discourse. Through this initiative, harmful practices linked to religious thinking are addressed in a safe and holistic manner, providing an opportunity to understand the impact of behaviour on the well-being and psychological development of children and in line with the *Maqasid al-Shari'ah* that governs all.

Research shows that adolescent girls who fall pregnant within two years of menarche or while their pelvic and birth canals are still developing face an increased risk of complications during pregnancy and childbirth, such as obstructed labour, which can lead to death (UNICEF, 2014b). There is also evidence to support the existence of the practice of exploiting women and girls with learning disabilities. Unable to protect themselves, they are subject to a higher risk of abuse and violence, with limited access to safeguarding measures either from family or the state (Sullivan and Knutson, 2000). The Prophet Muhammad (PBUH) said: 'There shall be no harm and no reciprocating harm. Whoever harms, Allah will harm him, and whoever makes things difficult [for others], Allah will make things difficult for him' (Sunan Ibn Majah, Book 36, *Hadith* 4077). Therefore, discouraging any harm done to a fellow human being is a message that needs to be shared more broadly.

One of the triggers of child marriage has been economic gain due to poverty among the poorest of households. The high incidence of child marriage in Afghanistan is directly linked to poverty and low levels of development. Afghanistan's legal minimum age of marriage is 16, yet, nationwide, 16 per cent of children are married before the age of 15 and 52 per cent are married before 18. Niger, which is the fifth poorest country in the world and where Muslims account for 98 per cent of the population also has one of the world's highest rates of child marriage, with three out of four girls getting married before the age of 18 (Idrissi, 2019). To achieve an end to child marriage a multidisciplinary response is required in which development agencies and faith leaders work together through an innovative approach to transformative change. Bostrom and Lofstedt (2003) report that an interdisciplinary panel of scholars found that, for psychological well-being, a child needs a strong attachment to parents and families but also a 'deep connection to moral and spiritual meaning' of the kind generally provided by religious traditions. Innovative approaches need to be explored to unearth the cultural practices that expose children to harm in a safe and holistic manner.

Conclusion

The Prophet Muhammad (PBUH) said: 'Verily, your blood, your property are as sacred and inviolable as the sacredness of this day of yours, in this month of yours, in this town of yours' (Muslim, Book 15, *Hadith* 159). This was part of the last speech delivered by the Prophet Muhammad (PBUH) to his followers, emphasizing rights, justice, and protection. The responsibility of safeguarding and protecting children is incumbent upon all, regardless of faith, colour, or creed, particularly in times of crisis. A number of tools, methods, and approaches have been discussed as well as religious scriptures illustrating the need for children to be shown affection, compassion, and love, while highlighting the long-term impact of emotional, physical, sexual, and psychological abuse. However, humanitarian actors have had limited discussions around the *Maqasid al-Shari'ah*, which can prove to be a key framework in Muslim communities to address rights and the dignity of human life. A number of verses of the *Qur'an* and sayings of the Prophet Muhammad (PBUH) demonstrate the importance that Islam places on parents and caregivers providing a nurturing and loving environment, while supporting and strengthening norms and values that relate to respect and to non-violent, non-discriminatory, and compassionate behaviour. There is still further need to explore and expand on the role played by culture and faith, which in some parts of the world are intrinsically seen as being one and the same. Using the Social Ecological Model, every sphere affecting children needs to be considered, from equipping parents with the skills to be positive role models to influencing policymakers and securing long-term funds for socio-economic support and growth for the hardest-to-reach and poorest families. Equally, working closely with faith actors can also influence behavioural change within families and communities which put children at risk of violence in all its forms.

This would require a multifaceted approach involving academics, practitioners, governments, and – crucially – faith and community leaders working together for sustainable change by creating robust local protection mechanisms and referral pathways that families and their children can access safely, and that consider in particular the needs of women and girls. If faith and community leaders, including women and voices of children, are involved in the process they will be likely to own the process and help design it so that it is fit for purpose – and therefore become advocates for it. This mechanism would reflect intersectional challenges, making it more accessible to all. Additionally, this collaborative approach would work closely with governments to enforce legislation protecting the rights of children as framed by the *Maqasid al-Shari'ah*, holding to account all those who try to violate it.

Notes

1. See <https://www.jasserauda.net/new/pdf/maqasid_guide-Feb_2008.pdf>.
2. See <https://www.unicef.org.uk/what-we-do/un-convention-child-rights/>.
3. See <https://www.refworld.org/pdfid/44eaf0e4a.pdf>.

4. See the Convention on the Rights of the Child at <https://www.ohchr.org/en/professionalinterest/pages/crc.aspx> [accessed 6 May 2019].
5. The Social Ecological Model considers the complex interplay between individual, relationship, community, and societal factors. It allows us to understand the range of factors that put children at risk of violence or protect them from experiencing or perpetrating violence.
6. The age of 18 is the minimum legal age for marriage for women without parental consent in 158 countries. Girls younger than 18 are allowed to marry with parental or other consent in 146 countries, and 52 countries allow girls under 15 to marry. In contrast, 18 is the legal age for marriage without consent for males in 180 countries. Boys younger than 18 are allowed to marry with parental or other consent in 105 countries, while 23 countries allow boys under 15 to marry (UNFPA, 2012: 12).
7. See 'What is the minimum age of marriage for girls with parental consent?' at <https://www.worldpolicycenter.org/policies/what-is-the-minimum-age-of-marriage-for-girls-with-parental-consent>.
8. Both spouses must have the capacity to marry, which means attainment of puberty and comprehensive maturity (including sound judgement). They must also be capable of consenting (see *Shafqat*, 31).
9. A *maulvi* is a religious teacher.

References

Abu 'Abdullah Muhammad (1968) *Sa'd, Al-Tabaqat Al-Kubra*, Volume 2, edited by Ihsan 'Abbas, Dar Sadir, Beirut.

Ala'ddin b. (1981) *Husamuddin Mutaqi, Kanzul 'Ummal fi Sunann Al-Aqwal wa Al-Af'al*, Volume 16, edited by Bakri Hayani, Mu'sassat Al-Riasala, Beirut.

Alavi, H.R. (2008) 'Nearness to god: a perspective on Islamic education', *Religious Education* 103 (1): 5–21 <https://doi.org/10.1080/00344080701807361>.

al-Ghazali, M. (2018) *Al Mustasfa Min ilm Al Usul: On Legal Theory of Muslim Jurisprudence*, Volume 1, translated by Ahmed Zaki Mansur Hammad, CreateSpace Independent Publishing Platform.

Ali, F., Belembaogo, A., Hegazi, S. and Khaled, N. (2005) *Children in Islam: Their Care, Upbringing and Protection*, Al-Azhar University and United Nations Children's Fund (UNICEF), Cairo.

Almugahed. N, Pertek, I. S and Fida, N. (2017) Integrating Protection: An Integrated Approach to Gender-Based Violence and Child Protection, Key Findings from Mali, Niger and Pakistan, 2016-2017. <https://www.islamic-relief.org/publications/> [accessed 22nd May 2020].

Ashur, M. al-Tahir Ibn (2006) *Ibn Ashur: Treatise on Maqasid al-Shari'ah*, Volume 1, translated by M. El-Tahir El-Mesawi, International Institute of Islamic Thought (IIIT), London and Washington DC.

Auda, J. (2008) 'Maqasid Al-Shariah a beginners guide', Muslim-library.com <https://www.muslim-library.com/dl/books/English_Maqasid_alShariah_A_Beginners_Guide.pdf> [accessed 22nd May 2020].

Barbour, R. (1970) 'John Bowlby: attachment and loss', *British Journal of Psychiatry* 116 (530): 102–3.

Bostrom, A. and Lofstedt, R. (2003) 'Communicating risk: wireless and hardwired', *Risk Analysis* 23 (2): 241–8.

Durrant, J. and Ensom, R. (2012) 'Physical punishment of children: lessons from 20 years of research', *Canadian Medical Association Journal* 184 (12): 1373–7.

Fazl-Ul-Karim (1993) *Revival of Religious Learning, Imam Ghazzali's Ihya Ulum-In-Din*, Volume 1, Darul Ishaat, Karachi.

Fikree, F.F. and Pasha, O. (2004) 'Role of gender in health disparity: the South Asian context', *BMJ* 328 (7443): 823–6.

Handicap International (2015) *Disability in Humanitarian Context: Views from Affected People and Field Organisations*, Handicap International, Geneva <https://handicap-international.ch/sites/ch/files/documents/files/disability-humanitarian-context.pdf>.

Hillis, S., Mercy, J., Amobi, A. and Kress, H. (2016) 'Global prevalence of past-year violence against children: a systematic review and minimum estimates', *Pediatrics* 137 (3): e20154079.

Holtzhausen, L. (2011) 'When values collide: finding common ground for social work education in the United Arab Emirates', *International Social Work* 54 (2): 191–208.

Idrissi, M. (2019) 'Child marriage in Niger is a cultural issue, not an Islamic one', *Guardian*, 8 March <https://www.theguardian.com/global-development/2019/mar/08/child-marriage-in-niger-is-a-cultural-issue-not-an-islamic-one>.

Islamic Relief Worldwide (2016) '*One cut too many: policy briefing on female genital mutilation and cutting*', Islamic Relief Worldwide, Birmingham <https://www.islamic-relief.org/wp-content/uploads/2018/03/FGM-CSW62.pdf> [accessed 20 September 2018].

Islamic Relief Worldwide (2017b) *An Islamic Human Rights Perspective on Early and Forced Marriages: Protecting the Sanctity of Marriage*, Islamic Relief Worldwide, Birmingham <https://www.islamic-relief.org/publications/> [accessed 5th June 2020].

Jensen, R. and Thornton, R. (2003) 'Early female marriage in the developing world', *Gender and Development* 11 (2): 9–19.

Lahaie, C., Earle, A. and Heymann, J. (2013) 'An uneven burden', *Research on Aging* 35 (3): 243–74 <https://doi.org/10.1177/0164027512446028>.

Lipka, M. (2017) 'Muslims and Islam: key findings in the US and around the world', Pew Research Center <http://www.pewresearch.org/fact-tank/2017/08/09/muslims-and-islam-key-findings-in-the-u-s-and-around-the-world/> [accessed 22nd May 2020].

Lockhat, H. (2004) *Female Genital Mutilation: Treating the Tears*, Middlesex University Press, London.

MacMillan, H.L., Boyle, M.H., Wong, M.Y., Duku, E.K., Fleming, J.E. and Walsh, C.A. (1999) 'Slapping and spanking in childhood and its association with lifetime prevalence of psychiatric disorders in a general population', *Canadian Medical Association Journal* 161 (7): 805–9.

Miles, M. (1996) 'Walking delicately around mental handicap, sex education and abuse in Pakistan', *Child Abuse Review* 5 (4): 263–74.

Nguyen, M.C. and Wodon, Q. (2015) 'Impact of early marriage on literacy and educational attainment in Africa', in Q. Wodon (ed.), *Child Marriage and Education in Sub-Saharan Africa*, World Bank, Washington DC.

O'Leary P.J. and Squire, J. (2012) 'Child protection in humanitarian emergencies', in R. Sheehan, H. Rhoades, and N. Stanley (eds), *Vulnerable Children and the Law: International Evidence for Improving Child Welfare, Child Protection and Children's Rights*, Jessica Kingsley Publishers, London.

Rajabi-Ardeshiri, M. (2009) 'The rights of the child in the Islamic context: the challenges of the local and the global', *International Journal of Children's Rights* 17 (3): 475–89.

Squire, J. and Hope, K. (2013) *Child Protection in Islamic Contexts: A Roundtable Discussion, Reflection and Suggestions for Applied Practice*, Foundation Terre des Hommes, Lausanne.

Sullivan, P. and Knutson, J. (2000) 'Maltreatment and disabilities: a popu-lation-based epidemiological study', *Child Abuse and Neglect* 24 (10): 1257–73.

Thomas, E. (2018) *Children with Disabilities in Situations of Armed Conflict*, Discussion Paper, United Nations Children's Fund (UNICEF), New York <https://www.unicef.org/disabilities/files/Children_with_Disabilities_in_Situations_of_Armed_Conflict-Discussion_Paper.pdf> [accessed 6th June 2020].

UNFPA (2012) *Marrying Too Young: End Child Marriage*, United Nations Population Fund (UNFPA), New York.

UNICEF (2009) 'What are the Social Ecological Model (SEM), Communication for Development (C4D)', United Nations Children's Fund (UNICEF), New York <https://www.unicef.org/cbsc/files/Module_1_SEM-C4D.docx> [accessed 22nd May 2020].

UNICEF (2012) *Partnering with Religious Communities for Children*, United Nations Children's Fund (UNICEF), New York <https://www.unicef.org/about/partnerships/files/Partnering_with_Religious_Communities_for_Children_(UNICEF).pdf>.

UNICEF (2013) *Children and Young People with Disabilities: Fact Sheet*, United Nations Children's Fund (UNICEF), New York <https://www.unicef.org/disabilities/files/Factsheet_A5__Web_REVISED.pdf>.

UNICEF (2014a) *Female Genital Mutilation/Cutting: What Might the Future Hold?*, United Nations Children's Fund (UNICEF), New York.

UNICEF (2014b) *Ending Child Marriage: Progress and Prospects*, United Nations Children's Fund (UNICEF), New York.

UNICEF (2015) 'Child protection in emergencies: a toolkit for practitioners in Pacific Island countries', United Nations Children's Fund (UNICEF), New York <https://www.unicef.org/pacificislands/Child_protection_toolkit.pdf> [accessed 14th March 2020].

UNICEF (2017), *A Familiar Face: Violence in the Lives of Children and Adolescents*, United Nations Children's Fund (UNICEF), New York <https://data.unicef.org/wp-content/uploads/2017/10/EVAC-Booklet-FINAL-10_31_17-high-res.pdf>.

UNICEF (2018) *A Future Stolen: Young and Out of School*, United Nations Children's Fund (UNICEF), New York.

UNICEF (2019) 'Education in emergencies', United Nations Children's Fund (UNICEF), New York <https://www.unicef.org/education/emergencies> [accessed 22nd May 2020].

UNICEF USA (2019) 'Child refugees', United Nations Children's Fund (UNICEF) USA, New York <https://www.unicefusa.org/mission/emergencies/child-refugees> [accessed 5th June 2020].

von Jhering, R. (2001 [1913]) *Law as a Means to an End* [*Der Zweck im Recht*], translated by I. Husik, 2nd edn, The Lawbook Exchange, Clark NJ.

WHO (1997) 'Female genital mutilation: a joint WHO/UNICEF/UNFPA statement', World Health Organization (WHO), Geneva.

WHO (2016) 'Child maltreatment', World Health Organization (WHO), Geneva <https://www.who.int/news-room/fact-sheets/detail/child-maltreatment> [accessed 14th March 2020].

WHO (2018) 'Adverse Childhood Experiences International Questionnaire (ACE-IQ)', World Health Organization (WHO), Geneva <https://www.who.int/violence_injury_prevention/violence/activities/adverse_childhood_experiences/en/> [accessed 14th March 2020].

About the author

Neelam Fida is the Child Protection and Inclusion Advisor and Safeguarding Lead for Islamic Relief Worldwide. She holds a degree in Psychology and has skills and expertise in research, mentoring, counselling, social behaviour network therapy, and strategic planning. Neelam is the lead investigator on safeguarding and PSEA (Protection against Sexual Exploitation and Abuse), overseeing a global team. She has done extensive work on ending violence against children and led on the organization adopting faith-sensitive approaches to child protection programming.

CHAPTER 9

An Islamic approach to peacebuilding: putting theory into practice

Sylvia Brown and Haroon Kash

Violent conflict continues to exact a high cost on societies around the world, many of whose religious values shape their understanding of conflict and peace. Conflict prevention and peacebuilding approaches that recognize the centrality of faith to local communities and work with religious values and local faith actors may be more effective than secular approaches in some contexts. However there is little information available about how INGOs can best support these faith-based approaches. Islamic Relief has developed a holistic vision of peacebuilding, based on a number of values and principles central to Islamic philosophy, which has been operationalized by designing 'nexus' programmes that incorporate a blend of human-itarian, development, and peacebuilding activities. Some of these activities are secular while others support the religious values of local faith actors such as mercy, compassion, forgiveness, and equality, and Islamic traditions of conflict resolution and reconciliation in Muslim communities. INGO support to Islamic-based peace-building contains potential risks as well as rewards.

Keywords: peacebuilding, development, peace, conflict, Islamic Relief, Kenya, Mandera, Yemen, Sudan, Darfur, INGO, local faith actor, nexus, Islam

Introduction

Conflicts around the world continue to take their toll on the lives of many people and societies. Sadly, in recent years there has been a significant increase in protracted and intractable conflicts resulting in prolonged human suffering, huge economic and financial costs, and large-scale displacement and refugee flows.[1] The Global Peace Index's 2018 quantitative dataset found that tensions, conflicts, and crises around the world resulted in a gradual, sustained fall in peacefulness for the fourth consecutive year, in marked contrast to the longer-term trend of a decline in global armed conflict (IEP, 2018). The economic impact of violence on the global economy in 2017 was $14.76 trillion in purchasing power parity terms,[2] which equates to $1,988 for every person on the planet (ibid.: 4). This represents a 16 per cent increase since 2012, corresponding with the start of the Syrian war and an increase in violence following the Arab Spring (ibid.).

http://dx.doi.org/10.3362/9781788530613.009

Many of the deadliest current conflicts are in predominantly Muslim countries (Syria, Yemen, Afghanistan, Iraq, and Somalia) and these are proving to be some of the most difficult to resolve. Conflict in these Muslim-majority countries has religious dimensions, which is also a growing trend in armed conflict globally. Baumann et al. (2018: 1) argue that 'conflicts in which one or more of the issues has a religious dimension are increasing and now account for a majority of all armed conflicts'. There are two basic ways in which religion can play a role in conflict: as the identity marker of the conflict parties; and as an influence on the issues that conflict parties fight about (ibid.). However, the authors point out that while religion is itself not usually the issue, parties can enter into a conflict over specific religious issues or be mobilized across religious identity (ibid.).

Baumann et al. (2018: 1) argue that conflicts without religious aspects and conflicts fought about non-religious issues are not increasing over time, indicating that classical conflict resolution approaches may be working for these types. They also suggest that classical conflict resolution approaches may not be sufficient for conflicts with a religious dimension and that disentangling the religious from the political components or adapting conflict resolution tools to better deal with differences in religious beliefs may be important.

The concept of peacebuilding dates back many centuries, but its current manifestation within the international development sector can be attributed to its recognition within peace studies. Galtung (1976), in his essay 'Three approaches to peace', called for a structural approach to peacebuilding involving reforming social structures to remove the causes of war and establishing mechanisms for peace that the social system could draw upon as alternatives to war (HPCR, 2019). Similarly, Lederach (1997: 20) defines peacebuilding as 'a comprehensive concept that encompasses, generates, and sustains the full array of processes, approaches, and stages needed to transform conflict towards more sustainable, peaceful relationships'. Thus, while the term 'peacekeeping' is applied more narrowly to mean an often militaristic enforcement of an end to hostilities, in its academic origin 'peacebuilding' is a broad term encompassing the reform of social structures and a wide variety of other activities that aim to transform societies experiencing high levels of violent conflict into societies with institutionalized mechanisms for sustaining peaceful relationships.

Said and Funk (2002: 37–8, quoted in Bouta et al. 2005: 11) reason that religion 'is deeply implicated in individual and social conceptions of peace, because it addresses some of the most profound existential issues of human life, such as freedom/inevitability, fear/security, right/wrong and sacred/profane'. Yet within the scope of peacebuilding efforts it was not until the late 1990s that the role of religious peacebuilding and practice was given recognition (Marshall and Saanen, 2007). A series of meetings[3] between leaders of major world faiths captured the importance of the role that faith could play within the development sector and was consequently the impetus for driving the 'peacebuilding from faith' perspective to a wider audience. These meetings were also instrumental in linking the challenges in the Millennium Development Goals (MDGs) to the ideas and work of religious leaders and institutions. The MDGs have now been replaced by the Sustainable Development Goals (SDGs), with a target of achieving these goals by 2030. However violent conflicts are now perceived to 'pose a significant threat to the 2030 agenda' (Schafer, 2018). At the World Humanitarian Summit in May 2016, various stakeholders pledged to address global conflicts, recognizing that: 'An end to human suffering requires political solutions, unity of purpose and sustained leadership and investment in peaceful and inclusive societies' (UN, 2016: 2).

Although peacebuilding scholars and practitioners have subsequently sought to integrate authentic, indigenous, and local methods of conflict analysis and intervention with the generic Western-based conflict resolution models developed in the United States and Europe, their implementation in Muslim communities has been problematic (Abu-Nimer, 2001). Westendorf (2015: 4) argues that 'international structures, organizational incentives, bureaucratic imperatives, and the global peace-building culture all contribute to the perpetuation of the technocratic model of peace building'. Thus, part of the problem may be that technocratic models of conflict resolution do not speak to communities' religious values or customary ways of understanding conflict and peace. Mufti (2014) is more critical of the underlying motives of the global peacebuilding culture, arguing that the West, in pursuing the objectives of peacebuilding, is in fact 'altering, modifying, and/or reforming the Islamic societies towards its specific hegemonic agenda'. Whether concern stems from a pragmatic point of view or from a perceived (or real) need to counter Western hegemony, the scale of conflict in the Muslim world suggests a need to consider what an Islamic approach to peacebuilding could offer in these contexts.

There has been increasing recognition recently among some of the United Nations (UN) agencies that faith-based actors play a fundamental role in fostering resilience, preventing violent conflict, and sustaining peace (Trotta and Wilkinson, 2019). For example, the UN High Commissioner for Refugees' (UNHCR's) Global Compact on Refugees recognizes the importance of faith-based actors in conflict prevention and reconciliation, while the UN Office on Genocide Prevention and the Responsibility to Protect issued a 'Plan of Action for Religious Leaders and Actors to Prevent Incitement to Violence that Could Lead to Atrocity Crimes' (ibid.). Elsewhere, research on 'tradition- and faith-oriented insider mediators' (TFIMs) stresses the value of 'insiders', such as local faith actors, because of their deep local knowledge and connections to peacebuilding processes (Mir and Vimalarajah, 2016). However, several studies also warn of the challenges and risks involved in engaging local faith actors in peacebuilding, arguing that this should not necessarily be seen as the default option (Trotta and Wilkinson, 2019).

While there is recognition that faith-based actors may be important in conflict prevention and peacebuilding, Bouta et al. (2005) argue that the institutional development of Muslim peacebuilding actors has lagged behind that of Christian and multi-faith actors. This largely stems from differences in the way in which Muslim societies and Christian societies in the West are organized, with Western societies more individualistic, professional, and bureaucratized while kinship, tribalism, and family ties are more dominant in Muslim societies (ibid.). The interaction between Christian missionary churches and secular organizations, as well as the spread of mass communication through the internet, has particularly assisted in the development of Christian peacebuilding actors, while Muslim equivalents have received less visibility and outside support (ibid.).

Abu-Nimer (2001) further argues that a misconception of Islam not being a peaceful religion has emerged in scholarly discussion within security, war, and strategic studies. He states that 'progress has been hampered by a well-publicized Western assumption that Islamic religion and culture contradict the principle of peacebuilding, conflict resolution, nonviolence and democracy' (ibid.: 217). This chapter does not seek to enter the debate about if or how Islamic religion and tradition justify war or violence. This is an intense debate that far more qualified scholars, such as Abu-Nimer (ibid.), have written about extensively. However, it does seek to open a window to interested scholars and practitioners into the world view and peacebuilding practices of a global Muslim faith-based organization (FBO): Islamic Relief Worldwide.

Islamic Relief Worldwide is an international non-governmental organization (INGO) founded in the UK in 1984 by a group of medical doctors and activists. It is the international headquarters of Islamic Relief, which is a large multi-mandate family of organizations operating in over 40 countries. Islamic Relief is inspired by its Islamic faith, but it works with people in need regardless of race, political affiliation, gender, or belief. In 2013, Islamic Relief commissioned research to inform about conflict transformation from an Islamic perspective; this was published in *Understanding an Islamic Framework for Peacebuilding* (Kadayifci-Orellana et al., 2016). Since then, Islamic Relief has engaged in several conflict prevention or peacebuilding programmes that have sought to apply these academic findings.

Little (2005: 14) suggests that there is a growing interest in the 'Track II' type of diplomacy, the so-called 'unofficial endeavours' of middle- and community-level actors. He promotes what he calls 'the hermeneutics of peace', a framework 'grounded in the conviction that the pursuit of justice and peace by peaceful means is a sacred priority, and it is employed as a way of examining the texts, traditions, and practices of one religion or another for their contribution to the promotion of justice and peace' (ibid.: 15). The discussion that follows here is from this perspective. It is an exploration of the 'hermeneutics of peace' within Islam and the unofficial peacebuilding endeavours of Islamic Relief, and is organized as follows.

The first section summarizes the conceptual links between Islamic principles and peacebuilding concepts, as presented in the publication *Understanding an Islamic Framework for Peacebuilding* (Kadayifci-Orellana et al., 2016). This is followed by an explanation of how Islamic Relief has put these principles into practice. The next section presents three case studies from Kenya, Sudan, and Yemen, and then we draw out some of the opportunities and challenges that an FBO such as Islamic Relief faces in its peacebuilding work, to give scholars and practitioners a greater understanding of which conditions and approaches best promote the peaceful resolution of political, social, and other conflicts. The discussion ends with our conclusions.

Conceptual links between Islamic principles and peacebuilding

'For many communities, faith shapes the way they view the world and how they understand their place within it' (Bradley, 2009: 112). In Islamic traditions, conflict is viewed as a normal social condition because, as the *Qur'an* states, differences between people is part of God's plan for humanity (*Qur'an*, 49: 13). The *Qur'an* is rich in promoting and recognizing the diversity and coexistence that exist within and among communities: 'And if your Lord had so willed, He could surely have made mankind one *Ummah* [nation or community following one religion, i.e. Islam], but they will not cease to disagree' (*Qur'an*, 11: 118). Ordinarily, differences are expected to be resolved through non-violent means. The history and acts of the Prophet Muhammad (Peace Be Upon Him) demonstrate the level of respect that was afforded to other religions, customs, and practices, much of which was conducted through relationships built on and encouraged through constructive dialogue. Peace is also overwhelmingly referenced within the *Qur'an* through messages of 'tolerance, forgiveness, conciliation, inclusiveness and peace' (Hayward, J., 2011).

Among Muslim communities, Islamic scripture and religious teachings contain extensive sources of values, beliefs, and strategies for the peaceful resolution of conflicts (Abu-Nimer, 2001). For example, the *Misaq-e-Medina* (Constitution of Medina) is an example from the seventh century of how to peacefully govern relations between Muslim and non-Muslim believers for the future good and peace of the whole community (the *Ummah*). The Treaty of Hudaybiyyah is another example. The Prophet Muhammad (PBUH) and his followers yearned to perform the *Umrah* (lesser pilgrimage) to Mecca but were prevented from entering Mecca at a place called Hudaybiyyah by the Meccans. Negotiations took place, which culminated in the Treaty of Hudaybiyyah, within which it was agreed that there would be no war for the next 10 years and that the pilgrims would return to Medina but would be allowed to return to Mecca to perform the pilgrimage the following year. Although the agreement was disadvantageous to the Muslims, the Prophet (PBUH) agreed to sign it to promote a peaceful resolution to the problem. The Treaty of Hudaybiyyah demonstrated the peaceful and patient nature of the way in which the Prophet (PBUH) dealt with conflict. It is still considered by Muslims to be an excellent example of being faithful to the principles of *'pacta sunt servanda'* ('agreements must be kept'), which are considered to be key components of peacebuilding initiatives (Zoli et al., 2017).

The *Qur'an* is unambiguous in stating that Muslims are prohibited from offensive violence, but if defensive warfare should become unavoidable they must act within a code of conduct comparable to the Western 'just war' doctrine (Hayward, D.J., 2011). Muslims are permitted to fight in self-defence and to defend others who are oppressed because oppression is considered to be worse than a conflict that ends continual discord (Salek, 2014). Where violence is permitted, Muslims are obliged to react proportionately, justly, and with restraint (ibid.): 'If anyone kills a person – unless in retribution for murder or spreading corruption in the land – it is as if he kills all mankind, while if any saves a life it is as if he saves the lives of all mankind' (Qur'an, 5: 32). A number of verses in the Qur'an and accounts of the Prophet Muhammad's (PBUH) life in the Sunnah detail the rules of war that must be obeyed, such as treating prisoners of war well, non-combatant immunity, and prohibitions on looting, unsanctioned killing, and retaliation (Salek, 2014).

In the research publication that Islamic Relief commissioned in 2016, Kadayifci-Orellana et al. (2016) argue that eight Islamic principles and values of peace and conflict resolution form a theological basis for peacebuilding practice in the Muslim world (Box 9.1).

The eight principles described in Box 9.1 give guidance to Islamic Relief's conflict transformation work. The organization's philosophical approach is stated in its toolkit, *Working in Conflict: A Faith-based Toolkit for Islamic Relief*, which states: 'We believe that faith is a powerful agent for change – one which is often under-emphasised. When people have faith, their principles are often supreme guiding motivations. Islamic principles and teachings can positively encourage people to address competing priorities, avoid violent conflict and accept compromise' (Salek, 2014: 14).

Box 9.1 The eight Islamic principles and values of peace and conflict resolution

1. **Pluralism, diversity, and human solidarity through the principle of *tawhid* (the oneness of God)**
   In Islam, since there is believed to be a single source of all creation, the whole of humanity is believed to be descended from a single mother and father (Adam and Eve). The concept of the *Ummah* (one nation) applies to the whole of humanity and calls for social solidarity and collective action, principles that are also used in peace movements and non-violent resistance to injustice. Diversity and pluralism within the *Ummah* are also argued to be central principles in God's design, according to the Qur'an, and these principles are central to conflict resolution and peace.

2. **Universality, dignity, and sacredness of humanity through the principle of *fitrah* (the original nature of human beings)**
   The sanctity and dignity of human life are explicitly stated in the Qur'anic principles of *fitrah*, which also reject any notion of innate sinfulness, arguing instead that the essential nature of the human spirit at birth is good, regardless of religious, ethnic, racial, or gender backgrounds. *Fitrah* also means that everyone has free will to reason and choose their own actions. The relationship to conflict resolution and peacebuilding is that the sanctity of life should be preserved because all people have the potential to change through reason and compassion – nobody is born evil.

3. **Social empowerment by doing good (*khayr* and *ihsan*) through the principle of *khilafah* (stewardship)**
   From an Islamic point of view, conflict, violence, and injustice are related to the problem of evil, and since evil is understood to be something that can be discerned by the intellect, Muslims are obliged to shun evil and do good. The link with *khilafah* is that, since human beings are understood to be stewards of God's world, collectively

---

(Continued)

Box 9.1 Continued

they are responsible for bringing peace and order to the world and resisting violence in all its manifestations.

4. Pursuit of justice, equality, and fairness through the principle of *adl* (justice)

The Qur'anic notion of justice is that it is universal and equal for all humans, and peace cannot be attained without justice. Justice, including social and economic justice, is seen as the central component of peace and Muslims are asked to work to correct injustice. This fits well with peacebuilding approaches which recognize that unjust structures of social, political, and economic systems are often a major source of conflict.

5. Transformation of relationships and re-humanization through the principles of *rahman* and *rahim* (compassion and mercy)

Compassion and mercy are central to the *Qur'an* (almost all chapters start with the recitation '*Bism Allah al-rahman al-rahim*' ('We begin in the name of Allah who is compassionate and merciful') and were key qualities of the Prophet Muhammad (PBUH) and the Prophet Moses (PBUH). As such, the *Qur'an* asks Muslims to be merciful and compassionate themselves, irrespective of ethnicity, religion, or gender. These principles, when enacted, prevent the dehumanization of an opponent (which is a key process in war that enables atrocities to take place) and are tools to facilitate the re-humanization of the 'other' in a process of conflict resolution.

6. Reconciliation and healing through the principles of *afu* and *musamaha* (pardoning and forgiveness)

Reconciliation and healing are also central principles in the *Qur'an*, which stresses that forgiveness is of a higher value than maintaining hatred or vengeance or seeking retribution. The *Qur'an* states: 'The recompense of injury is an injury the like thereof: but whoever forgives and thereby brings about a reestablishment of harmony, his reward is with God; and God loves not the wrongdoers' (*Qur'an*, 42: 40). Pardoning and forgiving facilitate the healing of wounds and memories from conflict and a transformation in the relationship between former opponents to one of peace.

7. Non-violent and creative solutions to problems through the principle of *sabr* (patience)

Patience (*sabr*) is one of the core subjects of Islamic scriptures and it is critical to an Islamic conception of peace, for example through the verse 'And we shall surely bear with patience all the harm you do us' (*Qur'an*, 14: 12–13). This does not mean that Muslims are expected to remain silent or passive in the face of injustice or oppression (several verses urge non-violent struggle to right these wrongs); rather, it means that Muslims must resist responding with violence and be patient while seeking to conquer people's hearts and minds through Islam's philosophy.

8. Quest for peace through *hubb* (love) and *mawadda* (the principle of loving kindness)

Loving kindness is an important concept in peacebuilding for the transformation of relations between enemies into friendships based on respect and understanding. According to Islamic tradition, love is the source and cause of all creation and is often associated with peace, mercy, and forgiveness, so transforming enmity into love is believed to be a sign of the mercy of God.

Source: Kadayifci-Orellana et al. (2016).

From principles to practice: Islamic Relief's approach to faith-based peacebuilding

When Islamic Relief has sought to implement these principles in peace-building, four particular approaches have consistently emerged: first, the adoption of a holistic, rather than a narrow, approach to designing a peace-building programme; second, a focus on inclusivity and respect for diverse perspectives; third, activities that focus on building a rational understanding of the causes of conflict and the behaviour of opponents in order to rehumanize them; and finally, support for Islamic practices of mediation and reconciliation. Each is explained in more detail below.

A holistic approach to peacebuilding

Islamic Relief's framework for development is based on a holistic understanding of human development according to Islam: 'In Islam, the goal of development is to create an environment that enables people to enjoy spiritual, moral and socio-economic well-being' (Salek, 2014: 19). In order to work towards this environment, Islamic Relief has adopted the *Maqasid al-Shari'ah* (objectives of *Shari'ah*), which places human dignity at the centre of an Islamic framework for development. Islamic Relief also strongly believes in a holistic approach to peacebuilding. This belief is based on the principle of *adl* (justice), without which peace cannot be attained according to the *Qur'an*. The *Qur'an* adopts a broad interpretation of justice, including social and economic justice, and this implies structural reform to address structural violence (Abu-Nimer, 2001). SDG 16 ('Promote peaceful and inclusive societies') also recognizes that justice is critical to peacebuilding. The targets in SDG 16 contain a number of references to the transformation of governance structures, such as promoting the rule of law, ensuring equal access to justice, and establishing inclusive and accountable decision-making institutions.

In practice, pursuing a holistic approach has meant designing peacebuilding programmes that blend short-term humanitarian assistance, longerterm support, and context-specific activities of conflict prevention, conflict resolution, and peace support. This is known as the 'triple nexus'. A triple nexus approach can blur conceptual boundaries between development, humanitarian, and peacebuilding and potentially result in an incoherent programme. Thus, a nexus approach to conflict prevention and peacebuilding means working only on either development issues that are causes of conflict or humanitarian issues that are the effects of conflict. Programme goals and outcomes are defined in terms of peace, and all programme activities – whether development, humanitarian, or peacebuilding – have to work coherently towards these peace outcomes.

Islamic Relief works with local government – both to ensure that programming fits in with their own structural reform strategies and local planning priorities, and to help communities voice concerns to government officials over issues such as resource access and distribution. Programme designs also often have built-in humanitarian assistance activities to address the immediate needs of those affected by conflict, such as food aid to displaced people or funding to rebuild damaged infrastructure including schools, health facilities, and water and sanitation structures. Peacebuilding activities may include some religiously informed initiatives, such as discussion of what the *Qur'an* says about particular issues, and about building peace in general, but they also use secular activities such as sports tournaments where there is no religious message at all. This approach works across the 'triple nexus' of development–humanitarian–peacebuilding operations, which has gained increasing prominence in development circles since the World Humanitarian Summit in 2016.

When members of Islamic Relief work with local government agencies and officials to address conflict issues it is often in the role of a trusted, neutral third party, creating a dialogue between community groups, leaders, and local government officials and helping each group interpret the language and procedural norms of the other. The purpose of these dialogues is often to improve poor relations between the state and society, helping communities voice their concerns to government and helping the government be more responsive to local communities and transparent about the way it operates. This approach supports structural reform of governance and Muslim communities' pursuit of *adl* (justice).

Where approved by the state, Islamic Relief staff also work with customary authorities. Obtaining state approval first is not because of any ideological bias towards the state but simply because it would be impossible for the organization to work with customary authorities otherwise. For example, in Kenya there is an approved hybrid governance model in which traditional clan leaders and governance systems have an agreed role. Faith leaders also have traditional roles to play in these systems. Working with traditional and religious leaders to advance peace locally is therefore both a values-based choice and a pragmatic choice. Working with a wide array of formal and customary governance actors is a reflection of the principle of *khilafah* (stewardship), in which human beings are understood to be stewards of God's world and are therefore collectively responsible for bringing peace and order.

Inclusivity and respect for diversity

The principles of diversity and pluralism within the *Qur'an* lay the foundation for Islamic Relief to advocate for the inclusion of marginalized groups, voices, and opinions in processes of governance reform and peacebuilding. The concept of *shura* (consultation) is central to Islamic governance. *Shura* involves equality and expression of opinion, although there is much debate about who and when to consult in different situations. Islamic Relief focuses on the inclusion of women in particular, which is articulated in its Gender Justice Policy,[4] an approach that is also compatible with SDG 5 ('Achieve gender equality and empower all women and girls'). This goal recognizes that 'gender equality is not just a fundamental human right, but a necessary foundation for a peaceful, prosperous and sustainable world' (UN, 2019).

With these principles in mind, Islamic Relief's peacebuilding work often directly targets marginalized groups, with the goal of bringing them into improved governance structures and local consultations about peace and conflict issues. This enables new voices, who might typically be marginalized in traditional peacebuilding processes, to gain greater recognition and public legitimacy.

Promoting women and youth inclusion in community conflict prevention and peacebuilding processes can be a very sensitive issue, depending on the local history and context, because it challenges entrenched norms of patriarchy and gerontocracy and because there are different interpretations of *shura*. A good context and gender analysis helps identify where and when there is room to push for greater inclusion and respect for diversity and where there is not.

Transforming relationships and rehumanizing 'others'

In places where there is violent state–society conflict, improving state–society relations is important for rehumanizing Muslim communities in the eyes of state actors and for preventing state-sponsored 'collective punishment' or mass violence against Muslim citizens.[5] Rehumanizing the 'enemy' is important in other forms of conflict, such as inter-clan conflict, too. A typical activity for a community peace group in Islamic Relief's approach is to conduct a community conflict analysis. This exercise seeks to demystify the root causes, proximate causes, and dynamics of the conflicts that communities are experiencing and rationalize the behaviour of the 'enemy'. Since individual behaviour is understood in Islam to be a result of free will, and since humans are believed to be essentially good in spirit (*fitrah*), it is possible to understand an opponent's behaviour. It is also desirable because this understanding helps rehumanize them, which is an essential step in building peace. The Islamic scholars and faith leaders with whom Islamic Relief works also help rehumanize the 'other' through their public prayers, teaching, and other public messaging work. This public messaging includes teaching on the principles of *hubb* (love), *mawadda* (loving kindness), *rahman* (compassion), and *rahim* (mercy).

Islamic mediation and reconciliation

Faith-based mediation has been seen as a powerful contributor to conflict resolution and peace in recent research (Silvestri and Mayall, 2015). Islamic Relief recognizes the importance of Islamic mediation and reconciliation to the Muslim communities with whom it is engaged, especially in places where formal justice systems are out of reach, too lengthy, or too culturally distant from local communities. It also respects the 'credit of trust' that many local faith leaders possess, which is deeply meaningful for peacebuilding work. As Weingardt (quoted in Silvestri and Mayall, 2015) argues, there are three main reasons for this credit of trust: first, reference to theology can justify peaceful conflict resolution in a comprehensive and legitimate way; second, faith leaders are viewed by conflict parties as being able to consider not just the 'facts' of a dispute but also the underlying and profound issues of morality, responsibility, reconciliation, and forgiveness; and third, faith leaders are often perceived to be less driven by self-interest than secular actors, and more considerate of the general interest of all. They also typically display authority, trust, professionalism, cultural proximity, and an experiential closeness to conflict actors (Cox et al., 1994, quoted in Silvestri and Mayall, 2015).

Islamic mediation, called *Suluh*, aims to build consensus on an issue through dialogue and is a communal process with the wider community, rather than simply between the individual victim and perpetrator (Abdi and Mason, 2019). However, one of the challenges with Islamic mediation is that a focus on restoring social harmony can undermine an individual victim's rights to justice, especially when the victim has little power. Users of customary justice systems, particularly women and marginalized populations, are often more vulnerable to nepotism, discrimination, and sanctions that violate internationally accepted human rights standards (IDLO, 2019). The dilemma of trading off individual rights in order to improve conditions of violent insecurity for all is often challenging to resolve, especially for external actors such as INGOs. Islamic Relief aims to navigate this dilemma by incrementally pushing for greater respect for individual human rights where situations allow and developing policy positions on specific issues to justify this.[6] The goal is not large-scale transformation of customary processes, because this is likely to be destabilizing. It is more about pushing the parameters of dialogue to include greater representation of all groups in a society and working towards establishing more equitable traditions.

Islamic Relief staff do not take on the role of mediator in Islamic mediation, but rather the role of a trusted third party and sometimes a witness. As Abu-Nimer (2001: 246) states: 'the role of the third party, as an integral part of peacebuilding intervention, is mainly to facilitate communication, reduce tension, and assist in rebuilding relationships'. As a trusted third party, Islamic Relief may facilitate mediation by arranging transportation for disputing parties, paying for some of the meeting costs for formal dispute resolution dialogues, and supporting related public communications about peace processes.

The rituals of reconciliation are important to Muslim communities, such as the slaughter of livestock and communal feasting to restore harmonious social relations between warring parties, and collective prayer led by religious leaders from both warring parties. Islamic approaches additionally place importance on finding 'internal' peace within oneself and in one's relationship with God. This is a reflection of Islamic teaching: that an outward expression of Islamic teaching and practice (the ritual) is underpinned by an inner acceptance (belief or 'Iman'). This inner acceptance is fundamental, and without it the outward expression is meaningless and without conviction. Sheherazade Jafari and Abdul Aziz Said state that 'within an Islamic peace-making framework, inner personal transformation is connected to societal conflict transformation' (Aroua, 2013: 45). The principles of pardoning (*afu*) and forgiveness (*musamaha*) are the ultimate goal of reconciliation in the *Qur'an*, both internally, within oneself, and publicly, to really achieve peace. Islamic Relief recognizes the importance of these Islamic principles in conflict resolution and supports the rituals of reconciliation.

Islamic Relief's faith-based peacebuilding in practice

Peacebuilding is not the core work of Islamic Relief, which has traditionally focused more on humanitarian programming. However, there is growing interest within the organization in moving into the peacebuilding sector because there is recognition that Islamic Relief is one of the few INGOs able to access remote Muslim communities. Furthermore, the ever increasing humanitarian caseload requires interventions that tackle the root causes of conflict as well as its effects. Islamic Relief has now engaged in six peacebuilding interventions around the world, three of which are presented below.

Comparative advantages and challenges for a Muslim FBO working on peacebuilding

What is the comparative advantage that an FBO such as Islamic Relief brings to peacebuilding programmes? In addition to the organization's collective experience and the three case studies discussed above, our response to this is informed by our individual experience working in this field over several years. It should therefore be considered as impressions rather than hard evidence. As with all peacebuilding activities, it is challenging to measure the specific impact of faith-based actors (Bouta et al., 2005). With this caveat in mind, our experience suggests that the following points are significant.

First, because Islamic Relief is an FBO, it respects the position, authority, and wisdom of religious leaders, which secular organizations may not view with the same level of trust. This does not mean that all religious leaders are supported by Islamic Relief staff. Indeed, the choice of religious leader with whom the organization is willing to work can be extremely complex and sensitive. However, it does mean that Islamic Relief is willing to engage in a partnership with identified local faith actors. By cultivating long-lasting partnerships with local faith actors, Islamic Relief is able to intervene in a range of sensitive issues: for example, gender-based violence and child protection.

Gopin (2000, quoted in Silvestri and Mayall, 2015) is critical of secular conflict resolution approaches for ignoring religious values and approaches, arguing instead for a much greater understanding of how religious values, institutions, and practices have traditionally approached issues of conflict and peace. However, there are a number of challenges to the establishment of fruitful partnerships between international actors and local faith actors (LFAs): a lack of evidence of the impact of local faith actors' roles; a lack of information about the different peace initiatives implemented by local faith actors around the world, and a corresponding lack of coordination to create normative practices among international actors in their engagement with LFAs; difficulty in navigating the diversity among LFAs, including their political orientation; and a lack of trust, knowledge, and capacity for international engagement with LFAs, both among secular agencies and LFAs themselves (Trotta and Wilkinson, 2019: 6).

Box 9.2 Conflict prevention and peacebuilding in Mandera, Kenya

In 2018, Islamic Relief commenced a three-year conflict prevention and peacebuilding project in Mandera County in Kenya. Mandera County borders Somalia and Ethiopia in the north-east of Kenya. The population is approximately 2 million people, who are almost entirely ethnic Somali and Muslim. Most people practise livestock and/or agricultural farming as either their main or secondary occupation. The Somali community is organized into traditional clan structures. Clan networks extend across the porous borders – indeed, the border is largely invisible in this pastoral region. There is a low population density, but despite this there are increasing pressures on pasture land and water access, due to increasingly regular droughts.

There are two main types of organized, violent conflict in this region: inter-clan conflict and terror group conflict (of which Al-Shabaab is the largest group). Inter-clan conflicts are most commonly triggered by political events, competition over scarce water and pasture, cattle rustling, or escalated violent attacks by one clan member on another. These conflicts do not have religious dimensions, but there are extensive cross-border connections between clan networks. Such conflicts can be deadly and create a lasting context of insecurity: for example, in 2013 clan conflict between the large Garre and Degodia clans left 95 people dead and 17,000 displaced.

The second type of conflict in Mandera County is terror group conflict, which became a serious problem after the fall of the Islamic Courts Union in Somalia in 2006. It is an increasing issue on the Kenyan side of the border because Somalia-based terror groups have begun to target Kenyan sites and security forces in response to the Kenyan military's intervention Operation Linda Nchi in Somalia in 2011 (Lind et al., 2017). This type of conflict does have religious dimensions and attacks in Mandera County are targeted towards Christian Kenyans. Groups such as Al-Shabaab operate across the entire triangle border region (Somalia–Kenya–Ethiopia) and clan conflict is at times intertwined with terror groups in complex ways. Both types of conflict are very much cross-border, transnational conflicts with networks and linkages extending all the way to the port of Mogadishu and Nairobi.

Islamic Relief's conflict prevention and peacebuilding project aimed to address the underlying context of insecurity as well as more proximate causes of inter-clan conflict. It did not seek to address terror group conflict directly, as Islamic Relief believed that this was beyond their mandate and too dangerous to get involved in without extensive security management systems.

The target groups for the ongoing project are youth and women, the groups marginalized from formal political and traditional conflict management structures. The project incorporates a blend of livelihood activities for women and youth to address their economic disenfranchisement, which is a contributing factor in youth recruitment into armed groups. It also implements a range of conflict prevention or peacebuilding activities, including mixed-team sports tournaments combined with public peace messaging, support to clan dispute resolution dialogues, and support to women's peace groups and youth peace groups. The women's peace group set up a conflict early warning mechanism in the county using WhatsApp; this has become a thriving and successful locally owned peace structure. One of the benefits of the mechanism is that Somali women with low levels of literacy can record and listen to voice messages on the WhatsApp group. The project has also helped build a hybrid network between community and government stakeholders to assist peace management.

One activity that is particularly popular is the radio talk shows that Islamic Relief has set up. Somali people have a strong oral tradition and listening to the radio is very popular. Islamic Relief Kenya has set up (and pays for) a series of monthly radio talk shows with Star FM (a local station) that focus on particular relevant conflict issues. For example, if there is mass pastoral movement from the Kenyan to the Somalia side of the border,

(Continued)

Box 9.2 Continued

due to drought in Kenya, then a radio session will focus on this issue, bringing in clan leaders to inform people about the arrangements that have been agreed between them for the pastoralist movement. Or if a violent incident between clan members might escalate, then participants will be invited who can appeal for a de-escalation of tension, provide insight, and reassure the community about the steps being taken to deal with the incident. Each session has around six speakers and always considers the balance of clan representation and linguistic (Somali and Oromifa) representation, so that discussion is not biased towards any one group.

Sometimes Islamic Relief has encouraged traditional and non-traditional religious leaders and scholars to participate in the radio programme. Traditional male religious leaders are an important moral authority in this region, but their messages are generally limited to Friday sermons in the mosque. Islamic Relief's peacebuilding specialists suggested that joining the radio talk show was the best way to support their peace messaging. The radio talk show now helps these religious leaders to reach a far larger audience across the widely dispersed pastoral communities in Mandera with their theological peace messages.

Female Islamic scholars are emerging as an important form of non-traditional religious leadership in Mandera County. Islamic Relief has worked with talented female Islamic scholars and *madrasa* teachers who are participants in a peace advocacy campaign organized by Islamic Relief and Mandera Women for Peace (a local community-based organization). Islamic Relief invited them to discuss a range of local peace and conflict issues and women's rights issues on the radio talk show.

The context and gender analysis conducted by the peacebuilding project in Mandera revealed a history of strong women's leadership in peacebuilding, and so supporting female peacebuilders and religious scholars was not too contentious. Despite young people having been highly vulnerable to violence (both as perpetrators and as victims), there has been much less history of youth involvement in peacebuilding in Mandera County. However, there was widespread recognition among the project communities that marginalized youth pose a serious threat to social order. Dialogues with clan leaders and local faith actors revealed a willingness to open up traditional clan dialogue and *shura* (consultation) processes to the youth cohort in order to address their social and political marginalization, which Islamic Relief was able to facilitate.

The religious leaders, scholars, and teachers involved in this project are a type of tradition- and faith-oriented insider mediator (TFIM). Through the radio talk show, their traditional sermons in the mosque, and their *madrasa* teaching, they use Islamic theology to address local conflict issues. They are also attempting to change local behaviour patterns towards a culture of peace and respect for customary and formal dispute resolution mechanisms, rather than a culture of using firearms to settle grievances. They provide spiritual guidance, moral authority, and trust in legal processes, to which they are also trusted witnesses at times. Beyond the radio programme, they also provide the spiritual guidance and public rituals to aid reconciliation. For example, in inter-clan dispute resolution meetings, public prayer acts as an oath of commitment to the peace agreement. Prayer can also assist peacebuilding by providing a break or spiritual nourishment when peace dialogues become stuck, or by helping build 'inner peace' within oneself while publicly working on outer peace (Abdi and Mason, 2019).

Islamic Relief's work in Kenya aims to support both traditional and informal faith leaders in these types of peacebuilding practices. The radio talk show is still running, and although it has not yet been part of formal evaluation, project monitoring and community feedback have found that it is popular across the triangle border region where the Somali pastoralists roam and that it appears to be having a positive impact on preventing conflict and reducing inter-clan tensions.

Box 9.3 Islamic Relief's community conflict resolution and reconciliation in Darfur

In 2012, Islamic Relief was awarded funding by the UN Development Programme (UNDP) Darfur Community Peace and Stability Fund to implement a community conflict resolution project. This two-year project engaged with representatives from the non-Arab pastoralists, Arab farmers, internally displaced persons (IDPs), and local religious leaders or imams to rebuild broken community conflict resolution and reconciliation structures. The project considered the needs of IDPs, nomadic communities, and host communities in El Geneina and Kreinik localities in West Darfur. While the vast majority of people in these areas were Muslim, inter-ethnic conflict tended to occur over the use of scarce water and pasture between Arab farmers and non-Arab pastoralists, pastoralist encroachment onto farmland, and a lack of grazing areas. Conflicts were also being reported between IDPs and host communities, due to the perception that IDPs were given preferential assistance to acquire drinking water by humanitarian organizations, while the host communities, who were also very poor, received little outside help. The health centre constructed by Islamic Relief in the IDP camp had been torched twice and donors were fatigued with the situation. Furthermore, previous efforts to involve host communities in the long-term management of the NGO-funded water hand pumps and boreholes had failed, making it difficult for NGOs to exit the area and work with more vulnerable populations elsewhere.

Like the project in Kenya, this programme integrated development and peacebuilding activities, which in this case comprised Water and Sanitation for Health (WASH), health, education, livelihoods, and conflict resolution and reconciliation. The project aimed to establish community reconciliation committees that would also develop community plans, based on needs identified by the community. These committees were also trained in peacebuilding skills by the head of the peacebuilding research centre at the University of El Fasher in North Darfur and colleagues from the University of Zalingei in Central Darfur. Part of the training (which Islamic Relief staff also attended) covered 'Conflict Transformation from an Islamic Perspective'; this was delivered by a highly respected local *sheikh* (leader) over three days.

The community plans formed the basis for community interaction with formal government and NGOs such as Islamic Relief, which helped meet the identified needs. Meanwhile, the reconciliation committees were trained to solve disputes according to customary law before passing on any unresolvable cases to the local police. This was accompanied by peace education programmes in schools. An integrated approach, which provided water, healthcare, and school structures to all communities in the area, along with these 'softer' peacebuilding activities, worked particularly well. For example, when mobile health teams went out into the rural areas to provide healthcare to remote communities, people from pastoralist and non-pastoralist communities congregated around the mobile health clinic to engage in dialogue. Or when women went to fetch water for domestic use, instead of having to walk long distances (which puts them at risk of attack and an escalating cycle of violence) and wait in line for hours (which had previously prompted fights among the women), the additional boreholes and solar-powered pumps made it a much quicker, more peaceful task and freed up time for women to engage in other activities.

When it was evaluated after one year, there had been no further community disputes leading to violence or arson since the start of the project. One of the important factors in the success of the project in West Darfur was reportedly the work of the local imams. These were highly respected customary leaders who played a crucial role in conflict prevention, dispute resolution, and dispensing justice. The combination of theologically rooted guidance together with their moral authority, skill, and legitimacy makes local faith leaders well equipped to be effective peacebuilders. Islamic Relief staff were able to reach out to these religious leaders in a way that secular organizations probably could

---

(Continued)

> **Box 9.3** Continued
>
> not have done. Initially, Islamic Relief was not wholly trusted as it was assumed to be allied with the Sudanese government; however, the organization built trust and members of the Muslim community reported that they felt that Islamic Relief understood its cultural values and needs well. Islamic Relief's staff were also able to capitalize on their social capital within the community to advocate for gender justice with the reconciliation committees and the imams.

Figure 9.1 Singing for peace in schools in West Darfur
Source: Islamic Relief.

Box 9.4 Islamic Relief's conflict transformation and peacebuilding programme in Yemen

Although this project was implemented six years before the publication of Islamic Relief Worldwide's *Understanding an Islamic Framework for Peacebuilding* (Kadayifci-Orellana et al., 2016), it is included because it was the pioneering project that shaped the conversation in Islamic Relief about the gap in Islamic approaches to peacebuilding by INGOs. It is also a good example of how an Islamic FBO can engage in peacebuilding work within a very sensitive context where INGOs are regarded with deep suspicion.

The conflict transformation and peacebuilding programme in Yemen was funded jointly by the UK's Department for International Development and the Dutch government in 2007 and it aimed to build the conflict resolution skills of key stakeholders in the Sana'a, Saa'da, Lahj, and Aden governorates. These stakeholders included local and central government departments, tribal leaders, local councils, imams, students, female mediators, and NGO leaders. Although participants felt that the training should have been longer than three days, after receiving the intensive training in conflict resolution, 80 per cent of the 633 participants stated that they had utilized the skills they had developed in their work, resolving a wide array of disputes including land disputes, blood revenge/family disputes, industrial disputes, water disputes, health service disputes, education disputes, and religious disputes.

What was different about this peacebuilding training was that it contained explicit references to Islamic theology, which reportedly helped it to resonate more deeply among

(Continued)

Box 9.4 Continued

the Muslim participants. The training included Islamic views on violence, the importance of dialogue from an Islamic perspective, and a discussion of both the Universal Declaration of Human Rights and human rights according to Islam. Human rights according to Islam (*huquq*) share similar aspirations with the Universal Declaration of Human Rights in terms of improvements in the lives of individuals, but they are embedded in the 'perfection of one's self, reason, life, family and property' (Soliman, 2009). Like the Universal Declaration of Human Rights, they are applicable to everyone, regardless of race, colour, language, belief, sex, religion, political affiliation, social status, or any other consideration. The evaluation conducted by Islamic Relief stressed the value of this approach:

> Overwhelmingly the participants found the understanding and references from Islamic teachings helpful and in some cases crucial to altering people's behaviour and attitudes away from resorting to violent conflict and encouraging compassion and forgiveness. Faith in Islam is deeply rooted in Yemeni culture, although there is often inadequate understanding of faith teachings in relation to harming others and human rights. Teachings from Imams have not always emphasized the principles of seeking peaceful resolution of conflict at a national and international level. Several Imams said that they had integrated the knowledge gained into their preaching as well as in their resolving conflict. (FitzGibbon, 2009: 14)

The evaluation of this project also suggested that there was much more that could be done in using Islamic theology and jurisprudence to advocate for greater respect for human rights, constitutional democracy, and peaceful conflict resolution, which encourages further development of this programme (either in Yemen or elsewhere) (FitzGibbon, 2009: 15). Given the descent into war in Yemen in the years following this programme, despite the best efforts of the peacebuilders who were supported through this intervention, there is arguably an even greater need for this kind of intervention in Yemen now.

The value of an FBO in this case was its ability to use authentic faith-based references to translate the technical language of Western-based peacebuilding tools into a language that resonated more closely with Yemeni stakeholders' Islamic values. In Yemen in particular, the influence of highly conservative Saudi Salafi teachings was a major barrier to organizations seeking to improve basic human rights in the country. People whose vested interests were perceived to be under threat were broadcasting a counterargument that 'the real interests of those working for greater rights is to undermine the religious values of the Muslim community and create moral disintegration and social instability' (FitzGibbon, 2009: 15). The evaluator of this programme in Yemen stated that, in his opinion, a Muslim organization can much more effectively undermine these claims than a secular organization (ibid.).

Religion can act as a source of tension between people as well as a source of peace (Trotta and Wilkinson, 2019). The practice of Islam is very closely intertwined with local cultural norms and traditions and these vary significantly between subnational regions, even from village to village in some places. These differences can be very sensitive, to the point that Muslim national staff from one region of a country may feel quite unfamiliar with cultural and Islamic practices in another region. Therefore, humility and sensitivity to cultural differences are essential attributes for staff working on peacebuilding programmes.

Second, since a faith organization such as Islamic Relief is an outsider in the contexts in which it works, it brings new ideas to communities. Research evidence suggests that a '*cultural proximity*' syndrome persists among Muslim communities, in that they believe that FBOs, and specifically Muslim NGOs, 'can more efficiently and successfully work among Muslim populations' than their secular counterparts (El Karhili and Jassem, 2018). This cultural proximity has meant that local communities and local faith actors have been willing to consider the new ideas or alternative perspectives that Islamic Relief staff bring to communities. One example of this was in Islamic Relief's peacebuilding programme in Yemen. In Yemen in 2007, there was intense condemnation of the promotion of what was thought to be 'Western' human rights by Saudi Salafi teachings, but because Islamic Relief Yemen was perceived to be culturally close to Muslim communities, the organization found itself in a position to promote greater respect for human rights where others could not.

An FBO such as Islamic Relief can also capitalize on a trusted partnership developed with local faith actors and local communities to translate the language of secular human rights into a more locally acceptable equivalent. For example, while Islamic Relief staff work to help local communities achieve the SDGs, they frame their peacebuilding work in language that resonates more meaningfully with those communities, such as the language of the Islamic faith. In effect, Islamic Relief member organizations act as 'brokers'[7] between the world views of local Muslim communities and international norms agreed among aid, development, and peacebuilding agencies.

Third, an FBO can mobilize external financial resources to support the practicalities of conflict prevention and peacebuilding, while simultaneously mitigating concerns about the ulterior motives of foreign donors. When funding is mobilized through *zakat* donations (the provision of alms), the nature of the donation is well understood by Muslim communities. But when funding comes from foreign donors (whether governmental or private), it can be viewed with intense suspicion. As Kirmani et al. (2008: 10) argue: '[M]any secular or Christian FBOs and donor agencies are at times viewed with suspicion and are often themselves fearful of working in Muslim areas, due to hostility stemming from religious, ethnic or political issues.' These suspicions are often centred on the ulterior motives of the donor, the suspicion that financial power will be used to interfere in local affairs, and concerns about 'neo-colonialism' of Muslim societies by Western INGOs with roots in Christian philosophy. Although the funding for the conflict prevention and peacebuilding project in Kenya came from the Swedish government, the fact that it was channelled through a Muslim organization appeared to help alleviate these concerns within the local community to some extent.

While there are some clear strengths and opportunities for the delivery of a peacebuilding programme through a Muslim FBO there are also a number of challenges or dilemmas. First, trust and access to communities are not automatic – they take time and extensive consultation to build, and project durations need to be lengthy to allow this to take place. Depending on the nature of government in each context (whether peacebuilding is a devolved or centrally managed activity, for example), it may be necessary to build relationships at both a subnational and a national level. In our experience at Islamic

Relief, it is often easier to build trust at a local level with local government officials, members of the security forces, and communities than it is to build trust at a national level. This is because local-level actors are present and involved in community consultations conducted by Islamic Relief staff.

At the local level, Islamic Relief's country offices work jointly and transparently with local government and customary governance actors (e.g. *Jirga*[8] or clan leaders) on peacebuilding programmes, to prevent any misunderstanding. In our experience, we have found that there is a reasonably shared understanding of the context and a willingness from both local government and customary leaders to try new things and welcome outside support from Islamic Relief. However, where conflict has religious overtones – especially conflicts involving radical Islam – there is sometimes a wariness among communities about the nature of Islamic Relief and staff need to work extra hard to explain the organization's principles of neutrality.

National government departments often have very different, even contradictory considerations compared with those of their local counterparts. Some national government departments view peacebuilding through a militarized lens, preferring military solutions and viewing INGO involvement with intense suspicion. National government officials may also be more sensitive about the actions of Islamic-inspired organizations, worrying that they will incite religious protest, aggravate religious divisions, or be a front for political Islam.

Second, maintaining neutrality in engagement is challenging. While Islamic Relief wishes to remain neutral and unbiased in its peacebuilding support to communities it must consider its own reputational risk and abide by domestic and international laws such as counterterrorism legislation. As a result, some actors are inevitably left out of community engagement – often the actors with the most polarizing viewpoints who are probably the actors who most need to be engaged in peacebuilding. As Islamic Relief has stated elsewhere, possible challenges to engaging with local faith actors include the risks of proselytization, discrimination based on gender, ethnicity, or religious beliefs, and links to violent groups (LWF and IRW, 2018). This is something that Islamic Relief has to be constantly aware of in its choice of partners.

There is also a tension between engagement and legitimization. The support the organization provides, such as radio time, legitimizes some actors over others in the community, which has an effect on the dynamics of conflict and peace. To manage this dilemma and help staff make choices based on the best available information at the time, Islamic Relief prioritizes context sensitivity. A context-sensitive approach allows staff to better judge the possible implications of their choices and monitor the effects of their action on the context. For example, it enabled staff in Mandera, Kenya, to see that it was important to give equal time and space to representatives of all the different clans and language groups to talk on the radio programme.

There is also a neutrality dilemma regarding the provision of support to state-building processes and the strengthening of state institutions in response to borderland insecurities. In these contexts, attempts to replace customary governance institutions with state-based ones are often major drivers of violence (Plonski and Yousuf, 2017). To address this dilemma, Islamic Relief works only in contexts where local government actors and customary governance providers have already agreed to jointly prevent conflict and build peace. While this may be perceived as providing a 'peace dividend' to customary actors who have submitted to the will of the central state, the practical limitations of Islamic Relief's global work prevent it from engaging in peacebuilding programmes with actors who are in armed conflict with state forces.

Third, it is a challenge to develop peacebuilding programmes that are scalable and replicable elsewhere, because the dynamics of conflict are unique to the local context – and this implies a need for very locally specific solutions. As Westendorf (2015: 5) argues, for peacebuilding efforts to be successful they have to be 'custom-designed to suit the specific functions of the process, the context in which it operates, and the needs of the local population'. Islamic Relief is still testing its organizational approach to peacebuilding programming. It has not yet developed a clear framework of religiously informed strategies that can be applied across multiple contexts. It is also unsure how far to take a theologically driven model of peacebuilding. As Woocher (2011) points out, conflicts emerge and escalate based on an incredible diversity of local contexts and conditions. Islamic Relief is cognisant that in most, if not all, places, Islamic Relief staff (either at international level, country level, or subnational level) are not best placed to advise local community and faith leaders on particular religious texts to invoke, or the conflict resolution strategies to deploy, based on the situation at the time. Doing so would easily invite accusations of heresy or neo-colonialism. Instead, Islamic Relief currently takes the approach advocated by Gopin (2000, quoted in Silvestri and Mayall, 2015) of working with faith and other community leaders as partners, rather than seeking to impose a particular view from above, however religiously educated it might be.

Conclusion

This chapter has sought to highlight the conceptual approach and peace-building practice of a Muslim FBO, Islamic Relief, in order to widen understandings of peacebuilding beyond secular, technocratic approaches and Christian-based philosophies. As Bouta et al. (2005) argue, there is not one Islamic tradition of peace and peace-making traditions; there are various different approaches in the Muslim world representing the diversity of lived experiences of Islam. Yet in many of the remote and conflict-affected places where Islamic Relief works, there is a lack of knowledge and understanding about Islamic texts and a misunderstanding that Islam is incompatible with 'Western' political structures and universal norms of human rights. Thus, while we see that there is a challenge in developing scalable and replicable peacebuilding programmes because the dynamics of a conflict are unique to the local context, we also see that there is more that could be done in terms of using Islamic theology and jurisprudence to advocate for greater respect for human rights, constitutional democracy, and peaceful conflict resolution. A faith-based INGO such as Islamic Relief effectively straddles two worlds: the world of international development, with its SDGs and human rights norms, and the world of local Muslim communities and customary structures where Islam is intertwined with governance, peace, and conflict. It is therefore in a unique position to marry the two, but it has to be mindful of being associated with perceived Western hegemonic agendas.

As a trusted third party, Islamic Relief occasionally acts as a witness to local peace agreements. It also acts as a broker of meaning between local communities and state actors, helping to strengthen state–society relations to improve security and address some of the underlying causes of conflict in fragile places (such as poor governance and the lack of basic services). The 'brokerage' role of NGOs, community leaders, and other actors who move between different worlds and translate their languages is currently receiving significant scholarly interest (see Meehan and Plonski, 2017).

Islamic Relief is still developing its experience and organizational thinking around how to support local Muslim communities in fragile contexts to transform into relatively just societies with stronger mechanisms for preventing and managing conflict. The case studies demonstrate that Islamic Relief has chosen to engage in peacebuilding only in conflicts in Muslim-majority countries that do not have strong religious dimensions. It also engages with customary conflict resolution processes only where customary and formal governance actors have agreed a hybrid model of governance. As yet it has little experience in peacebuilding where conflicts contain religious dimensions, although there is some interest in the organization in engaging in inter-faith peacebuilding work in collaboration with Christian INGOs. Islamic Relief's convening power as a trusted third party to Muslim communities may be its most valuable asset in this work, but it would need careful thought and preparation.

Until now, explicit consideration of how to work with local faith actors on peacebuilding has been absent from discussions (Trotta and Wilkinson, 2019). This chapter seeks to remedy this gap in knowledge by highlighting the practical experience and conceptual background of Islamic Relief's peace-building work. However, there is still a need for more rigorous evaluation of Islamic Relief's peacebuilding programmes to give more weight to these preliminary findings.

Notes

1. See <https://www.agendaforhumanity.org/cr/1>.
2. 'Purchasing power parity' is a currency exchange rate that buys exactly the same basket of goods in each currency, thereby eliminating disparities caused by exchange rates on global money markets.

3.   Leaders of major world faiths met at Lambeth Palace in London in February 1998 and in Washington DC in November 1999, which led to the creation of World Faiths Development Dialogue (WFDD), now based out of Georgetown University's Berkley Center for Religion, Peace and World Affairs.
4.   Islamic Relief Worldwide's Gender Justice Policy is available at <https://www.islamic-relief.org/gender-justice>.
5.   For example, in the postcolonial era, collective punishment has been an enduring feature of Kenyan 'securitization' of its Somali-majority regions in Mandera, Wajir, and Garissa counties, which became especially brutal during and immediately after the Shifta War (Lind et al., 2017).
6.   See the following examples of Islamic Relief Worldwide (IRW) publications: *An Islamic Human Rights Perspective on Early and Forced Marriages*; *One Cut Too Many: Islamic Relief Policy Brief on Female Genital Mutilation/ Cutting (FGM/C)*; *The Rights of Forced Migrants in Islam*; and *Gender Justice*. They are all available on the IRW website at <https://www.islamic-relief. org/publications/>.
7.   According to Meehan and Plonski (2017: 2), 'brokers' are 'network specialists' whose ability to straddle multiple knowledge systems and life worlds enables them to act as gatekeepers who transmit or interpret messages across these spaces.
8.   A *Jirga* is a customary tribal governance system used by Pashtun tribes in Pakistan and Afghanistan.

References

Abdi, D.I. and Mason, S.J. (2019) *Mediation and Governance in Fragile Contexts*, Kumarian Press, Boulder CA and London.

Abu-Nimer, M. (2001) 'A framework for nonviolence and peacebuilding in Islam', *Journal of Law and Religion* XV: 217–65.

Aroua, A. (2013) *The Quest for Peace in the Islamic Tradition*, Kolofon Press, Oslo.

Baumann, J., Finnbogason, D. and Svensson, I. (2018) 'Rethinking mediation: resolving religious conflicts', *Policy Perspectives* 6/1, Center for Security Studies (CSS), ETH Zurich, Zurich.

Bouta, T., Kadayifci-Orellana, S.A. and Abu-Nimer, M. (2005) *Faith-based Peacebuilding: Mapping and Analysis of Christian, Muslim and Multi-faith Actors*, Netherlands Institute of International Relations Clingendael and Salam Institute for Peace and Justice, The Hague and Washington DC.

Bradley, T. (2009) 'A call for clarification and critical analysis of the work of faith-based development organisations (FBDOs)', *Progress in Development Studies* 9 (2): 101–14.

El Karhili, N.E. and Jassem, M.H. (2018) 'Muslim NGOs and sectarianization', *Maydan*, 30 November <https://www.themaydan.com/2018/11/muslim-ngos-sectarianization/>.

FitzGibbon, A. (2009) *Final Project Evaluation Report: Conflict Transformation and Peace Building Project. Sana'a, Saa'da, Lahj and Aden Governorates, Yemen*, Islamic Relief Worldwide, Birmingham.

Galtung, J. (1976) 'Three approaches to peace: peacekeeping, peacemaking, and peacebuilding', in J. Galtung, *Peace, War and Defense: Essays in Peace Research*, Volume 2, pp. 282–304, Ejlers, Copenhagen.

Hayward, D.J. (2011) *Qur'anic Concepts of the Ethics of Warfare: Challenging the Claims of Islamic Aggressiveness*, Cordoba Foundation, London.

HPCR (2019) 'Peacebuilding initiative', Program on Humanitarian Policy and Conflict Research (HPCR), Harvard University, Harvard, Cambridge MA <http://www.peacebuildinginitiative.org/index34ac.html> [accessed 16 April 2019].

IDLO (2019) *Navigating Complex Pathways to Justice: Engagement with Customary and Informal Justice Systems*, International Development Law Organization (IDLO), Rome.

IEP (2018) *Global Peace Index 2018: Measuring Peace in a Complex World*, Institute for Economics and Peace (IEP), Sydney <http://visionofhumanity.org/reports>.

Kadayifci-Orellana, S.A., Abu-Nimer, M. and Mohammed-Saleem, A. (2016) *Understanding an Islamic Framework for Peacebuilding*, Islamic Relief Worldwide, Birmingham <http://library.iracademy.org.uk/understanding-an-islamic-framework-for-peacebuilding/>.

Kirmani, N., Khan, A.A. and Palmer, V. (2008) *Does Faith Matter?: An Examination of Islamic Relief's Work with Refugees and Internally Displaced Persons*, Islamic Relief Worldwide, Birmingham.

Lederach, J.P. (1997) *Building Peace: Sustainable Reconciliation in Divided Societies*, Institute of Peace Press, Washington DC.

Lind, J., Mutahi, P. and Oosterom, M. (2017) '"Killing a mosquito with a hammer": Al-Shabaab violence and state security responses in Kenya', *Peacebuilding* 5 (2): 118–35.

Little, D. (2005) *Proceedings of the Workshop Religion, Politics, Conflict and Humanitarian Action Faith-based Organisations as Political, Humanitarian or Religious Actors*, Graduate Institute of International Studies, Geneva.

LWF and IRW (2018) *A Faith-sensitive Approach in Humanitarian Response: Guidance on Mental Health and Psychosocial Programming*, Lutheran World Federation (LWF) and Islamic Relief Worldwide (IRW), Geneva and Birmingham.

Marshall, K. and Saanen, M.V. (2007) *Development and Faith: Where Mind, Heart and Soul Work Together*, World Bank Publications, Washington DC.

Meehan, P. and Plonski, P. (2017) 'Brokering the margins: a review of concepts and methods', Working Paper 1, 'Borderlands, Brokers and Peacebuilding in Sri Lanka and Nepal: War to Peace Transitions Viewed from the Margins' project, SOAS and University of Bath <https://eprints.soas.ac.uk/25820/1/1488349944_BROKERING%20THE%20MARGINS%20-%20Patrick%2BMeehan%20and%20Sharri%20Plonski%20February%202017.pdf> [accessed 24th June 2020].

Mir, M. and Vimalarajah, L. (2016) *Tradition- and Faith-oriented Insider Mediators (TFIMs) as Crucial Actors in Conflict Transformation: Potential, Constraints and Opportunities for Collaborative Support*, Network for Religious and Traditional Peacemakers, Helsinki.

Mufti, S.I. (2014) 'Peacebuilding and conflict resolution in Islam', Islamicity.org, 12 November <https://www.islamicity.org/6351/peacebuilding-and-conflict-resolution-in-islam/> [accessed 24th June 2020].

Plonski, S. and Yousuf, Z. (2017) 'Bringing in the margins: peacebuilding and transition in borderlands', Political Settlements Research Programme (PSRP) Report, Conciliation Resources, London.

Salek, L. (2014). *Working in Conflict: A Faith-based Toolkit for Islamic Relief,* Islamic Relief Worldwide, Birmingham.

Schafer, H. (2018) 'The drivers of conflict: where climate, gender and infrastructure intersect', World Bank Blogs, 5 March <http://blogs.worldbank.org/dev4peace/drivers-conflict-where-climate-gender-and-infrastructure-intersect> [accessed 24th June 2020].

Silvestri, S. and Mayall, J. (2015) *The Role of Religion in Conflict and Peacebuilding,* British Academy, London.

Soliman, H. (2009) 'The potential for peacebuilding in Islam: toward an Islamic concept of peace', *Journal of Religion, Conflict, and Peace* 2 (2).

Trotta, S. and Wilkinson, O. (2019) *Partnering with Local Faith Actors to Support Peaceful and Inclusive Societies,* Joint Learning Initiative on Faith and Local Communities and International Partnership on Religion and Sustainable Development (PaRD), Washington DC and Bonn.

UN (2016) *Agenda for Humanity: Annex to the Report of the Secretary-General for the World Humanitarian Summit,* United Nations (UN), New York <https://agendaforhumanity.org/sites/default/files/AgendaforHumanity.pdf> [accessed 29 May 2019].

UN (2019) 'Sustainable Development Goals', United Nations (UN), New York <https://www.un.org/sustainabledevelopment/sustainable-development-goals/>.

Westendorf, J.-K. (2015) *Why Peace Processes Fail: Negotiating Insecurity after Civil War,* Lynne Rienner, Boulder CO.

Woocher, L. (2011) *Conflict Assessment and Intelligence Analysis: Commonality, Convergence, and Complementarity,* United States Institute of Peace, Washington DC.

Zoli, C., Bassiouni, M.C. and Khan, H. (2017) 'Justice in post-conflict settings: Islamic law and Muslim communities as stakeholders in transition', *Utrecht Journal of International and European Law* 33 (85): 38–61.

About the authors

Sylvia Brown is Conflict Advisor at Islamic Relief Worldwide. She has an MA in International Development, specializing in poverty, conflict, and reconstruction, and a PhD in Development Studies, focusing on youth participation in armed opposition groups in Myanmar's borderlands. Sylvia has experience of governance, refugee, development, human rights, peacebuilding, and borderland issues in Myanmar, Pakistan, Kenya, Indonesia, and the Philippines and has worked with civil society organizations, INGOs and the UN. She is also an experienced management consultant, specializing in local government reform in the UK.

Haroon Kash is currently the Head of Programme Funding at Islamic Relief Worldwide and has extensive experience of working in the international development sector on both humanitarian and development initiatives. He has a particular interest in and has recognized the need for and importance of faith-based programme interventions.

CHAPTER 10

Walking gently on the Earth: Islamic environmentalism and Muslim FBOs

Ajaz Ahmed Khan and J.R.A. Williams

Islam entrusts humankind with a sacred responsibility to protect and conserve the environment for present and future generations. This chapter outlines the major Islamic environmental principles and assesses the extent to which these influence the activities of British Muslim faith-based humanitarian aid and development organizations. It concludes that, despite the strong Islamic environmental ethic, environment-related programmes and advocacy are not generally prominent among their activities. Nevertheless, there is increasing recognition that referencing Islamic environmental teachings may be an effective method to stimulate individual consciences and motivate behavioural changes among Muslim populations to address issues such as land degradation, deforestation, and climate change.

Keywords: Islam, environment, stewardship, climate change, Muslim faith-based organizations

Introduction

There is a strong environmental ethic in Islamic teachings that emphasizes a respect for creation and a command to maintain the natural balance. Islam entrusts humankind with a sacred responsibility to protect and conserve the environment. There are numerous verses in the *Qur'an*[1] and the words and actions of the Prophet Muhammad (Peace Be Upon Him) that praise the natural world, describing the relationship between man and nature, including plants and animals and their environment (Izzi Dien, 2000; Khalid, 2002; Abdul-Matin, 2012; Manoiu et al., 2016; Aboul-Enein, 2018). In fact, Islam considers the creation of the environment to be greater than that of humankind. The *Qur'an* (40: 57) states: 'The creation of the Heavens and the Earth is greater by far than the creation of mankind; though most people do not know it.' Recognizing the important role of religious beliefs in promoting moral codes of conduct and the potential of faith communities and faith-based organizations (FBOs) to promote environmental stewardship, the United Nations Environment Programme (UNEP) launched the Faith for Earth initiative in 2017 and declared: 'Tapping into the spiritual wealth of people and their beliefs accelerates people's engagement and their organizational

http://dx.doi.org/10.3362/9781788530613.010

drive to contribute.'[2] In a similar vein, the renowned Islamic philosopher Seyyed Hossain Nasr has developed an 'Islamic' environmentalism (Hancock, 2018), which argues that 'reawakening a sacred concern for nature is required to halt global environmental degradation' (Nasr, 2015).

Recent research highlights the extent of environmental degradation and its adverse impacts, particularly on people living in poverty. According to the Intergovernmental Science-Policy Platform on Biodiversity and Ecosystem Services (IPBES, 2019), nature is declining globally at unprecedented rates. Around 1 million animal and plant species are now threatened with extinction, many within decades, more than ever before in human history. Since the beginning of the twentieth century the average abundance of native species in most major land-based habitats has fallen by at least 20 per cent. More than 40 per cent of amphibian species, almost one-third of reef-forming corals, more than one-third of all marine mammals, and 10 per cent of insect species are also threatened (ibid.). Furthermore, an estimated 18.7 million acres of forests are lost annually through deforestation. The main causes are clearing land for agriculture or grazing,[3] or to use the timber for fuel, construction, or manufacturing. Deforestation impacts on both people and animals. Some 250 million people living in forests and savannah areas depend on forests for their livelihoods (FAO, 2018), and 80 per cent of the world's animals and plants live in forests.[4] One-third of the Earth's land is severely degraded and 24 billion tonnes of fertile soil are being lost each year due to soil erosion (UNCCD, 2017). More than 90 per cent of people worldwide live in areas that do not meet the World Health Organization's (WHO's) standards for healthy air and air pollution is the fifth leading risk factor for mortality worldwide (Health Effects Institute, 2019). Globally, one in three people do not have access to safe drinking water and more than half of the world does not have access to safe sanitation services (WHO and UNICEF, 2019).

Climate change is adversely impacting the livelihoods of poor people around the world as unpredictable seasons, rising sea levels, and erratic rainfall contribute to floods, droughts, and poor crop yields (IPCC, 2018). At the same time, efforts to meet commitments to limit global warming are not being fulfilled. The World Economic Forum (2020) reports that the most pressing threats to the world all relate to the environment. They include extreme weather events, failure to mitigate and adapt to climate change, natural hazards, biodiversity loss, and human-made environmental disasters. The same report states:

> global temperatures are on track to increase by at least 3°C towards the end of the century – twice what climate experts have warned is the limit to avoid the most severe economic, social and environmental consequences. The near-term impacts of climate change add up to a planetary emergency that will include loss of life, social and geopolitical tensions and negative economic impacts. (World Economic Forum, 2020: 6)

Despite the prominence accorded to the environment in Islam and the adverse impacts of environmental degradation on the poor, environment-related programmes and advocacy comprise only a relatively small proportion of the activities of Muslim FBOs[5] in the UK. This chapter examines the reasons for this and specifically some of the efforts made by Muslim FBOs to incorporate Islamic teachings into their environment-related programmes. We first begin by describing the key Islamic environmental principles.

Islamic environmental principles

The most important principle in Islam is *tawhid*, or the unity of God. This affects every component of Islam, including environmental ethics. *Tawhid* means that God is the owner and creator of everything in the universe and that creation is a unified, complete, and interdependent whole. The *Qur'an* (4: 126) states: 'It is to God that everything in the Heavens and Earth belongs: God is fully aware of all things.' Furthermore, God's creation obeys His rules, or 'laws of nature', and this maintains perfect balance and measure. The *Qur'an* (54: 49) says: 'We have created all things in due measure.' Humankind, who has been given free will, is instructed not to disrupt this balance: 'He has raised up the sky. He has set the balance, so that you may not exceed the balance: weigh with justice and do not fall short in the balance' (*Qur'an*, 55: 7–9). As Khalid (2005) observes, Islam considers the natural world to be held together because it is in a state of dynamic balance or *mizan*. In several verses of the *Qur'an*, creations are described as a sign, or *ayat*, of God. For example, 'There are signs in the Heavens and the Earth for those who believe' (*Qur'an*, 45: 3); and 'Another of His signs is the creation of the Heavens and Earth, and the diversity of your languages and colours. There truly are signs in this for those who know' (*Qur'an*, 30: 22). Therefore, exploitation of, damage to, and pollution of the natural world are tantamount not only to upsetting the natural balance but also to destroying the signs of God.

The Prophet Muhammad (PBUH) considered all of God's creations to be equal before God and he believed that not only animals and insects but also trees and rivers, stones and mountains have rights. Therefore, abusing one of God's creations, whether it is a living being or a natural resource, is a sin. In fact, Islam considers that animals are communities like human beings and have similar rights: 'all of the creatures that crawl on the Earth and those that fly with their wings are communities like yourselves' (*Qur'an*, 6: 38); and 'the Earth, He has assigned it to all living creatures' (*Qur'an*, 55: 10).[6] There are numerous verses in the *Qur'an* as well as a rich tradition in the *Sunnah*[7] highlighting the importance of animal welfare. This leads Abdul Rahman (2017: 2) to conclude: 'Animals are seen to have their own lives and purpose, valuable to themselves and to Allah above and beyond any material value they may provide to humanity.' The Prophet Muhammad (PBUH) stressed the importance of caring for animals when asked 'Is there a reward for us in serving the animals?' He said, 'Yes, there is a reward for serving any animate [living being]' (Bukhari, Book 78, *Hadith* 40).[8]

Another important principle guiding Islamic teachings on the environment is that humankind has been entrusted with the trusteeship, or *khalifah*, of the

Earth. The *Qur'an* (6: 165) says: 'It is He (God) who has made you successors on the Earth.' As such, Islam considers that humankind will be held accountable for its treatment of the Earth and all living species. Trusteeship involves preserving the environment for the benefit of present and future generations.[9] An often quoted *hadith* states: 'The world is beautiful and verdant, and verily God, be He exalted, has made you His stewards in it, and He sees how you acquit yourselves' (Muslim, Book 49, *Hadith* 12). At the same time, according to Islamic law, the basic elements of nature – land, water, air, fire, forests, and sunlight – belong to all living things, not just human beings.

While Islam encourages humankind to make use of natural resources, this should be in a sustainable manner, without inflicting harm on other creatures or the environment or disrupting the ecological balance. In this regard, it has been argued that the prophetic declaration 'There should be neither harming nor reciprocating harm' (Ibn Majah, Book 12, *Hadith* 33) and the key Islamic legal principle that 'averting harm takes precedence over the acquisition of benefits' are of immense significance in the relationship between humankind and nature, particularly in discussions regarding the impact of climate change (Parvaiz, 2005). Islam advocates living in harmony with the environment, moderation, avoiding excess and being wasteful, and respect for life in all its forms. Should humankind ignore its responsibility for safeguarding the natural world, the *Qur'an* (30: 41) warns that it will suffer the consequences associated with environmental degradation and overexploitation of natural resources.

Another major Islamic principle is moderation, or *wasatiyyah*. This principle advocates against waste and promotes the conservation of resources, even if they are in abundant supply. The *Qur'an* (6: 141) says, 'but do not be wasteful: God does not like wasteful people'. Even when carrying out the compulsory ritual cleansings in preparation for daily prayers, which is one of the five pillars of Islam, Muslims are encouraged to use the minimum amount of water.[10] This is illustrated by the following *hadith*: 'The Prophet Muhammad (PBUH) passed by Sa'd when he was performing ablution, and he said: "What is this extravagance?" He said: "Can there be any extravagance in ablution?" He said: "Yes, even if you are on the bank of a flowing river"' (Ibn Majah, Book 1, *Hadith* 460). In effect, Muslims are encouraged to avoid being wasteful even when there is an abundance of resources available.

To protect flora and fauna, the Prophet Muhammad (PBUH) established sacred areas, known as *haram* and *hima*, in which resources were protected. To promote sustainability, the areas surrounding wells and water sources, for example, were designated as *haram* to safeguard the water from pollution. *Hima* (or 'protected place') applied to wildlife and forestry and referred to an area of land where grazing and the felling of trees were restricted or where certain animals such as horses and camels were protected. Yazdani (2015) observes that the Prophet Muhammad (PBUH) established a *hima* south of the city of Medina in present-day Saudi Arabia, which prohibited hunting within a four-mile radius and harm to trees or plants within a 12-mile radius.

The prohibition on felling trees and hunting animals remains in place within the boundaries of the sacred cities of Mecca and Medina in Saudi Arabia. In recent years, in some Muslim-majority countries, there has been a revival of interest in the concept of *hima* to potentially protect natural resources and promote animal conservation (FAO, 2019). It is worth mentioning, as Khalid (2002: 2) points out that traditionally the environment was not an issue or subject for separate treatment in life; rather, it was intrinsically related to all aspects of life. He cites the example of Abu Bakr, the first caliph of Islam, who prohibited Muslims from cutting down trees or plants even in times of war. He instructed his armies: 'Do not drown or burn date-palm trees. Do not cut down a fruit bearing tree. Do not demolish a church. And do not kill any children or old people or women' (narrated by Al-Bayhaqi in Sunan Al Kubra 9: 85, *Hadith* 17904).

Finally, in this brief discussion of environmental principles, Islam attaches particular merit to planting trees, as highlighted, for example, in the following *hadith*: 'If the Final Hour comes while you have a palm cutting in your hands and it is possible to plant it before the Hour comes, you should plant it' (reported in Al-Adab Al-Mufrad by Imam Bukhari, Book 1, *Hadith* 479). In effect, the planting of the palm shoot is, in itself, a good deed, even if one does not anticipate any benefit from it. Islam also regards the planting of trees as a charitable act if a person or animal might subsequently benefit from it. The Prophet Muhammad (PBUH) said: 'There is none amongst the Muslims who plants a tree or sows seeds, and then a bird, or a person or an animal eats from it, but it is regarded as a charitable gift for him' (Bukhari, Book 41, *Hadith* 1); and also 'Whosoever plants a tree and it matures, Allah plants a tree in paradise for that person' (Ahmad bin Hanbal, Musnad, IV, 61).[11] More generally, Islam encourages the restoration of land, as underlined by the following *hadith*: 'Whoever revives a barren land, then it is for him' (Tirmidhi, Book 15, *Hadith* 60).

The environment programmes and advocacy activities of Muslim FBOs

Having described the main Islamic environmental principles and briefly outlined the extent of environmental degradation and its adverse impacts, particularly on people living in poverty, this section now examines the extent to which Muslim FBOs implement these principles in their environment-related programmes and advocacy, and whether and how they employ Islamic teachings for fundraising, promoting awareness, and implementing programmes.

Like other development organizations, all the leading Muslim FBOs[12] have committed themselves to aligning their 'policies, strategies and programmes with the Sustainable Development Goals'[13] (SDGs). The SDGs are the set of 17 agreed goals that were adopted by the 193 member states of the UN in September 2015 to fight poverty and promote sustainable development. Although they are all interconnected, six of the SDGs specifically address climate change, promoting the sustainable use of natural resources, and conserving and protecting the Earth's biodiversity.[14]

Specific programmes targeting the environment have not traditionally featured in the activities of Muslim FBOs, and most organizations continue to dedicate only a relatively small proportion of their budgets to environment-related initiatives. This is partly because Muslim FBOs, which are largely reliant on individual Muslim donors for financial support, consider that their donors would be less willing to fund such projects despite 'recognising the theological imperative to act as environmental stewards'.[15] Instead they focus on activities that are relatively easy to fundraise for such as sponsoring orphans, seasonal food distribution, and providing humanitarian aid in emergency situations.[16] As a senior staff member of one leading Muslim charity stated: 'Essentially our work reflects whatever is the easiest to fundraise for, rather than what is most needed.'[17] There is also some evidence that the importance of Islamic environmental ethics is not adequately communicated to British Muslims.[18] The senior programme director of another leading Muslim FBO remarked: 'We need to educate our supporters, from an Islamic perspective, on the importance of supporting environmental programmes in the same way we campaign for building mosques, providing food parcels during Ramadan and drilling boreholes to supply drinking water.'[19]

However there is some evidence that the situation is changing. Younger donors in particular are more willing to support environment-related activities, especially as issues such as climate change receive greater public attention.[20] The Muslim Action for Development and Environment (MADE) was established in 2009 to 'enable and empower young British Muslims to serve society and the environment through volunteering, fundraising and campaigning'.[21] On occasion, Muslim FBOs are being pushed to address environmental concerns in the countries where they work. As the chief executive of one leading Muslim FBO remarked: 'It is our field staff in countries such as Pakistan that are insisting that we become more involved in environment-related programmes, while in other countries it is local governments who are highlighting the issue.'[22]

A popular strategy used by Muslim FBOs to attract support and respond to need is promoting tree-planting campaigns by referencing the *Qur'an* and *ahadith*. For example, Human Appeal is working to:

> provide 545 farmers in Palestine with 40 olive trees each, allowing each farmer to restore one *dunum* [roughly one square kilometre] of land. Through this project, which benefits 5,190 people, we'll be planting 24,376 olive trees, providing over 5,000 hours of work to local labourers, and we'll be training 90 women in the production of olive-based items such as soap.[23]

Since the olive trees will provide harvests for many years, it stresses that the donation will be considered as *sadaqah jariyah*, or ongoing charity. Furthermore, it highlights that: 'Olives are considered a blessed fruit in Islam. They are mentioned seven times in the *Qur'an*, and the Prophet (PBUH) instructed us to use olive oil on our hair and skin.'[24] Muslim Hands has adopted a similar fundraising strategy for planting 30,000 olive trees in Palestine[25] and 10,000 indigenous fruit trees in Mirpur, Pakistan.[26] Muslim Hands has created a designated 'Environment Fund'[27] to fundraise for tree planting and other environmental initiatives, specifically among Muslim FBOs. While important, these remain relatively small-scale initiatives.

The Islamic Foundation for Ecology and Environmental Science (IFEES/ EcoIslam), which was registered as a charity in the UK in 1994, is a specialist Muslim environmental organization. It has undertaken pioneering work on raising awareness of environmental issues among Muslims and developing an Islamic approach to environmental protection and natural resource management. One of its most notable achievements was the Misali Ethics Pilot Project, which was implemented in Zanzibar in 1999 in collaboration with, and largely funded by, the secular organizations CARE International and the World Wide Fund for Nature (WWF), as well as the Alliance of Religions and Conservation. The project involved running educational workshops directed at local fishermen, provincial government officials, Islamic school or *madrassa* teachers, representatives from the Ministry of Agriculture, Livestock, and Natural Resources, and senior members from the office of the Islamic leader, or *Mufti*, of Zanzibar. The population of Zanzibar is almost entirely Muslim. The workshops used teachings from the *Qur'an* to inform participants about the importance of conservation and sustainability and to motivate them to act. In contrast to previous conventional conservation efforts, this initiative effectively stopped the fishermen from dynamiting the reef to catch fish and encouraged them to use more sustainable fishing practices. The project also developed a guide for Muslim scholars and teachers to enable Islamic environmental messages to be disseminated to a wider cross-section of the community (Khalid and Thani, 2007). Members of the IFEES/EcoIslam team revisited Misali and found that, 10 years after its completion, environmental approaches initiated by the project were still being implemented by a new generation of farmers and fishing people.[28] The materials developed by IFEES/EcoIslam were also used in workshops in various regions of Indonesia that were attended by hundreds of participants, including *ulema* (religious scholars), *ustaz* (Islamic teachers), and imams (religious leaders) (Mangunjaya and McKay, 2012). As in Zanzibar, the objective of the workshops was to motivate a 'change in behaviour among Muslims to better guard the environment' (ibid.: 292). While it continues to perform an environmental advocacy role, IFEED/EcoIslam has been unable to attract support for other environmental protection and natural resource management projects.

The world's largest Muslim FBO, Islamic Relief, was founded in response to a devastating drought in the Horn of Africa in 1984.[29] In 2007, Islamic Relief identified climate change as undoing 'the positive steps that some countries have taken towards development' and that it would have 'fatal consequences for those affected by serious disease, malnutrition, and instability caused by mass population movements'.[30] Today it remains 'inspired by Islamic teachings on justice and stewardship' and recognizes 'climate change as one of the greatest moral, social, and environmental issues facing humanity'.[31] Islamic Relief's website[32] highlights the requirement for community-based preparedness and climate change adaptation 'based on our practical insight into the lived realities of the people we serve'. It has developed a comprehensive climate change policy (Islamic Relief, 2019), which states that 'Islamic teachings make it imperative for all Muslims to be good stewards of the Earth. As an organisation guided by Islamic teachings and values we are serious about tackling climate change.' It also recognizes that this will support its mission to reduce poverty and suffering.[33] In contrast to most other Muslim FBOs, but in common with many of its secular and non-Muslim peers that also attract a greater proportion of their income from institutional donors, Islamic Relief has adopted a very active and visible advocacy role on climate change. Islamic Relief's engagement includes backing global climate strikes,[34] renewing calls on national governments to cut greenhouse gases,[35] and participation in events such as the annual Conference of the Parties (COP) to the UN Framework Convention on Climate Change,[36] to which it is an accredited observer organization. It was also the only Muslim development organization that was a signatory to an Interfaith Declaration on Climate Change, which states that 'our different faith traditions urge us to speak out and respond to the injustice of climate change' and argues that the legally binding Paris Agreement must be implemented.[37] Ahead of the COP 25 in 2019, it joined 'over 150 organisations, movements and unions in signing an open letter calling for a new fund to support survivors of climate disasters in the Global South'.[38] The letter was sent to environment ministers, heads of delegations, and the president of COP 25.

Islamic Relief's climate change policy commits to helping communities cope with the short-term impacts of climate change through development, adaptation, and risk reduction interventions, as well as advocating for community-based adaptation and resilience and pro-poor mitigation policies, which they suggest will limit long-term impacts and help create the conditions for sustainable, equitable, and global prosperity. In the three years leading up to 2017, Islamic Relief raised over £26 million (almost 9 per cent of the total amount of funding it received during this period) to address issues related to climate change in over 50 projects covering 14 countries (Islamic Relief, 2017). Most of these were about adaptation – building the capacity of individuals and communities in order to reduce their vulnerabilities. These projects include providing safe drinking water, sanitation facilities, and health interventions to improve hygiene practices and reduce the risk of disease, especially among women and children in Pakistan; long-term programmes in Bangladesh to enhance income, food, and livelihoods security, to provide basic services, and to develop local disaster risk reduction plans for households and communities that are particularly vulnerable to climate change so that they can achieve and sustain emergence from extreme poverty; a solar irrigation project improving community resilience, preparedness, and food security in north-east Kenya (this programme increased self-reliance among pastoralists who had repeatedly lost their herds to drought by helping them switch to fruit and vegetable farming); and a project in Ethiopia helping pastoralists to grow fodder through sustainable irrigated farming where pastures have been destroyed by repeated rain failures.[39]

Although other Muslim FBOs have not developed such comprehensive climate change policies, at the International Islamic Climate Change Symposium held in Istanbul in August 2015, Muslim organizations from across the world came together to issue an Islamic Declaration on Global Climate Change.[40] This emphasizes the importance of responding to climate change based on the values and teachings of Islam. The declaration recognizes that climate change is 'human-induced' and that the 'Earth's fine equilibrium [*mizan*] may soon be lost' if urgent measures are not taken to address the root causes of climate change, as well as environmental degradation and the loss of biodiversity. It calls on Muslims to follow the example of the Prophet Muhammad (PBUH) in conserving water, protecting trees and wildlife, and reducing waste and recycling. Among a range of measures, it demands phasing out greenhouse gas emissions, adopting renewable energy, and pursuing a more balanced and sustainable economic development model that respects environmental responsibilities. The climate declaration has been translated into 11 languages[41] and is regularly referenced in newspaper reports and articles, but its messages have yet to reach the wider Muslim world. A project to have it distributed and displayed in mosques worldwide has struggled to receive funding. This may be because of the preference of Muslim donors to fund emergency aid (Khan, 2012), or it could be because likely support might emanate from institutions considered inappropriate partners for Islamic FBOs, such as the National Lottery Community Fund or commercial sponsors compromised by environmentally damaging activities.

Another interesting initiative was the Humanitarian Academy for Development's Action on Climate and Consumption (ACC) project.[42] This was a multinational programme implemented during 2016–18 that aimed to explore, understand, and act on the ways in which religious affiliation can be a driver of behavioural change, with a specific focus on sustainable consumption and production. It asserted that religion is one of the major influences on values, attitudes, and behaviours in individuals and communities. ACC's overall goal was to enable positive changes in behaviour and social norms among Muslims that would contribute to carbon reduction, ecological awareness, and a demand for climate action. Engaging religious leaders, Muslim villages and neighbourhoods, women's groups, academics and intellectuals, and Islamic Relief's Muslim staff and their families, the project concluded that, while they gained more knowledge and information to be able to understand the challenges they face due to climate change, mostly it revealed the amount of work still to be done, especially in rural areas. Religious leaders in particular saw their role as important in 'awakening

Muslims from their deep sleep on environmental issues' (Rozo, n.d.) and in helping them to understand how climate change is happening and affects them in their everyday lives.

The ACC project commissioned a research paper, *Towards an Islamic Philosophy of Consumption* (Rush, 2018), that reconsidered consumption and sustainability from an Islamic perspective. It sets out to apply a 'radical reform' methodology to the issue of sustainable consumption. It does this by first establishing an interpretative frame using subsequent re-readings of the sources and a brief reconsideration of the history of encounters between Islamic societies and the question of consumption. It then suggests a toolkit for both Muslims and activists to join the struggle for a more just, ecologically balanced world in harmony with creation. Another study (Skirbekk and Pędziwiatr, 2018), concentrating mainly on the attitudes of Muslim leaders from Northern countries and South Asia, concluded that Muslim communities tend to be well aware of the issues of climate change. They are ready to slow down economic growth to minimize its effects and are in favour of raising taxes on those polluting the environment most heavily. Many of the Muslims surveyed see their religion as a source of powerful tools to help preserve the Earth and address the problems of climate change. Similarly, a survey in North America found that Muslim citizens understand the origins and threat of climate change and strongly support measures to address it (Christopher and Salar Khan, 2018). However, these optimistic findings are not experienced elsewhere, and, while they demonstrate a desire for action, this does not always lead to more successful fundraising for environment-related activities.

Several significant environmental campaigns led by Muslims have emerged over the last decade or so. MADE brought together young Muslims from across Europe in the Green Up My Community! campaign to support young Muslims to get their local mosques and communities thinking about environmental issues. On a larger scale, the Muslim Seven Year Action Plan on Climate Change for the global Islamic community was coordinated by the Alliance of Religions and Conservation (ARC). The Muslim Climate Action Network sought to bring together Islamic faith-inspired UK-based NGOs to tackle climate change and Global Muslim Climate Action attempted the same internationally. All these organizations have since closed. It has proven difficult to attract support for sustained initiatives that specifically target Muslim communities. One reason for this may be the general lack of institutions and hierarchy in Islam, making it difficult to focus on a particular message and communicate it across a decentralized community.

Since 2019 the secular environmental organization Greenpeace has been working with an alliance of groups and individuals on developing a project that aims to create a Muslim climate movement by exploring Islamic culture and religion as a vector of mobilization. One innovation of this project is to use faith messages centred on paid-for social media, with its potential for wide reach, in an ambitious project to mobilize young Muslims on issues of consumption, environmental protection, and climate action. The messages to be tested include the following:

- Creation is part of divine will – 'No leaf falls without His knowledge' (*Qur'an*, 6: 59) – and everything has or serves some function for the common good of the human family.
- Everything was created in an equilibrium – but greed, overconsumption, and conflict have resulted in the tipping of the balance, causing harm and suffering among the inhabitants of this planet.
- The planet is a bestowed trust given by Allah – it is incumbent on human beings to value life, nature, and all created species as a wholesome blessing given by God.
- The destruction of the planet is caused by human 'hands' – knowing no limits, not heeding the advice from Allah and His messenger, people have built technologies that exploit nature to its destruction.
- Our task is to remember our place – as stewards of Allah on Earth to safeguard the balance and prevent the destruction of the planet, and to maintain a good relationship with God, human beings, other species, and all forms of creation.
- Do good to others around you and you will be rewarded – to tread lightly on Earth and be gentle on those you interact with, whether they are persons or other species.
- Even the smallest good deed will be rewarded (Sofjan, n.d.).

It will be interesting to see whether this initiative, driven by Islamic teachings but sustained by a broad-based organization, will have a lasting effect.

Another challenge described by Indonesian/American environmental campaigner Nana Firman is that Muslims:

> do not draw the connections about what we learn in Islam and the practicalities of the faith, especially as it pertains to the environment. For example, there is an *ayah* [verse] in the *Qur'an* that describes the act of walking gently on the earth, but few associate this verse with leaving a small ecological footprint. (Hummel and Daassa, 2019: 30)

In a discussion paper for the Greenpeace project, Indonesian academic Dicky Sofjan[43] notes that, in recent times, humans have refashioned their world view and behaviours to conform to economic growth and consumption without due consideration for ecological sustainability. As a result, very few religious leaders, groups, or organizations are genuinely committed to addressing the problems of climate change and sustainable development. As Firman observes: 'There is a disconnection between the religion of Islam and what is being practiced in these communities' (Hummel and Daassa, 2019: 31). As the ACC project concluded: 'More in-depth reflection and analysis is needed to understand how Muslim faith can be a resource or an inspiration when tackling environmental issues in such situations' (Rozo, n.d.). In his recommendations to the Greenpeace project, Sofjan identifies distinct metanarratives. In the first, he assumes that Muslims are rationalist, functionalist, and instrumentalist actors. The second predicts that Muslims will not adjust their behaviours solely on incentives, but 'through good counsel and remembrance of their main duty, task and responsibility'. He identifies these approaches as suited to different audiences of believers – the first towards 'the general public, congregational mosque members, the youths and students', and the second towards 'government/ministerial officers, technocrats, religious leaders and scholars vying to be better Muslims' (Sofjan, n.d.).

One of these approaches may be for Muslim organizations to develop their engagement with various interfaith groupings that have created a space for religious and spiritual narratives in the consultations, debates, negotiations, and calls to action around climate change. The UK-based Faith for the Climate Network connects with and supports its 150 members in faith-based action for the climate. Similarly, GreenFaith has been mobilizing people of diverse religious and spiritual backgrounds globally for environmental action in the United States and is launching an international network to bring its dynamic approach of inspiration, education, organization, and mobilization to a wider audience. At the UN Framework Convention on Climate Change, the Interfaith Liaison Group provides a moral and ethical perspective and is becoming increasingly influential in critical negotiations. UNEP's Faith for Earth initiative was launched in November 2017 with three main goals: to inspire faith groups to advocate for the environment; to make faith organizations' investments and assets green; and to connect faith leaders with decision makers and the public. Membership of these bodies is problematic for Muslims, as there are few institutions that can claim to be representative of such a diverse and decentralized faith. But it is important both that Muslim voices are heard and that the resources offered by these interfaith alliances can help Muslims encourage, inspire, and equip their communities to work on climate change.

Conclusion

There is a strong environmental ethic in Islamic teachings that emphasizes a respect for creation, a command to maintain the natural balance, and that entrusts humankind with a sacred and collective responsibility to protect and conserve the environment for present and future generations. Despite the prominence accorded to the environment in Islam and the adverse impacts of environmental degradation on the poor, environment-related programmes and advocacy have generally not featured prominently in the activities of Muslim FBOs from the UK. This analysis has suggested various reasons why this may be the case, including a perceived reluctance on the part of donors to support environmental activities. It may also be because, despite their rapid growth, leading Muslim FBOs are generally less experienced and less well established than their secular and non-Muslim counterparts. Arguably their focus remains on providing emergency relief rather than promoting longer-term development.

As the chief executive of one leading Muslim FBO commented: 'As we evolve, I hope our programming will become more holistic, and our programmes less divorced from theology.'[44] Promisingly, organizations such as IFEES/EcoIslam have very effectively referenced Islamic teachings to motivate behavioural changes among Muslim communities. The largest Muslim FBO, Islamic Relief, has adopted an increasingly visible position and references Islamic teachings to advocate for measures to address climate change, while secular organizations such as Greenpeace also wish to use the influence of religion to promote greater environmental awareness among Muslims.

Notes

1. Aboul-Enein (2018: 23) identifies 88 verses in 42 Qur'anic chapters with a 'considerable emphasis placed on the importance of water resource management and water conservation, environmental justice, plant conservation, biodiversity, sustainability and environmental stewardship', while Manoiu et al. (2016: 210) observe that there are 750 (of 6,236) 'green verses' in the *Qur'an* that refer to 'various aspects of nature, the relationship between man and nature, vegetal and animal organisms and their environment'.
2. See <https://www.unenvironment.org/about-un-environment/faith-earth-initiative/why-faith-and-environment-matters> [accessed 27 January 2020].
3. It is reported that just four commodities – beef, soya beans, palm oil, and wood products – are responsible for the majority of tropical deforestation. See <https://www.ucsusa.org/resources/whats-driving-deforestation> [accessed 29 January 2020].
4. See <https://www.worldwildlife.org/habitats/forest-habitat> [accessed 29 January 2020].
5. 'Faith-based' is generally used to describe organizations that have an affiliation with a religious body; a mission statement with explicit reference to religious values; financial support from religious sources; and a structure where staff selection or decision making is based on religious beliefs and values. In this context, Muslim FBOs are non-governmental organizations founded by Muslims that receive most of their financial support from Muslims, and whose actions, to varying degrees, are inspired and legitimized by Islam.
6. Hancock (2018) observes that this position differs markedly from Christianity, where the creation story of Genesis 1: 1–2: 3 instructs humankind to 'fill the Earth and subdue it'. In contrast, she argues, the *Qur'an* does not give humankind dominion over nature. Other authors – for example, Sherkat and Ellison (2007) – argue that the Bible is replete with examples of pro-environment teachings.
7. The sayings and actions of the Prophet Muhammad (PBUH).
8. Interestingly, as scientific evidence recognizes the importance of bees as pollinators (Hung et al., 2018), there are also *ahadith* that prohibit the killing of bees. For example, 'The Prophet (PBUH) prohibited to kill four creatures: ants, bees, hoopoes, and sparrow-hawks' (Abu Dawud, Book 43, *Hadith* 495).

9. Pope Francis invoked Christian teachings of stewardship in his 2015 encyclical calling for action on climate change and other ecological threats. It was the first encyclical of Francis's papacy and the first in the history of the Catholic Church to focus on the environment.

10. It is worth noting that Islam considers water to be a community resource and right for all humankind. The Prophet Muhammad (PBUH) stressed this in the following *hadith*: 'Three things cannot be denied to anyone: water, pasture and fire' (Ibn Majah, Book 16, *Hadith* 2567).

11. Islamic depictions of Heaven describe lush, green gardens with flowing rivers and trees rich with fruit.

12. Imtiaz (2020) estimates that there are 129 Muslim FBOs in the UK with a focus on providing humanitarian aid and promoting development in poor countries. The largest, in terms of reported income, is Islamic Relief, followed by Human Appeal, Muslim Aid, Ummah Welfare Trust, Penny Appeal, Al-Khair Foundation, and Muslim Hands.

13. See, for example, <https://www.islamic-relief.org/sustainable-development-goals-adopted/> [accessed 28 February 2020]. Similar commitments are made by other leading Muslim FBOs.

14. SDG 6 calls to 'ensure access to water and sanitation for all'; SDG 7 is 'ensure access to affordable, reliable, sustainable and modern energy'; SDG 12 demands 'sustainable consumption and production patterns'; SDG 13 calls for 'urgent action to combat climate change and its impacts'; SDG 14 requires us to 'conserve and sustainably use the oceans, seas and marine resources for sustainable development'; and SDG 15 calls for us to 'protect, restore and promote sustainable use of terrestrial ecosystems, sustainably manage forests, combat desertification, and halt and reverse land degradation and halt biodiversity loss'. A full list of the SDGs can be found at <https://www.un.org/sustainabledevelopment/sustainable-development-goals/>.

15. Personal communication with Chief Executive Officer, Muslim Aid, 15 March 2020.

16. Personal communication with Chief Executive Officer, Muslim Charities Forum, 12 February 2020.

17. Personal communication with Chief Executive Officer of a leading Muslim FBO who did not wish to be identified.

18. See <https://yaqeeninstitute.org/afsan-redwan/when-the-earth-speaks-against-us-environmental-ethics-in-islam/> [accessed 14 March 2020].

19. Personal communication with Head of International Programmes, Al-Khair Foundation, 21 February 2020.

20. Personal communication with Media and PR Coordinator, Human Appeal, 28 February 2020.

21. See <https://www.linkedin.com/company/made-in-europe/about/> [accessed 14 March 2020].

22. Personal communication with Chief Executive Officer, Muslim Aid, 15 March 2020.

23. See <https://humanappeal.org.uk/donate/projects/livelihoods/olive-trees> [accessed 28 February 2020].

24. See <https://humanappeal.org.uk/donate/projects/livelihoods/olive-trees> [accessed 28 February 2020].

25. See <https://muslimhands.org.uk/latest/2016/11/olive-trees-for-palestine> [accessed 11 March 2020].
26. See <https://muslimhands.org.uk/latest/2019/03/make-mirpur-green> [accessed 11 March 2020].
27. See <https://muslimhands.org.uk/donate/greatest-need/environment-fund> [accessed 14 March 2020].
28. Personal communication with Mark Bryant, Director, IFEES/EcoIslam, 11 March 2020.
29. Muslim Aid was founded in 1985, also in response to the drought in the Horn of Africa.
30. *Partnership with the Needy* 31 (Spring 2007).
31. See <https://www.islamic-relief.org/category/what-we-do/our-changing-climate/> [accessed 14 March 2020].
32. See <https://www.islamic-relief.org/islamic-relief-global-strategy_2017-2021/> [accessed 14th March 2020].
33. See <https://www.islamic-relief.org/wp-content/uploads/2018/11/Climate Changeweb1.pdf>.
34. See <https://www.islamic-relief.org/we-want-action-now-to-avert-catastrophe-islamic-relief-backs-global-climate-strikes/> [accessed 16 March 2020].
35. See <https://www.islamic-relief.org/after-cop25-islamic-relief-reissues-urgent-call-to-cut-emissions/> [accessed 16 March 2020].
36. Most recently COP 25 from 2 to 13 December 2019 in Madrid.
37. See <https://www.islamic-relief.org/islamic-relief-calls-for-more-action-from-world-leaders/> [accessed 17 March 2020]. As of 11 December 2019, 30 FBOs had signed the declaration.
38. See <https://www.islamic-relief.org/islamic-relief-calls-for-loss-and-damage-fund-with-debt-relief/> [accessed 18 March 2020].
39. See <https://www.islamic-relief.org/wp-content/uploads/2019/04/Stories-from-Afar.pdf> [accessed 16 March 2020].
40. The full declaration is available at <http://www.ifees.org.uk/wp-content/uploads/2016/10/climate_declarationmMWB.pdf>.
41. The languages are Arabic, English, French, Turkish, Bahasa Indonesia, Kiswahili, Urdu, Spanish, Malay, German, and Italian.
42. See <https://had-int.org/case-study/action-on-climate-change-and-con sumption/> [accessed 14th March 2020].
43. Unpublished report extracted from a wider research consultancy commissioned by Greenpeace MENA from Dicky Sofjan of the Indonesian Consortium for Religious Studies (ICRS), Universitas Gadjah Mada (UGM), Yogyakarta, Indonesia.
44. Personal communication with Chief Executive Officer, Muslim Aid, 15 March 2020.

References

Abdul-Matin, I. (2012) *Green Deen: What Islam Teaches about Protecting the Planet*, Kube Publishing, Markfield, Leicestershire.
Abdul Rahman, S. (2017) 'Religion and animal welfare: an Islamic perspective', *Animals* 7 (2): 11.

Aboul-Enein, B.H. (2018) '"The Earth is your mosque": narrative perspectives of environmental health and education in the Holy Quran', *Journal of Environmental Studies and Sciences* 8: 22–31.

Christopher, C. and Salar Khan, M. (2018) *Muslim-American Views on Climate Change: A National Survey*, Office for Interfaith and Community Alliances and Islamic Society of North America, Washington DC.

FAO (2018) *The State of the World's Forests 2018: Forest Pathways to Sustainable Development*, Food and Agriculture Organization of the United Nations (FAO), Rome.

FAO (2019) *Trees, Forests and Land Use in Drylands: The First Global Assessment. Full Report*, FAO Forestry Paper 184, Food and Agriculture Organization of the United Nations (FAO), Rome.

Hancock, R. (2018) 'Faith and creation: possibilities of an "Islamic" environmental ethic', ABC Religion and Ethics, 11 September <https://www.abc.net.au/religion/islamic-environmental-ethic/10233070> [accessed 23 January 2020].

Health Effects Institute (2019) *State of Global Air 2019*, Health Effects Institute, Boston MA.

Hummel, D. and Daassa, M. (2019) '"Walking gently on the Earth": an interview with Nana Firman on Islamic environmental ethics', *Journal of Islamic Faith and Practice* 2 (1): 24–39.

Hung, K.J., Kingston, J.M., Albrecht, M., Holway, D.A. and Kohn, J.R. (2018). 'The worldwide importance of honey bees as pollinators in natural habitats', *Proceedings of the Royal Society B: Biological Sciences* 285: 20172140.

Imtiaz, A. (2020) 'An examination of the inquiries conducted on British Muslim charities by the Charity Commission', *Forum* 2 (Winter 2019/20).

IPBES (2019) *Summary for Policymakers of the Global Assessment Report on Biodiversity and Ecosystem Services*, Intergovernmental Science-Policy Platform on Biodiversity and Ecosystem Services, Bonn <https://ipbes.net/sites/default/files/ipbes_7_10_add.1_en_1.pdf> [accessed 30 January 2020].

IPCC (2018) *Global Warming of 1.5°C. An IPCC Special Report on the Impacts of Global Warming of 1.5°C above Pre-industrial Levels and Related Global Greenhouse Gas Emission Pathways, in the Context of Strengthening the Global Response to the Threat of Climate Change, Sustainable Development, and Efforts to Eradicate Poverty*, Intergovernmental Panel on Climate Change (IPCC), Geneva <https://www.ipcc.ch/site/assets/uploads/sites/2/2019/06/SR15_Full_Report_High_Res.pdf> [accessed 11 March 2020].

Islamic Relief (2017) *Climate Champions: Islamic Relief's Global Climate Action*, Islamic Relief Worldwide, Birmingham <https://www.islamic-relief.org/wp-content/uploads/2017/11/Climate-Champions.pdf> [accessed 16 March 2020].

Islamic Relief (2019) *Climate Change Policy: Understanding and Responding*, Islamic Relief Worldwide, Birmingham <https://www.islamic-relief.org/wp content/uploads/2018/11/ClimateChangeweb1.pdf> [accessed 17 March 2020].

Izzi Dien, M. (2000) *The Environmental Dimensions of Islam*, Lutterworth, Cambridge.

Khalid, F. (2002) 'Islam and the environment', in P. Timmerman (ed.), 'Volume 5: Social and economic dimensions of global environmental change', in T. Munn (ed.), *Encyclopedia of Global Environmental Change*, John Wiley & Sons, Chichester.

Khalid, F. (2005) 'Islamic basis for environmental protection', in J. Kaplan and B. Taylor (eds), *Encyclopedia of Religion and Nature*, Continuum Publishers, London.

Khalid, F. and A. Thani (2007) *Teachers Guide Book for Islamic Environmental Education*, Islamic Foundation for Ecology and Environmental Science, Birmingham.

Khan, A.A. (2012) 'Religious obligation or altruistic giving? Muslims and charitable donations', in M. Barnett and J.G. Stein (eds), *Sacred Aid: Faith and Humanitarianism*, Oxford University Press, Oxford.

Mangunjaya, F.M. and McKay, J.E. (2012) 'Reviving an Islamic approach for environmental conservation in Indonesia', *Worldviews: Environment, Culture, Religion* 16 (3): 286–305.

Manoiu, V.-M., Düzgüneş, E., Azzeddine, M. and Manoiu, V.-S. (2016) 'A qualitative exploration of the Holy Quran's environmental teachings', *International E-Journal of Advances in Education* 2 (5): 209–17.

Nasr, S.H. (2015) 'A religious nature: philosopher Seyyed Hossein Nasr on Islam and the environment [interview]', *Bulletin of the Atomic Scientists* 71 (5): 13–18 <https://journals.sagepub.com/doi/pdf/10.1177/0096340215599785> [accessed 2 February 2020].

Parvaiz, M.A. (2005) 'Islam on man and nature', in J. Kaplan and B. Taylor (eds), *Encyclopedia of Religion and Nature*, Continuum Publishers, London.

Rozo, P. (n.d.) 'Action on Climate and Consumption – ACC: a participatory action-learning facilitated process' (unpublished), Islamic Relief Worldwide, Humanitarian Academy for Development, and Kann Rasmussen Foundation.

Rush, M. (2018) *Towards an Islamic Philosophy of Consumption*, Humanitarian Academy for Development, Birmingham <https://had-int.org/tag/sustainable-consumption/#> [accessed 16 March 2020].

Sherkat, D.E. and Ellison, C.G. (2007) 'Structuring the religion-environment connection: identifying religious influences on environmental concern and activism', *Journal for the Scientific Study of Religion* 46 (1): 71–85.

Skirbekk, V. and Pędziwiatr, K. (2018) *Sustainability and Climate Change in Major Religions with a Focus on Islam*, Humanitarian Academy for Development, Birmingham <https://www.researchgate.net/publication/329656310_Sustainability_and_climate_change_in_major_religions_with_a_focus_on_Islam> [accessed 16 March 2020].

Sofjan, D. (n.d.) 'Islam and climate change' (unpublished), Greenpeace MENA (Middle East and North Africa).

UNCCD (2017) *Global Land Outlook*, United Nations Convention to Combat Desertification (UNCCD), Bonn <https://www.unccd.int/sites/default/files/documents/2017-09/GLO_Full_Report_low_res.pdf>.

WHO and UNICEF (2019) *Progress on Household Drinking Water, Sanitation and Hygiene 2000–2017: Special Focus on Inequalities*, World Health Organization (WHO) and United Nations Children's Fund (UNICEF), New York.

World Economic Forum (2020) *The Global Risks Report 2020*, World Health Organization, Geneva <https://www.weforum.org/global-risks/reports>.

Yazdani, J. (2015) 'Islam and the environment', Unity Center of Santa Clarita, 16 July <http://www.unity-center.org/ucscv-blog/352-islam-and-the-environment.html> [accessed 17 January 2020].

About the authors

Ajaz Ahmed Khan is Senior Microfinance Adviser with CARE International. He holds a PhD in Development Economics and has extensive experience of working in a diverse range of countries in Latin America, Eastern Europe, Asia, and Africa. He has written widely on microfinance and on Islamic microfinance in particular, as well as more generally on faith and development.

J.R.A. Williams has lived and worked in over a dozen developing countries, specializing in education and early childhood. Since 2016, as Senior Policy Advisor on Poverty Reduction, he has led on climate change for Islamic Relief Worldwide.

Index

Page numbers in *italics* refer to figures.

Abou-El-Wafa, A. 88, 90–1, 93–4, 99, 100, 103–4, 105–6
additionality and spiritual capital 61–2, 64–5
advocacy role of Muslim FBOs 74–5
  on behalf of poor 79–81
  environmental 201–8
Afghanistan: early forced marriage (EFM) 166
Agenda for Humanity 2
Akhuwat Islamic Microfinance, Pakistan 74, 79
Al-Azhar, Grand Imam of 8
al-Ghazali, A.H. 7, 8, 10, 49, 77, 154, 162
Al-Qaradawi, Y. 29, 30–1
alms tax *see zakat*
aman (asylum), violation of 105
Aminu-Kano, M. and FitzGibbon, A. 9–10, 11
Ammar, N.H. 135
Ashgabat Declaration on Refugees 88
asylum *see* refugees, asylum, and forced migration
attachment theory 162
Awqaf Corporation 28–9
awqaf (endowments) 58
Awqaf Properties Investment Fund (APIF) 35

Barbour, R. 162
basic physical needs, right to 102
Baumann, J. et al. 174
Bewley, A. 48
bonds (*sukuk*) 35
Bouta, T. et al. 174, 175–6, 192
British Muslims 202

Cairo Declaration on Human Rights in Islam 100

Canada, community-based protection of refugees 98–9
capital market investment 35
change, theory/theology of 65–6
Channels of Hope 50, 146
  child protection (CoH-CP) 165–6
charitable giving *see waqf; zakat*
'Charter for faith-based humanitarian action' 2
child abuse, violence, and exploitation
  linked to faith and culture 163–6
  protection against 161–2
child marriage *see* early forced marriage (EFM)
child protection in emergencies (CPiE) 156
child protection and safeguarding 153–5
  framework 155–7
  humanitarian instruments and Islamic principles, contrasting 157–66
  summary and conclusion 167
children's rights 104–5, 156, 157–66
climate change 198, 203–8
colonialism
  'neo-colonialism' 190
  postcolonialism 45, 123
community (*Ummah*) 177
community champions 143–4
community conflict analysis 182
community conversation (CC) 138–41, *144*
community interests and welfare (*Maslaha*) 7, 50
community-based protection of refugees, Canada 98–9
conflict *see* peacebuilding
consultation (*shura*) 181–2

corporal punishment of children
161–2
cultural practices *see* harmful
traditional/cultural practices
(HTPs); *specific practices*
cultural proximity 189–90
custodianship of Earth 53, 59, 93,
115–16
see also stewardship/trusteeship,
environmental
customary authorities and local
government 180–1, 192

Darfur: community conflict
resolution and reconciliation
187–8
dignity/human dignity 4–5, 9–10,
11, 48, *51*
forced migration 91, 96, 100
generosity, and loving welcome,
right to 98–9
human rights 60–1, 133–4
and gender 113, 115, 118–19
disabilities, children with 156,
160–1, 166
domestic violence 123–4, 126, 134–6
impact of interventions 141–2
dowry 144

early forced marriage (EFM) 126,
136–7, 155–6, 164–6
Mali: young changemaker refusal
to accept FGM and 124–5
as obstacle to education 116–17
education
children's right to 158–9
girls, obstacles to 116–17
women and children's access to
Ethiopia 145
Philippines 125
Eid and Ramadan festivals 73
endowments (*awqaf*) 58
Environment Programme: 'Faith for
Earth' initiative (UNEP) 46,
197–8, 208
environmental protection for
posterity 59–60
environmentalism and Muslim FBOs
197–9
Islamic principles 199–201

programmes and advocacy
activities of Muslim FBOs
201–8
summary and conclusion 208–9
equality
children's right to 159–60
respect for diversity 181–2
see also gender and gender justice
Ethiopia (IRE): sexual and gender-
based violence (SGBV) interventions 138–46

'faith blind spot' in aid structures 13
Faith for the Climate Network 208
faith-based organizations
(FBOs/NGOs)
additionality 65
environmentalism 46
gender justice 111, 112,
121–2, 123
harmonization 63
inclusion, engagement and
participation 62
localization 64
Muslim Platform for Sustainable
Development 13
poverty alleviation 1–3, 9
sexual and gender-based violence
(SGBV) 138
see also advocacy role of Muslim
FBOs; environmentalism
and Muslim FBOs; poverty
alleviation and Muslim FBOs;
specific organizations
faith/religion/spirituality principle
51–2
in development *10, 11, 51*
gender justice 115
Fatwa Committee of Ministry of
Awqaf, Kuwait 30, 31
female genital mutilation/cutting
(FGM/C) 126, 137–8, 156–7,
163–4
community interventions and
impact 141, 143–4
Mali: young changemaker refusal
to accept 124–5
as obstacle to education 116–17
feminist foreign policy (FFP)
122–4

Feminist International Assistance
Policy (FIAP) 123
finance *see* Islamic social finance;
microfinance
Fiqh Academy 30, 31
Firman, N. 207
food parcels 73
forced marriage *see* early forced
marriage (EFM)
freedom of religion, right to
100–1
funding, needs and gaps 13, 19, 20

GDP (OIC countries) and *zakat*
collection 25–8
gender and gender justice 111–12
change in theological understanding and practice 124–5
feminist foreign policy 122–4
general Islamic teachings on
non-discrimination 118–20
Maqasid framework 114–18
implementation 120–2
Muslim-majority countries and
human rights 112–14
summary and conclusion 126–7
gender-based violence (GBV) *see*
sexual and gender-based
violence (SGBV)
Ghafournia, N. 123, 134, 136
Global Compact on Refugees 175
Global Goals 1–2, 4, 5, 13
global level implementation of *zakat*
27–8, 30
Global Muslim Climate Action 206
Global Partnership 2
Global Peace Index 173
governance and management of
Islamic social finance 31–7
governments
local government and customary
authorities 181, 191–2
waqf management 28–9
zakat administration 32
Greenfaith 208
Greenpeace 206–8

Hadith 53, 76
see also Prophet Muhammad (PBUH)

harmful traditional/cultural practices
(HTPs) 46, 121–2, 126–7
see also specific practices
harmonization and spiritual capital
61, 63–4
health and healthcare 50, 53–4
HIV/AIDS 80
pregnant adolescent girls 166
pregnant women 158
hijrah (migration) 88, 90–1
HIV/AIDS 80
holistic approach to peacebuilding
180–1
host communities, integration of
forced migrants into 105–6
Human Appeal 72, 77, 79
olive tree planting programme,
Palestine 202–3
human dignity *see* dignity/
human dignity
human rights *see* rights/
human rights
Humanitarian Academy for
Development: Action on
Climate and Consumption
(ACC) 205–6
humanitarian tradition 52, 53
Hummel, D. and Daassa, M. 207

ICT access and gender justice 117
inclusion
and peacebuilding 181–2
and spiritual capital 61, 62
income
and expenditure of Muslim FBOs
69–70, 71, 72–3, 74, 77–8
national *see* GDP
zakat and poverty alleviation
27–8
intellect (*aqal*) principle 54–5
children's education 158–9
in development *10, 11, 51*
gender justice 116–17
intergenerational concerns
see posterity
Intergovernmental Science-Policy
Platform on Biodiversity
and Ecosystem Services
(IPBES) 198

International Conference on Refugees in the Muslim World (UNHCR/OIC) 90
International Islamic Center for Population Studies and Research (IICPSR) 138
International Organization for Migration (IOM): definition of forced migration 88
International *Shari'ah* Board of *Zakat* (ISBOZ), Kuwait 30, 31
intersectionality 123–4
investment and construction/ development
  waqf 29–30, 31, 34–5, 36
  zakat 30
Islamic Declaration of Gender Justice 112, 119, 123, 146
Islamic Declaration on Global Climate Change 205
Islamic Development Bank (IsDB)
  Awqaf Properties Investment Fund (APIF) 35
  poverty-defining elements 4
Islamic Foundation for Ecology and Environmental Science (IFEES) 50, 59–60, 203
Islamic law/*Shari'ah*
  human rights and gender equality 114
  integration of forced migrants 106
  and poverty 6, 7–8
  see also jurisprudence; *Maqasid al-Shari'ah*; *Maslaha* (community interests and welfare); Prophet Muhammad (PBUH); *Qur'an*
Islamic mediation and reconciliation 182–3
Islamic Relief/Worldwide 4–5, 71, 73, 74, 75, 77, 79–80
  environmentalism 203–6
  forced migration 89
  gender justice 112, 116, 118, 119, 121, 122, 124–5
  'Human Development in Islam' framework 9–12
  peacebuilding 176, 178–92

right to freedom of religion, Jordan and Lebanon 101
sexual and gender-based violence (SGBV) 137–8, 163
  and child protection, integrated approach to 165–6
  Ethiopia (IRE) 138–46
spiritual capital 50, 59–60, 64
waqf donation and investment, UK 29
Islamic Research and Training Institute (IRTI) and Thomson Reuters (TR) 28
Islamic social finance
  conceptual framework 20–4
  current status and potential 24–8
  expanding: jurisprudential considerations 29–31
  improving governance and management 31–7
  summary and conclusion 37–8

Jordan and Lebanon: Islamic Relief and right to freedom of religion 101
jurisprudence
  expanding social finance 29–31
  and management of *zakat* 24–8
  see also Islamic law/*Shari'ah*; *Maqasid al-Shari'ah*; *Maslaha* (community interests and welfare)

Kadayifci-Orellana, S.A. et al. 52, 176, 178–9
Kahf, M. 20–1, 22–3, 25, 28–31
Karam, A. 3
Kenya: conflict prevention and peacebuilding 185–6, 190, 191
Kuala Lumpur (FTKL): *zakat* administration 33–4
Kuwait: *zakat* administration 30, 31

land and property assets (*waqf*) 28–9, 34–5, 36–7
learning disabilities, children with 166

Lebanon and Jordan: Islamic Relief and right to freedom of religion 101
life principle 53–4
  in development *10, 11, 51*
  gender justice 115–16
Lings, M. 92, 97–8
Little, D. 176
loans
  qard hasan 78, 79
  zakat 30–1
  see also microfinance
local communities
  peacebuilding 181, 190, 191
  see also entries beginning community
local faith actors (LFAs) 184, 190, 191
local government and customary authorities 180–1, 192
local level trust building 190–1
localization and spiritual capital 61, 64

Majlis Ugama Islam Singapore (MUIS) 35
Malaysia
  myZakat crowd funding 37
  Waqaf Al-Nur (WANCorp) 36
Mali
  integrated approach to gender-based violence and child protection 165
  young changemaker refusal to accept FGM and child marriage 124–5
Maqasid al-Shari'ah
  child protection 154, 155, 162–3, 167
  gender 114–18
  and human rights 60–1
  objectives of 51–60
  peacebuilding 180
  poverty alleviation 7–8, 9–12, 13
  purpose and priorities of divine law 49–51
  rights of forced migrants 95–6
marriage by inheritance 145
Maslaha (community interests and welfare) 7, 50

mental and physical health 53–4
Metanexus Institute 43
microfinance
  Akhuwat Islamic Microfinance, Pakistan 74, 79
  encouraging 78–9
  mosques 65
  zakat 30–1
migrant and Muslim women: domestic violence 123–4, 134
migration (*hijrah*) 88, 90–1
mosques
  construction/reconstruction of 74
  microfinance organizations 65
Mufti, S.I. 175
Muslim Action for Development and Environment (MADE) 202, 206
Muslim Aid 69, 71, 72, 77, 79, 80
Muslim Charities Forum (MCF) 69–70
Muslim Climate Action Network 206
Muslim faith-based organizations (FBOs/NGOs) *see* advocacy role of Muslim FBOs; environmentalism and Muslim FBOs; faith-based organizations (FBOs/NGOs); poverty alleviation and Muslim FBOs; *specific organizations*
Muslim Hands 69, 71, 72, 73, 74, 77, 79
  environmentalism 203
Muslim Platform for Sustainable Development 13
Muslim Seven Year Action Plan on Climate Change 206
myZakat crowd funding, Malaysia 37

Nasr, S.H. 54–5, 198
national income *see* GDP
neutrality in peacebuilding brokerage 191–2
NGOs *see* faith-based organizations (FBOs/NGOs); Muslim faith-based organizations (FBOs/NGOs); *specific organizations*

Niger
early forced marriage (EFM) 166
integrated approach to gender-
based violence and child
protection 165
non-discrimination
Islamic teachings on 118–20
right to 99–100
non-profit organizations 31–2, 33
non-refoulement (forced return),
protection from 97–8
non-separation from family, right
to 104

OECD Development Assistance
Committee 3
Organisation of Islamic
Cooperation (OIC)
Ashgabat Declaration on
Refugees 88
asylum 95
Covenant on the Rights of the
Child in Islam (CRCI) 104–5,
155, 157–8
Fiqh Academy 30, 31
forced migrants 106–7
secularization 88–9
and UNHCR 90
zakat 25–8
orphans 73
'others', rehumanizing in
peacebuilding 182

Pakistan 65
environmentalism 202, 203
gender-based violence, engaging
faith leaders 125
gender-based violence and
child protection, integration
of 165
Palestine: olive tree planting
programme 202–3
patriarchy 119–20, 132, 136
peacebuilding 173–7
comparative advantages and
challenges for Muslim FBO
184–92
conceptual links between Islamic
principles and 177–9

principles to practice 179–84
summary and conclusion 192–3
Philippines: women's and children's
access to education 125
post-secularism/secularization 45,
88–9
posterity principle 59–60
in development *10, 11, 51*
gender justice 117
poverty (and poverty alleviation) 1–3
current approaches: dimensions
and definitions 4–5
and GDP in OIC countries 26
'Human Development in Islam'
framework 9–12
and Islam 5–8
rate 20
summary and conclusion 12–14
see also Islamic social finance;
wealth
poverty alleviation and Muslim FBOs
69–71
advocacy 79–81
empowerment through self-
reliance 75–8
encouraging microfinance 78–9
programme focus 71–5
summary and conclusion 81–2
Programme Partnership Agreement
(PPA), UK 9
property
and funds, right to 103–4
gender justice 117–18
and land (*waqf*) 28–9, 34–5, 36–7
see also wealth
Prophet Muhammad (PBUH) 22, 23,
70, 71, 73, 74, 76, 77, 78, 79
child protection 154–5, 158, 159,
160, 161, 162, 163, 164,
166, 167
environmentalism 199, 200, 201,
202–3, 205
forced migration/asylum 72, 87–8,
92, 93–5, 96, 97, 98, 102, 104,
106
gender justice 116, 120
peacebuilding 177
sexual and gender-based violence
(SGBV) 134–5, 136, 142

spiritual capital 49, 51–2, 56–7, 58, 65
protection, right to 96–7
psychosocial support 141

qard hasan (cash loan) 78, 79
Qur'an 5, 6, 7, 20, 22, 70, 73, 75–6, 78, 80–1
  child protection 154, 155–6, 159, 160, 161, 164
  environmentalism 197, 199, 200, 202–3
  forced migration/asylum 72, 87–8, 90, 91–2, 93, 94, 96–7, 98, 99–101, 102, 104, 105
  gender justice 115–16, 118–19
  peacebuilding 177–8, 180
  sexual and gender-based violence (SGBV) 133–5
  spiritual capital 44, 47–8, 49, 52, 53, 54, 55, 56–7, 59, 65

Ramadan and *Eid* festivals 73
Refugee Convention (1951) 89
Refugee *Zakat* Fund, UNHCR 33
refugees, asylum, and forced migration 87
  duty to provide asylum 93–4
  duty to seek asylum 91–2
  history of forced migration 87–8
  Islamic traditions in modern context 88–90
  persecution 90–1, 91–2, 93–4
  Prophet Muhammad (PBUH) and *Qur'an* 72
  responsibility for providing asylum 94–5
  rights of forced migrants 95–105
  solutions to displacement 105–6
  summary and conclusion 106–7
relationships, transforming in peacebuilding 182
resilience and spiritual capital 58
rights/human rights 8, 9–10, 50, 63
  asylum 93
  children 104–5, 156, 157–66
  forced migrants 95–105
  and gender justice 112–14, 119–20
  life 53

natural world 199
  and obligations of wealth redistribution 5–6
  sexual and gender-based violence (SGBV) 132–3
  social justice 60–1, 65, 81
  'Western' 190
  work 102–3, 118

Salek, L. 177–8, 180
scalable and replicable peace-building, challenge of 192
secular and faith-bases approaches 3
secularization/post-secularism 45, 88–9
self-reliance 75–8
self-sufficiency 4
sexual and gender-based violence (SGBV) 126–7, 131–2
  faith-based interventions 138–46
  forms of 134–8
  Muslim perspectives on 133
  and Qur'anic principles 133–4
  and religion in humanitarian and development contexts 132–3
  summary and conclusions 147–8
  see also specific forms
Shari'ah see Islamic law/*Shari'ah*; jurisprudence; *Maqasid al-Shari'ah*; *Maslaha*; Prophet Muhammad (PBUH); *Qur'an*
shura (consultation) 181–2
Siddiqi, M.N. 20, 21
social capital 43, 59, 62, 65
social justice 60–1, 65, 81
  see also rights/human rights
Sofjan, D. 207–8
Somali Region of Ethiopia
  see Ethiopia (IRE)
soul 47–8
spiritual capital 43–7
  implications for development practice 61–5
  Maqasid al-Shari'ah objectives 51–60
  Maqasid al-Shari'ah purpose and priorities of divine law 49–51
  and social justice 60–1
  spirit 47–9
  theory/theology of change 65–6

spiritual needs and poverty 8, 13
state-society conflict 182
stewardship/trusteeship
    environmental 197–8, 199–200,
    202, 204
    see also custodianship of Earth
sukuk (bonds) 35
Sustainable Development Agenda
    (2030) 2
Sustainable Development Goals
    (SDGs) 19, 20, 112, 116, 118,
    175–6, 180, 181, 190, 201–2
Syrian refugees, Turkey's responsi-
    bility for and rights of 102–3

trees, felling and planting of 200–1,
    202–3
'triple nexus' of development—
    humanitarianism—peace-
    building 180–1
Turkey: responsibility for and rights
    of Syrian refugees 102–3

Ummah (community) 177
Ummah Welfare Trust 74, 75, 77, 79
UN
    Convention of the Elimination of
        All Forms of Discrimination
        Against Women (CEDAW)
        113, 114, 118
    Convention of the Rights of the
        Child (UNCRC) 113, 155, 156,
        157, 158
    Framework Convention on
        Climate Change 204
    Maqasid objectives and gender
        rights 115
    Office on Genocide Prevention
        and the Responsibility to
        Protect 175, 208
    Security Council 122
    and spiritual capital 63
    Sustainable Development Agenda
        (2030) 2
UNCTAD: *World Investment Report* 19
UNDP: Human Development Index
    (HDI) 4
UNEP: 'Faith for Earth' initiative 46,
    197–8, 208

UNFPA 3, 138, 164
UNHCR
    forced migration/asylum 88,
        89, 90
    Global Compact on Refugees 175
    Refugee *Zakat* Fund 33
    service-led vs community
        response 46
    sexual and gender-based violence
        (SGBV) definition 131
UNICEF 153–4, 158, 159, 161,
    164, 166
    Arigatou and 8
    WHO and 198
UNITFR (Interagency Task Force on
    Religion) 3, 12
Universal Declaration of Human
    Rights (UDHR) 116

voluntary repatriation 106
vulnerable groups, rights of 104–5

Waqaf Al-Nur (WANCorp),
    Malaysia 36
waqf (property and land assets) 58
    current status and potential 28–9
    expanding: jurisprudential
        considerations 29
    gender justice 118
    improving governance and
        management 34–7
    principles, types and background
        22–3
wealth
    in development *10, 11, 51*
    and humanitarianism 52, 53
    protection and redistribution 5–6,
        55–8
    see also property; *waqf*
wealth tax *see zakat*
Westendorf, J.-K. 175, 192
women
    vulnerable, rights of 104
    see also gender and gender justice;
        sexual and gender-based
        violence (SGBV)
work 77
    right to 102–3, 118
World Bank 4, 5, 20

World Economic Forum 198
World Faiths Development
    Dialogue 2
World Health Organization (WHO)
    air, water and sanitation
        standards 198
    child abuse definition 161
    female genital mutilation/cutting
        definition 137, 163
    lifetime prevalence of physical/
        sexual violence 132
World Humanitarian Summit, UN
    121–2, 175, 181
World Vision 50, 165

Yemen, conflict transformation and
    peacebuilding programme in
    188–9, 190

zakat (charitable giving/wealth
    tax) 58
    current status and potential 24–8
    expanding: jurisprudential
        considerations 29–31
    gender justice 118
    improving governance and
        management 32–4
    poverty alleviation 3, 5, 9
    principles, types and background
        21–2
    Qur'an 6
    rights of forced migrants 102
    and *sadaqah* (prayers) 70
    vs foreign donations in
        peacebuilding 190
Zanzibar: environmental
    programme 203